ROBERT THE BRUCE'S IRISH WARS

THE INVASIONS OF IRELAND 1306–1329

ROBERT THE BRUCE'S IRISH WARS

THE INVASIONS OF IRELAND 1306–1329

SEÁN DUFFY (EDITOR)

TEMPUS

First published 2002

PUBLISHED IN THE UNITED KINGDOM BY:

Tempus Publishing Ltd
The Mill, Brimscombe Port
Stroud, Gloucestershire GL5 2QG
www.tempus-publishing.com

PUBLISHED IN THE UNITED STATES OF AMERICA BY:

Tempus Publishing Inc.
2 Cumberland Street
Charleston, SC 29401
Tel: 1-888-313-2665
www.tempuspublishing.com

Tempus books are available in France and Germany
from the following addresses:

Editions Alan Sutton
8 Rue du Docteur Ramon
37540 Saint-Cyr-sur-Loire
FRANCE

Sutton Verlag
Hochheimer Strasse 59
D-99094 Erfurt
GERMANY

British Library Cataloguing in Publication Data.
A catalogue record for this book is available from the British Library.

ISBN 0 7524 1974 9

Typesetting and origination by Tempus Publishing.
PRINTED AND BOUND IN GREAT BRITAIN.

Contents

Preface

The purpose of this collection is simple and its aims are modest. The best modern account of the involvement of Edward and Robert Bruce in Irish affairs is a lengthy article by Robin Frame, 'The Bruces in Ireland, 1315–1318', first published in 1974 in *Irish Historical Studies*, vol. 19, and since reprinted and updated in a collection of his papers published in 1998 under the title *Ireland and Britain, 1170–1450* (Hambledon Press, London). Other work on the Bruce invasion is not so readily available in print, and it seemed worthwhile, in publishing the rather unvarnished piece that forms Chapter 1 of this volume, to use the opportunity to reprint a number of other items on the subject that are less accessible than Professor Frame's masterly study.

Chapter 2 first appeared in *Cambridge Medieval Celtic Studies*, no. 21 (summer 1991); Chapter 3 in *Historical Studies IV. Papers read before the fifth Irish Conference of Historians*, ed. G.A. Hayes-McCoy (London: Bowes & Bowes, 1963); Chapter 4 in *The Scottish soldier abroad 1247–1967*, ed. G.G. Simpson, University of Aberdeen Mackie Monographs 2 (Edinburgh: John Donald and Maryland, USA: Barnes & Noble, 1992); Chapter 5 was originally broadcast by Radio Éireann (now RTE) in the winter of 1955–56 as a lecture in the 'Thomas Davis' series, and printed in *The Irish at war*, ed. G.A. Hayes-McCoy (Cork: Mercier Press, 1964); Chapter 6 remains in print but is an expensive purchase as Chapter X of the 1,000-page-plus *A new history of Ireland. II. Medieval Ireland 1169–1534*, ed. Art Cosgrove (Oxford: Clarendon Press, 1987; 2nd impression 1993); and Chapter 7 appeared as an article in *Scottish Historical Review*, xlii (1963).

Appendix A is an extract from our main source for the invasion, John Barbour's *The Bruce*, and if not technically the most accurate translation from the original fourteenth-century Scots verse (that is now available in the superb new edition by A.A.M. Duncan (Edinburgh: Canongate Classics, 1997)), it is perhaps the most fluent, by George Eyre-Todd (Edinburgh: Gowans & Gray, 1907). Finally, Appendix B contains the most important piece of correspondence to which the Bruce invasion gave rise, the letter from King Domnall O Neill to Pope John XXII, generally

Opposite 1. *After success over the English at Bannockburn in June 1314 it looked as though Robert Bruce might secure the independence of Scotland and his own claim to the throne; but the hope was illusory and hence his brother Edward was sent to Ireland to tighten the screw* known as the 'Remonstrance of the Irish Princes'; it survives in Walter Bower's *Scotichronicon*, now majesterially in print in nine volumes under the general editorship of D.E.R. Watt (Aberdeen: Aberdeen University Press, 1987–1998), at vol. 6, pp. 384–403, with elaborate notes by the leading authority on the subject, J.R.S. Phillips (at pp. 465–81), but as the cost of owning a copy of this splendid series will necessarily be beyond the means of many students of the subject, we print below the text of Edmund Curtis's spirited translation from *Irish historical documents 1172–1922*, eds E. Curtis and R.B. McDowell (London: Methuen, 1943).

Needless to say, many debts are incurred in putting together even a limited collection of essays such as this, and I am exceedingly grateful to all of the authors, editors, publishers, executors, and other agents who so willingly acceded to the request to reprint them here. I thank too Jonathan Reeve of Tempus, for his patience (rarely has a publishing house had a more apt title), and his colleagues for their professionalism in bringing the work together. Unless otherwise stated, the photographs are the possession of Linzi Simpson and her patience too has been sorely taxed and is much appreciated.

SD
Dublin
March 2002

1

The Bruce Invasion of Ireland: A Revised Itinerary and Chronology

Seán Duffy

The Bruce invasion of Ireland, lasting from 1315 to 1318, is one of the best documented episodes in medieval Irish history. We know the exact day in the early summer of 1315 on which Edward Bruce and his army landed in Ireland and the precise location (or locations) of the landing point; we know too the exact date on which his life ended and with it his attempt to conquer Ireland, and the very hill on which this fateful event occurred; and we know much of the turbulent and sometimes tragic events in between. It is a story familiar to many and recorded in a great variety of contemporary and later accounts. But these are often contradictory and over the succeeding centuries errors have crept into the version of events that is set down by even the most eminent of historians. Nearly 700 years on we are, in fact, still finding new sources of information, and rejecting as unreliable – and even as forgeries – documents previously thought to offer important insights into this remarkable episode. So, some purpose may be served, even now, from setting out a basic chronology of events, and an itinerary of Edward Bruce's movements, throughout the three and a half years in which his involvement in the affairs of Ireland looked set to change the course of its history.

The crushing defeat of the English at Bannockburn in June 1314 started a new phase in the Anglo-Scottish war that had been waged with varying degrees of intensity since 1296. It looked like Robert Bruce might at last achieve his objective of securing Scotland's independence and his own position as its acknowledged king.

Yet, little happened. The war dragged on, King Edward II still refusing to recognise either Scotland's independence or Bruce's right to rule.[1] In fact, there were some straws in the wind to suggest that recent Scottish successes might prove short-lived: Robert had recaptured the Isle of Man from the English in summer 1313, but by January 1315 it had been won back; since control of the Irish Sea was crucial to the strategies of both sides, this was a potentially disastrous development.[2] Therefore further action was required. There is some evidence that King Robert may have been at Tarbert, at the northern end of Kintyre, from about March 1315; there he had a castle, and was in close proximity to the Western Isles and the seaway to Ireland, and he may have been gathering galleys to transport the Scottish fleet to Ireland.[3] Before setting out for Ireland, on 26 April 1315, a Scottish assembly was held at Ayr, facing the Antrim coast, and this may have been a muster for the impending invasion by the king's brother Edward. Many of the leaders of the invading army would have been present at that assembly, having made their preparations for what would potentially be a long absence overseas. By the time they set sail it was late May and they embarked at Ayr, a Dublin-based chronicler reporting that Edward Bruce's invading fleet landed on the coast of County Antrim on 26 May.[4] At the same time, Robert Bruce himself set sail from Tarbert for the Western Isles along with his son-in-law, Walter Stewart, and he subjected their rulers to his authority, so that 'all the Isles, great and small, were brought to his will.'[5]

John Barbour, archdeacon of Aberdeen, who wrote a biography (in verse) of Robert Bruce some sixty years later, based on surviving records and recollections, stated that Edward's fleet put ashore at Larne ('Wolringis Fyrth') where Olderfleet Castle still stands, preserving a trace of the earlier Norse name.[6] The Dublin chronicle disagrees: it says that the commander of the fleet, Edward Bruce, disembarked at a place which it calls 'Clondonne'.[7] G.H. Orpen worked hard to reconcile the two accounts by suggesting that the latter is in fact Clondunmales, now Drumalys, a townland near Larne,[8] and this may well be the case. But it looks more like Glendun, considerably further up the Antrim coast, and it may be worth pointing out that many years later, in July 1327, when Robert Bruce came to Ireland again, he made a truce with the steward of the earldom of Ulster which was dated at Glendun ('Glendouyn').[9] And it must be said that the latter does seem quite plausible. The Bruces inherited an interest in the Glens. Robert Bruce's great-grandfather Duncan, earl of Carrick in greater Galloway, had been granted the barony of Upper Glenarm (stretching from Larne to Glenarm) a century earlier by King John. Others had since taken possession of it from his heirs, the Bruces, but the latter were intent on recovering it – Edward Bruce had been granted the earldom of Carrick by his brother just two years prior to the decision to invade Ireland – and the coastline at the foot of the Glens would therefore make a logical place at which to land.[10] There were up to 6,000 troops in the invading force (according to Archdeacon Barbour), so we can envisage any number of landing spots spread along the Antrim coast from Larne to Glendun – all the better to safeguard at least some of them from being wiped out by local opponents should they be set on upon arrival.

2. Castle Carra, County Antrim: built on lands near Cushendun to which the Bruces may have had a claim, Castle Carra must have fallen into Scots hands upon their arrival in Antrim in May 1315

This indeed happened: Barbour tells us that they arrived safely, in Larne Lough as he has it, without any opposition or attack upon them, and were sufficiently confident of success to send their ships home.[11] The Anglo-Irish government and the earl of Ulster, Richard de Burgh, seem to have been taken unawares by the landing, as the chief governor was in Munster and de Burgh in Connacht,[12] but the earl's most prominent tenants – the de Mandevilles, the Bissets of the Glens, the Logans, and the Savages – soon took to the field against them. However, they were defeated by the Scots, under the command of Thomas Randolph, earl of Moray. The leader of the Ulster forces, Sir Thomas de Mandeville, who was the Bruces' chief opponent in the province on behalf of his lord the earl, was forced to flee and to seek refuge further south, closer to the safety of Dublin.[13] The Scots had got the first of many subsequent tastes of victory in Ireland and proceeded to march on the town of Carrickfergus. The town itself fell easily into their hands and they billeted themselves there, though its heavily fortified and well-garrisoned castle was to remain under siege for many months – its capture was essential to Bruce's prospects of success.[14] The initial stages of the siege were overseen by Edward Bruce himself and delayed his progress for much of June 1315, but it provided the opportunity for his supporters among the native Irish of Ulster to come to his presence. Barbour states that ten or twelve Irish kings came and swore fealty to him and the Irish annals imply (without explicitly stating so) that it was at this point that Edward was proclaimed king of Ireland by the Irish:[15]

> [He] took the hostages and lordship of the whole province of Ulster without opposition and they consented to his being proclaimed king of Ireland, and

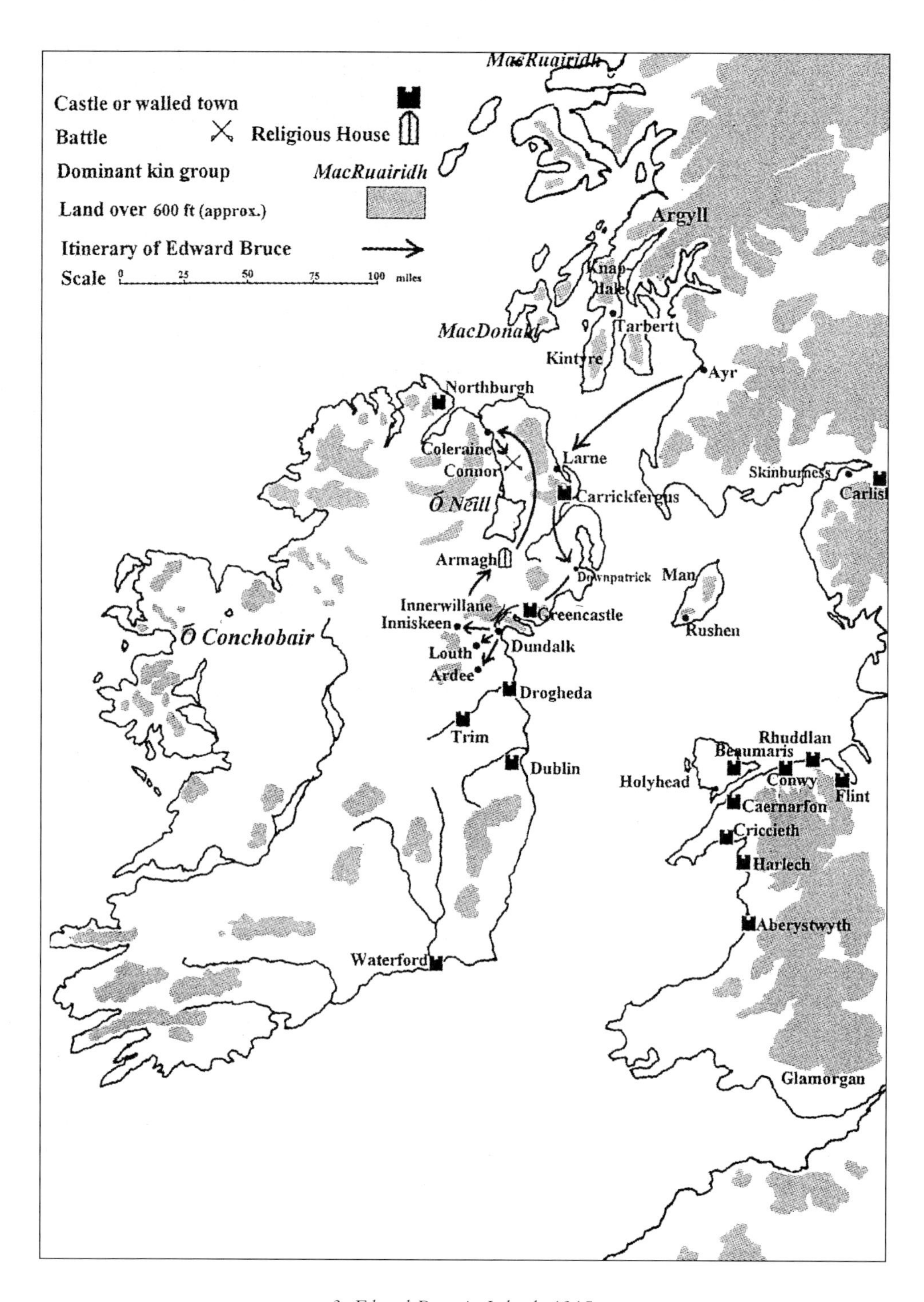

3. Edward Bruce in Ireland, 1315

4. Carrickfergus Castle: while the town of Carrickfergus fell easily before the Scots advance, the castle held out defiantly until September 1316

> all the Gaels of Ireland agreed to grant him lordship and they called him king of Ireland.

This latter point is significant because, influenced partly by the confused chronology supplied in some brief Latin annals compiled in Dublin and partly by a Gaelic text which has since turned out to be a nineteenth-century forgery, many scholars have stated that Bruce only became king of Ireland in the following year and that he was inaugurated king at Faughart, ironically the site of his disastrous defeat and death in 1318.[16] There seems no justification for such a view and all the evidence suggests that Edward and his Irish allies had intended that he become king from the start of his Irish adventure and that this was in fact enacted, at or near Carrickfergus, at some stage in June 1315.

But King Edward Bruce's delay to receive the voluntary submissions of the Irish and the hoped-for forced submission of Carrickfergus Castle, provided the opportunity for the Dublin government to begin to organise itself against him and he may have grown to regret it. He headed south along the Six Mile Water, known as Magh Line to the Irish, and burned the settlement at Rathmore near Antrim town.[17] A.A.M. Duncan has struggled above and beyond the call of duty to suggest that the latter is another Rathmore in County Meath, but this is most improbable:[18] it is placed before the march further south on Dundalk and Ardee, and the very fact that Rathmore in Moylinny belonged to Bruce's enemies, the Savages, is ample reason for taking the annals at their word.[19] Barbour then reports that Bruce went south via a pass of which he says, 'in all Ireland there is none narrower', and which in manu-

5. This standing stone overlooking Dundalk seems to point the way to 'the Gap of the North' directly overhead, through which the Scots forces made their way for the first time in June 1315

scripts of *The Bruce* is spelt Innermallan and Enderwillane. He adds that, as Edward Bruce was travelling south, two of the Irish who had earlier submitted to him, Mac Duilechain of Clanbrassil and Mac Artain of Iveagh, lay in wait for the Scots to prevent them getting through, but were overcome by Bruce's troops who successfully forced the pass and headed towards Dundalk. The same place is mentioned in a court record dating from 1282 which refers to an individual who, having made peace with Mac Artain of Iveagh, 'escaped from Ulster by the pass of Imberdoilan to Dublin'.[20] Likewise, in 1345, the chief governor (justiciar), in entering Ulster, 'by a pass called Emerdullan', was attacked and heavily defeated by Mac Artain.[21] In other records of the period it is spelt Humberdoylan, Endulan and Aberdulan, and by the 1350s Mac Artain was styled 'keeper' of the pass and charged travellers a shilling to secure safe-conduct through it.[22] The traditional way south out of Ulster was along an old route between Newry and Dundalk, through the Moiry Pass via Jonesborough and Kilnasaggart, and this must be what is intended.

Dundalk was the most substantial town that the Scots had yet approached and their actions there are significant. The town had been established by the de Verdon family, who were still its lords and fierce opponents of the Bruces.[23] On the route south through the 'Gap of the North' Bruce would have come close to their massive fortress of Castleroche, the manor of which was reported in 1316–17 as being, 'so burned and destroyed by the Scots and Irish that no profit could be received',[24] and then he would have seen on the horizon the magnificent site of their original castle, perhaps still in occupation, at Castletown Mount, but seems to have ignored it and

6. The drumlin hills of south County Armagh line the Moiry Pass through which was the primary route in and out of Ulster until modern times

instead, on 29 June, he stormed the relatively poorly defended town.[25] There was some local resistance but not enough to withstand the assault and the town was severely damaged. John Clyn was a Franciscan friar based at Kilkenny who later pieced together a set of annals for this period, and he therefore took particular offence at the fact that the Scots did not even forego burning the town's friary, and in fact set fire even to its books, vestments and altar ware.[26] The ferocity of Bruce's assault on Dundalk suggests perhaps an animosity towards its lords, the de Verdons (whose head, the elderly Theobald, was then in England, where he died a year later), and this is evidenced later in his campaign, but it was a choice of enemy that was to come back to haunt him and to play a central part in his downfall and death.

The chief governor at the time of Bruce's assault was Edmund Butler, father of the first earl of Ormond, and he assembled the feudal host of Leinster and Munster and headed north to oppose Bruce. The man who had suffered most to date was the earl of Ulster, Richard de Burgh; he was also lord of Connacht and this, as already stated, is where he was when the Scots had landed in his earldom. Now he assembled his Connacht tenants, along with the fighting men of Feidlim Ó Conchobair of Connacht, and they too marched to oppose Bruce. One should not read too much into Feidlim's decision at this stage to oppose the Scots: he was just one of the claimants to the all but defunct kingship of Connacht and at this stage could not afford to jeopardise the possibility of securing de Burgh's support. In any case, Butler's army and de Burgh's army – the latter by way of the towns of Roscommon and Athlone – converged, about 22 July, somewhere in the Sliabh Breagh hills to the south of Ardee. The Scots army, and their Irish allies, were at this stage at Inniskeen,

7. Castleroche, County Louth: the imposing sight of the de Verdon fortress at Castleroche must have been a cause of trepidation for Bruce's army on their march towards Dundalk

some ten miles to the north. Between them lay the village of Louth, the location of an important Augustinian abbey, and the earl of Ulster moved his army north to Louth on the following day where he set up camp. His cousin, William Liath de Burgh, attempted to catch the Scots unawares and some skirmishing took place between them in which a small number were killed on both sides, but Bruce wisely refused an open battle against what was in effect the feudal host of the English colony in Ireland, and, adopting the advice of his leading Irish ally, Domnall Ó Néill, he retreated northwards to Coleraine in modern County Derry.[27]

We do not know precisely what route the Scots and Irish army took north. Logically, we would expect them to have travelled west of Lough Neagh, through territories friendly towards Ó Néill, and the annals of Inisfallen do indeed confirm that they passed through the ecclesiastical city of Armagh.[28] The Anglo-Irish forces would be on safer territory east of the Bann which they had heavily settled, and sure enough the justiciar, Edmund Butler, was later reported to have been in the vicinity of Carlingford which suggests activity further east.[29] In any case, the chief governor chose not to pursue Bruce further north and the task of ridding the earldom of the Scottish threat was left to its earl, along with Feidlim Ó Conchobair. Arriving at Eas Craoibhe near Coleraine, the Scots burned the latter town, with the exception of the Dominican friary (spared because it was probably founded by an Irish ally of the Bruces, Ó Catháin perhaps), and threw down the bridge over the river Bann to prevent their enemy crossing over. The two armies, camped on either side of the river, stood facing each other for some time, the earl waiting for the water level to fall in order to cross, and hoping that the Scots would eventually begin to run short

8. For all its impregnability, the manor lands of Castleroche were afterwards reported as having been 'burned and destroyed by the Scots and Irish'

of food supplies. The latter did indeed occur, Inisfallen reporting that in the Scots camp, 'four quarters of a sheep fetched two shillings sterling'. But the Irish of those parts, notably Ó Néill, Ó Catháin and Ó Floinn, came to the Scots' aid, and de Burgh, beginning to feel the pinch himself, withdrew the best part of forty miles to Antrim town, 'desiring to secure plentiful supplies for his army'.[30] Meanwhile, a rival of Feidlim Ó Conchobair, his cousin Cathal, took advantage of the latter's absence to have himself proclaimed king of Connacht, and Feidlim made the decision to return home to contest the kingship, no doubt weakening de Burgh's forces somewhat. It is also reported that 3,000 men (an exaggeration, no doubt), under the earl's cousin Walter, son of Sir Walter Cattus de Burgh, deserted from him at this point and returned to Connacht.[31]

The earl of Ulster was now in a vulnerable position, particularly if the Scots chose to cross the Bann in pursuit. This they managed with the help of four ships supplied by the Scots sea-captain, Thomas Dun.[32] An initial skirmish occurred in which several of Bruce's forces and some Anglo-Irish, including John Staunton and Roger of Holywood, were killed, while George de Rupe (i.e., Roche) was wounded.[33] This, though, was soon followed by a more serious encounter: the earl moved his forces from Antrim town to the episcopal seat of Connor, but the Scots and their Irish supporters, including Ó Néill, charged them before they were as yet ready and, although some Scots were killed, including one of the leaders of the invading force, John de Bosco, the latter army prevailed, and the earl was forced to flee. His cousin, William Liath de Burgh, was wounded and captured and ultimately transported to Scotland, probably by the earl of Moray who returned home

9. The original de Verdon settlement at Dundalk had been on Castletown Mount, perhaps the original Dún Dealgan associated with Cú Chulainn in the early saga literature but, as the surviving motte and fosse indicate, it was substantially remodelled for their use

on 15 September 1315 in part to raise further troops but with several ships full of captured booty.[34] The Dublin chronicler dates the battle of Connor to 10 September, and this is the date normally accepted, but one of its veterans soon afterwards gives the date as 1 September.[35] It was a humiliating experience for the great Richard de Burgh, who retreated to Connacht and was subsequently described by the Irish annals as, 'a wanderer up and down Ireland, with no power or lordship';[36] as for the other Anglo-Irish survivors of the defeat, they withdrew to the still uncaptured Carrickfergus Castle which the Scots now began to besiege in earnest. Sometime later, in October or early November, some English sailors arrived secretly in the town under cover of darkness and killed forty Scots, whose tents they managed to steal, but the siege was maintained.[37]

On the very day of the battle of Connor, the Dublin government was sent a letter from King Edward II, by now finally realising the gravity of the threat that the Scots posed to his lordship of Ireland, in which he ordered the justiciar and chancellor of Ireland to convene a meeting of the Anglo-Irish magnates at which the king's special envoy to Ireland, John de Hothum, would discuss certain urgent matters of state with them.[38] The outcome of this seems to have been a parliament which gathered in Dublin on 27 October.[39] Its deliberations have not survived, but certainly nothing conclusive seems to have been agreed on. Less than three weeks later, on 13 November, Bruce and the bulk of his army went on the offensive again. The delay had been caused by the need to wait for the earl of Moray to return with reinforcements, and the 500 men he brought with him from Scotland were enough to

10. The first de Verdon burial ground was presumably located at the medieval parish churchyard of Castletown, near Dundalk, seen here with a later tower house in the background

encourage Edward to launch another southern campaign. He marched south, again via Dundalk, where once more there was some resistance – we are told that 'some gave them [the Scots] the right hand' – and by 30 November Bruce was at Nobber in County Meath. He left a garrison there and advanced on Kells.[40] Here his opponent was Roger Mortimer of Wigmore, who had married the granddaughter of Geoffrey de Joinville, lord of Trim, and thus came to inherit a substantial lordship in east Meath. It is perhaps no coincidence that the other half of the great lordship of Meath founded in 1172 by Hugh de Lacy was now in the possession of the de Verdons, another target of Bruce's aggression, and that one of the very few Anglo-Irish families attracted to Bruce's cause were the de Lacys, a cadet line of the family now reduced to a rump of their former status but no doubt anxious to recover the full estate which Mortimer and the de Verdons had won from them through marriage. Roger Mortimer was a figure of like status to the earl of Ulster and he was intent upon resisting the Scots, but his army, though large, was less than loyal, and fled the field of battle on or about 6 December. Mortimer had to retreat to Dublin, and thence to England, while his lieutenant Walter Cusack sought refuge in Trim Castle, making sure that this noble fortress did not fall into enemy hands.[41]

Doubt has occasionally been cast on the date and significance of the battle of Kells, and indeed on whether it happened at all. But it is worth noting the measures that the king's envoy, John de Hothum, now ordered to be put in place for the defence of Dublin: these included the demolition of the bell-tower of the parish church of St Mary del Dam (at the western end of Dame Street, just inside the city walls) for stone to repair the castle's walls 'against certain perils that were

11. Friar John Clyn recalls how the Franciscan friary at Dundalk, founded by the de Verdons, was a particular target of the wrath of the Scots

feared', and the purchase of lead for repair of the castle's towers; the bulk supply of foodstuffs, as well as thousands of crossbow bolts and hides and stones (presumably for catapults), for storage in the castle; and an insistence on the records and monies of the exchequer being brought back from that building (at the junction of Exchequer Street and South Great George's Street) to the castle every night. Most of these instructions were to take effect from 9 December 1315, and must surely have been deemed necessary because Roger Mortimer had just arrived in the city with the bleak news of the Scots success.[42]

Bruce, however, contented himself with burning Kells and turned instead west into Westmeath, heading as far as Granard in County Longford, where he burned the manor of the Anglo-Irish Tuit family and the Cistercian monastery at Abbeylara which the latter family had founded:[43] it is probably no coincidence that when Bruce's leading Irish ally, Ó Néill, wrote to the pope in 1317 to seek papal support for the invasion (the famous 'Remonstrance of the Irish Princes'), among the injustices against the Irish which the letter cited was the claim that the monks of Abbeylara (Granard) had no difficulty in hunting the Irish with spears by day and saying Vespers by evening.[44] An English settlement had been established on the modern Cavan-Westmeath border at Finnea, which the Scots also torched before turning south into Uí Fheargail (O Farrell) country in Angaile (Annaly, County Longford), now also dotted with English settlements which they raided, including a castle at Shrule held by tenants of the de Verdons, before reaching the de Verdons' own manor of Loughsewdy, the caput of their half of the lordship of Meath. Here, Bruce added insult to injury by setting up home in the manor house for Christmas. He only left when all its supplies had been consumed, and razed it to the ground on his departure.[45]

It is noticeable that none of the Meath manors still in de Lacy hands, such as Rathwire, were destroyed by Bruce, suggesting that the de Lacys were already recruited to his cause. They were certainly in contact with him at this point, although when subsequently charged with collusion they claimed that they had in fact 'patriotically' guided the Scots away from soft English targets in Meath and took them on a meandering journey through Irish lands further west, delaying them from reaching Leinster for a fortnight and in the process causing them to lose both men and horses. It was a rather lame excuse but a jury accepted it, and the de Lacy faction was restored to the peace for a fine of £200.[46] And there might just be something to their claim to have brought the Scots (though, perhaps unintentionally) through lands belonging to hostile Irish. The Scots army next appears on record in Tuath Dá Maige, the Tethmoy area of County Offaly, where the leading Anglo-Irish power was the de Bermingham family, no friends of the de Lacys. In order to get to Tethmoy, the Bruce army would have had to traverse Clann Máelugra (Clanmaliere) in modern Counties Offaly and Laois, the territory of the Uí Díomasaigh (O Dempseys), an Irish family who were generally on good terms with the Dublin government in this period. Now, Archdeacon Barbour preserves a story in his account of the Bruce invasion about an Irish king called 'Ydymsy', who had sworn an oath of fealty to Edward Bruce and, 'had begged him to see his land and [there]

12. The town of Galway was a de Burgh foundation, established in the early thirteenth century by an earlier Richard, grandfather of the earl. The photograph shows a medieval ogee-headed window from a house in Barrack Lane in the town

13. Geoffrey de Joinville inherited by marriage half of the great de Lacy lordship of Meath, which had Trim Castle at its core, and which then passed to the Mortimers. The photograph shows, under excavation, the mural tower on the walls of Dublin which was called after de Joinville and which he may have used as a residence

would be no lack of food or anything else that could help him'. Bruce trusted him, and was led to a location near the banks of a river, where Ydymsy told him to set up camp while he went and got victuals; but far from helping the Scots, he had dammed up the river and by removing the dam during the night Bruce's camp was flooded so that he and his men nearly drowned. So Barbour says.[47] Unfortunately, he places the incident at the time of the battle of Connor and somewhere in the vicinity of the Bann, which is clearly wrong; but 'Ydymsy' must surely be O Dempsey, and since the latter would not be well known outside Ireland, we must assume that Barbour is recording a genuine incident, however exaggeratedly, and albeit at a misplaced time and location.

It seems likely, therefore, that in the early days of January 1316, while crossing from the lordship of Meath into Leinster, Bruce was the target of a treacherous plot by an erstwhile ally, but he was soon back in control of his fortunes. Marching through Tethmoy he came into County Kildare, into the lands of the head of the Leinster Geraldines, John fitz Thomas, second only to Richard de Burgh among the ranks of the resident Anglo-Irish baronage. We know that Bruce assaulted the Geraldine castle at Rathangan before moving on to Kildare itself, where he spent three days trying unsuccessfully to force the castle into submission. Unfortunately for Bruce, the constable of the castle had known of his intentions and spent over £200 in provisioning and garrisoning it so that the castle could withstand a siege.[48] Although two of the constable's kin were killed, the Scots knew that there was little to be gained from exhausting their resources in a lengthy siege, and so pushed further south as far

14. After Roger Mortimer's ignominious defeat at the battle of Kells in December 1315 he fled to Dublin and left Trim Castle in the charge of Walter Cusack. The photograph shows the keep of the castle under excavation, with the barbican gate in the background

as Castledermot, County Kildare, before swinging north again, travelling by way of Athy and Reban till they came within sight of the great mound of Ardscull. By now the colonists had assembled to deal with the threat. They were led by the justiciar, Edmund Butler, and by the local Geraldine lord John fitz Thomas and his son, along with their cousin, Maurice fitz Thomas, head of the Munster Geraldines and later first earl of Desmond; also among their leaders were two members of the Power clan, John le Poer, baron of Dunoil (Dunhill, County Waterford), and Arnold le Poer, seneschal of Kilkenny, and two leaders of the Roches, David and Miles de la Roche, as well as another Munster baron, Maurice de Rocheford. On 26 January they finally got to face the invaders in the open field.[49] What is generally called the battle of Ardscull was in fact fought at a place called Skerries, not far from Ardscull, about three miles north-east of Athy. John de Hothum, Edward II's messenger, was present on the occasion and sent his master a brief and tactful account of what transpired,[50] although neither it nor the annals that report the battle are very specific. The reason for this is clear: the size of the government's army apparently far exceeded that of Bruce, and victory should have been theirs, but it seems that a quarrel broke out among its leaders, presumably regarding tactics, and the result was that they left the field of battle to the Scots allowing the latter to claim a victory of sorts despite incurring heavier losses. Friar Clyn claimed that only five English were slain (we know that these included Hamon le Gras and William de Prendergast) but that the Scots lost about seventy men (including Fergus of Ardrossan and Walter of Moray), who were brought for burial to the Dominican priory in Athy.[51]

15. Kildare cathedral: not much of the current fabric of Kildare cathedral is old enough to have witnessed the passage of the Scots through the town in January 1316, but the south trancept and part of the tower probably did

In the aftermath of the battle of Skerries, the Scots army retired into Laois, still largely in Irish hands, where they were among friends and, in its boggy terrain, safe for the time being from possible cavalry assault. Not that they had much to fear: the justiciar had fled to Dublin, presumably accompanied by de Hothum. The fear lingered that the Scots might try to push home their advantage by seeking to storm the colony's capital, and this seems to lie behind a decision made in early February that the justices of the bench would postpone the anticipated sitting of their court until after Easter, 'because of the Scots'.[52] The other leaders of the Skerries fiasco also retired to lick their wounds in Dublin, although leaving their troops behind in the neighbourhood of Castledermot in case the Scots forged south again. Here they were joined by the lord of Thomond, Richard de Clare, and in a formal assembly held in the city on 4 February 1316 they renewed their oaths of loyalty to their king, swearing to defend his rights in his lordship of Ireland, and to do their utmost to destroy the Scots on pain of forfeiting their bodies, lands and chattels should they resile from that commitment. John de Hothum presided over these proceedings and on 15 February he wrote to Edward II informing him of developments and, since the treasury was empty because of the great expenditure on resisting the Scots and the fall-off in revenues because of the crisis in the country, he felt compelled to ask the king to subsidise the government's activities to the tune of £500 – in haste![53]

While the government was in a state of panic, Bruce himself had no great cause for celebration. If his aim was, as seems to have been the case, to make himself king throughout all Ireland, he had enjoyed only limited success to date. His natural allies, the native Irish, were by no means universal in their support, but far worse than this

16. Kildare: this largely overlooked remnant of the medieval fortifications of the town of Kildare may have suffered the assault of the Bruce army in January 1316

disappointment was the battle against the elements that Bruce was now facing. The autumn of 1315 saw the first of a series of disastrous harvests that afflicted not just Ireland but much of Europe, a combination of bad weather and crop failure that led to one of the worst famines Europe ever saw, and one of the bleakest episodes in medieval Irish history. It was Edward Bruce's great misfortune that his invasion should have coincided with such an unforeseen calamity. Of course, it was not entirely without benefit to him since he was pursuing a scorched-earth campaign against his enemies and the famine added to their woes, making it more difficult to put an army into the field against him, and more expensive to feed them: the Dublin chronicler tells us that in the spring of 1316, wheat (that might normally be expected to cost five or six shillings a crannock) was selling for eighteen shillings.[54] But Bruce was even more vulnerable. He was the one campaigning overseas, dependent on the backing of Irish allies who had committed their support to him before famine struck but were now in a struggle for their very survival: it would hardly be surprising if their enthusiasm for the Bruce adventure rapidly waned or if they began to blame Edward Bruce himself for the desperate state of affairs facing the country throughout his occupation.

It was undoubtedly the famine, the sheer inability to feed his troops, that prevented Bruce from pushing home the advantage after his victory at Skerries. While John fitz Thomas was in Dublin (and soon to be rewarded for his loyalty in the face of the Scots by a grant of the title earl of Kildare), the Scots attacked and burned his great fortress at Lea, just east of Portarlington, County Laois, and by 14 February had come within sight of another great Geraldine castle at Geashill, which

17. Lea Castle, County Laois: John fitz Thomas's magnificent castle at Lea in County Laois is testimony to the control he exerted in this frontier area close to the Irish, but Edward Bruce consigned it to the flames in 1316

they were preparing to assault. But by this stage the government army was assembling in the neighbourhood of Kildare. Bruce's forces, depleted by the rigours of a winter campaign in a hungry landscape, were not prepared to risk another battle in open field. To avoid the possibility of having their avenue of retreat cut off, they rapidly took a north-westerly route and turned up shortly afterwards in Fore, County Westmeath, where many of them were reported to have died of hunger and exhaustion. There was no option but to retreat to their base in north-east Ulster before any further harm came their way, and so they continued on their weary march and were back in their northern refuge before the end of February.[55] Here they were safe, if uncertain perhaps about what course to take next.

We know that the earl of Moray was again now sent back to Scotland to seek reinforcements from King Robert and did not return for almost a year. Then Edward Bruce, as befitted someone claiming to be king of Ireland, held proceedings which involved trying and executing some of his Ulster opponents, and which one source claims was an actual parliament.[56] It is recorded that he paid a brief visit to Scotland himself in mid-Lent, which in 1316 would have fallen on 21 March, and that he brought with him as a prisoner one of the more prominent of his Ulster enemies, Alan fitz Warin: Archdeacon Barbour tells us that the latter had been captured the previous autumn at the battle of Connor and we know that Edward II later pardoned him, in common with many Ulstermen, for eventually defecting to the side of the Scots.[57] There was still some resistance to Bruce's rule in Ulster. Sir Thomas de Mandeville had not given up hope of recovering his position there and the fact that Carrickfergus Castle still held out against Bruce was cause for

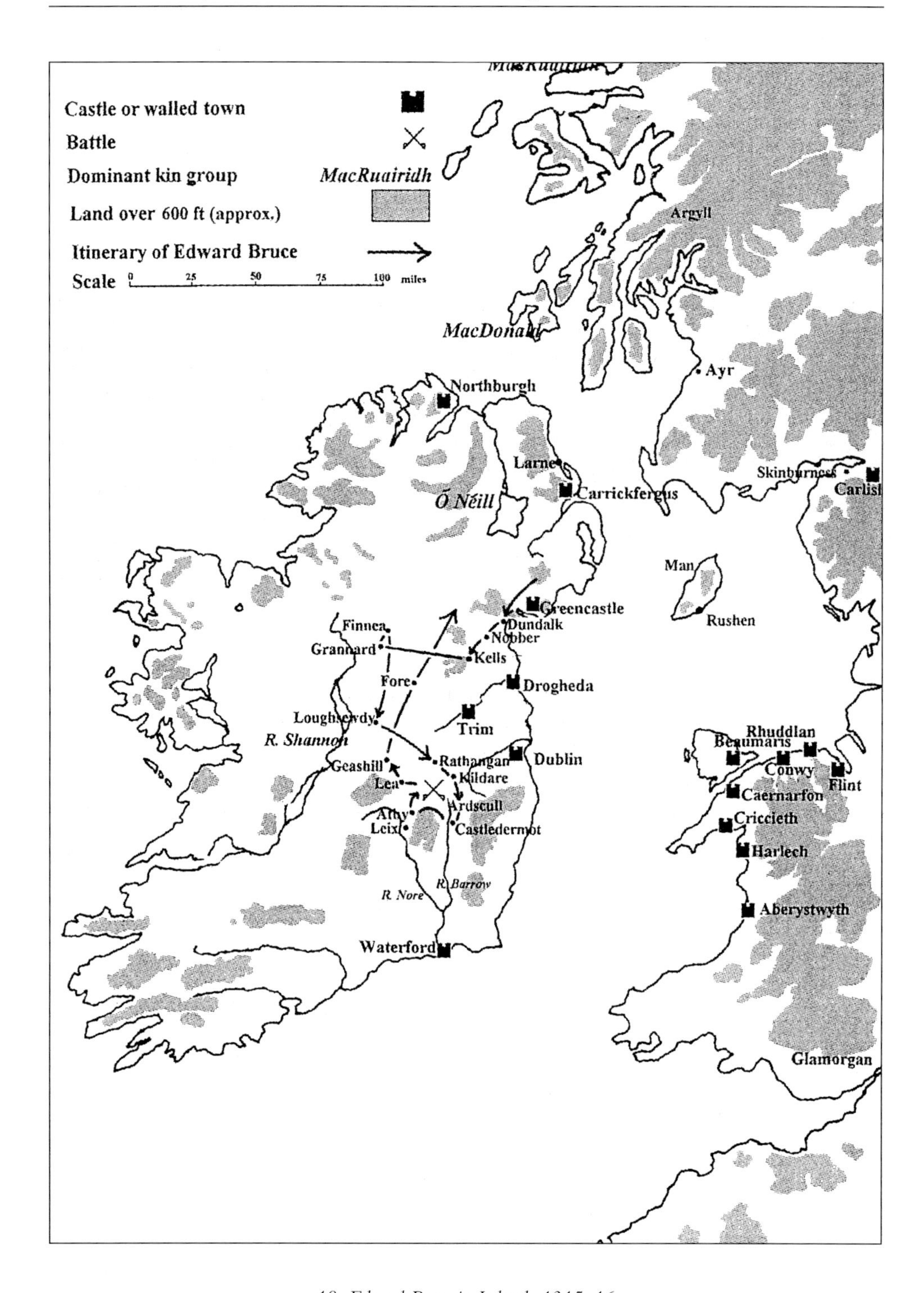

18. *Edward Bruce in Ireland, 1315–16*

19. These de Verdon lands north of Dundalk were the subject of the predations of raids by the native Ó hAnluain (O Hanlon) dynasty in 1316

hope. So, in Easter Week 1316 de Mandeville set out from Drogheda and, sailing up the east coast, landed at Carrickfergus where he did battle with the Scots, upwards of thirty of whom he is said to have killed, causing the other besiegers to flee. Another encounter took place just outside the gates of the castle on Easter Saturday, and again some Scots are reported as being killed, but so too was Sir Thomas. Nevertheless, the castle itself continued to elude Bruce. We are told by the Dublin annalist that he came to the defenders of Carrickfergus and demanded its surrender, which they agreed to, asking him to send thirty men to receive it from them; this he did, but the garrison allegedly imprisoned them. So hungry were those inside that they are said to have been reduced to chewing skin and eating the corpses of their captives. Finally, at midsummer 1316, while Thomas Dun was increasing the pressure on Carrickfergus by besieging it from the sea, a one-month truce was agreed, allowing the castle's constable the opportunity to visit Edward Bruce who was then at Coleraine. The end of this lengthy siege was in sight, and by September 1316 news had reached Dublin that the garrison had opened the castle gates to Bruce, having received guarantees as to their own safety (which Bruce honoured).[58] In the meantime, he had managed to capture and lose again Greencastle in County Down, although his men were successful in the west of the province in that year, taking the fortress of Northburgh in Inishowen which the earl of Ulster had recently constructed with a view to guarding the passage through Lough Foyle to Derry.[59]

The Dublin annals claim that, at some point prior to the fall of Carrickfergus (possibly in late July 1316), Robert Bruce had arrived in Ulster to help his brother,

20. Kindlestown Castle, County Wicklow, built to protect the southern approaches to Dublin; the manor lands of Kindlestown Castle were probably among those burned by the O Tooles and O Byrnes during the Bruce wars

but we have no other evidence for it and, even if true, he cannot have stayed long: on 30 September 1316, Edward Bruce was at Cupar in Fife, in the presence of King Robert and the earl of Moray, and, styling himself 'Edward, by the grace of God, king of Ireland', formally agreed to his brother's grant to Moray of the Isle of Man.[60] It seems likely that the reason Edward's consent to this grant was sought was because he had designs on Man himself. The Isle of Man had been acquired by the Scots from the Norse under the terms of the treaty of Perth in 1266. The then king, Alexander III, was sufficiently proud of the acquisition to give his heir, also Alexander, the title 'lord of Man'. Following the deaths of both, Man was occupied by the earl of Ulster who handed it over to Edward I in 1290, and it was only recaptured by the Scots, under Robert Bruce himself, in 1313, although Scots enemies of the Bruces retook the island just months before Edward's Irish invasion.[61] When, at the Ayr assembly in April 1315, the latter was ratified as Robert's heir presumptive (in the absence as yet of a royal son) he could reasonably have assumed that the precedent set by Alexander III would stand, and that he could claim Man for himself, if he won it back. One English chronicler, well-informed about events connected with the Isle of Man, does specifically state that it was Edward's intention to be, not just king of Ireland, but 'conqueror of the Isles',[62] and therefore his brother's decision to give Man instead to the earl of Moray may have been a sore point, sufficient to cause him to leave Ireland at a crucial juncture in order to sort out the matter.

If his aim was to have Robert change his mind about Man, Edward's mission home was a failure, but it is more than likely that his agreement to allow the earl of Moray

21. The medieval Castle d'Exeter at Slane lay in the path of Robert and Edward Bruce and an estimated army of 20,000 Scots and Irish in mid-February 1317, which is said to have ravaged the countryside roundabout

to retain Man was given only after receiving guarantees that more resources would be ploughed into his Irish adventure. Thus Edward Bruce returned to Ireland, presumably in October 1316, and prepared for the next stage of his struggle, in the knowledge that his brother, Robert the Bruce, was soon to join him. Help was certainly needed. Apart from his own visits home to Scotland, he does not appear to have left the confines of what is now County Antrim since his disheartened return there in late February. His Irish supporters were doing their best to keep the pressure on the English, though perhaps only for their own benefit. We know that in 1316 the Uí Anluain (O Hanlons) of Armagh ravaged the area around Dundalk,[63] and that Ó Domnaill (O Donnell) levelled Sligo Castle which had only recently been rebuilt by the earl of Ulster. There is no evidence that Ó Domnaill was an ally of Bruce, and every reason to doubt it in fact, since he was no friend to Domnall Ó Néill, Bruce's mainstay. But in Connacht, Feidlim Ó Conchobair had been won over to the Scots cause, and having established himself as supreme over his rivals and been inaugurated as king, he launched a major offensive against the English settlements in the province. Unfortunately for him, though, in July 1316 the captured William Liath de Burgh had managed to secure his release by the Scots in exchange for his son, and he rallied the English against Feidlim and defeated and killed him, and countless others, at the battle of Athenry on 10 August.[64]

There was better news for Bruce elsewhere. The Irish of the Wicklow mountains, O Byrnes and O Tooles, had also taken the opportunity to rebel, and it was reported by the Dublin annalist that they had 'burned all the southern lands', namely Bray, as well as the ports of Arklow and Wicklow and the important royal fortification at Newcastle McKynegan, 'and all the adjacent vills'.[65] It may be that these were just the ordinary run-of-the-mill disturbances for which the area was noted, but that was not the perception that was abroad at the time. Contemporaries believed that it was the arrival of the Scots that produced the disorder. Here is what a Wicklow colonist said of the effects of the Scots' invasion on his locality:[66]

> ... The Scots enemies of the lord king arrived in this land, since whose arrival the Irish of the Leinster mountains, manifestly unable to restrain themselves, put themselves at war against the lord king, just as the other Irish in this land did, and they hostilely invaded, burned, and totally destroyed the aforesaid lands and tenements of the lord king at Bray and indeed all other lands and tenements of divers lieges of the lord king in those parts.

It was, after all, the deliberate intention of Edward Bruce to provoke such a reaction when he brought his armies into the valley of the river Barrow in the early days of 1316. After his victory at Skerries in County Kildare he made his way into Laois and, as we saw, spent some time dwelling among the Irish there. This had the desired effect: later, we are told, 'The O Mores burned and devastated Laois in Leinster',[67] and expeditions to quell these and other outbursts were necessary in 1316 and 1317, using up scarce government resources.[68]

Soon the trouble spread further afield. Maurice fitz Thomas, head of the Munster Geraldines, had to contend with a rebellion of the Irish of Desmond, described in the following terms by a local jury:[69]

> ... When the Irish of the surname of Odoneganes, who are the men and tenants of the aforesaid Maurice fitz Thomas, heard of the coming of Edward Bruce and of other Scots into the parts of Ireland, at the time when the Scots came as far as Skerries, the said Irish of the surname of Odoneganes and all the other Irish of the parts of Desmond hostilely rose up against the lord king, openly making war against the said lord king and his lieges, hostilely committing arsons, homicides, robberies and very many other evils, both in the land of the said Maurice fitz Thomas and of other lieges of the lord king in the county of Limerick.

It is clear that the jury believed this to be no ordinary rebellion, but an impassioned outburst occasioned by the Scots presence. And it was in an effort to stir up just such emotions that King Robert himself came to Ireland.

Edward certainly needed assistance if he was to make his position more secure. In October 1316, the Irish treasurer was empowered by Edward II to promise £100 for 'any deed committed against Edward de Brus, a rebel being in the land of Ireland, by which he may lose life or limb'.[70] Not long after he returned to Ireland, on 1 November 1316, 300 of Bruce's men-at-arms are said to have been killed in Ulster by John Logan and Hugh Bisset of the Glens, while on 5 December Logan and John de Sandall captured one of Edward's lieutenants, Sir Alan Stewart, whom they imprisoned in Dublin Castle.[71] It looked like the tide might have been turning against Edward, so Robert's presence was desperately needed. Archdeacon Barbour tells us that the king set sail for Carrickfergus from Loch Ryan in Galloway, and Friar Clyn adds that he arrived about Christmas.[72] The Irish annals also record the king's arrival, placing it at the start of their entry for 1317, and noting that Robert brought with him a great army of galloglass, 'to help his brother Edward and to expel the foreigners from Ireland'.[73] A council of war was held to plan their next action, and the decision was taken to launch a major offensive through Ireland, from one end to the other, as Barbour puts it.[74] By late January-early February they were on the move. They took their way south again through the Moiry Pass and, joined by what the Dublin annalist calls 'the army of Ulster', presumably Ó Néill and his subordinates, they allegedly numbered in total 20,000 men by the time they reached the vicinity of Slane in County Meath in mid-February, ravaging the countryside as they went. The earl of Ulster was at his manor of Ratoath and may have attempted to ambush the Scots (if Barbour is to be believed), but his opposition proved futile and he and his family fled to Dublin, and took refuge in St Mary's Cistercian abbey.[75]

Not surprisingly, the people of Dublin, aware that the invincible Robert Bruce was advancing on the city, began to panic. On 21 February, the mayor, Robert de Nottingham, went to St Mary's abbey and forcibly seized Richard de Burgh and some of his family and imprisoned them in Dublin Castle.[76] Obviously, the suspicion was that the earl could not be trusted and was in collusion with the Scots, but Edward II does not seem to have doubted de Burgh and ordered an inquiry into his imprisonment. To be on the safe side, he directed that the earl be given a safe conduct to England, although this did not happen even though the earl's release was not secured until 8 May, when the panic had abated. It was not an entirely unreasonable fear. Apart from the fact that this once mighty earl had proved a very feeble opponent of the Bruces since their arrival in Ireland, he had an association with their family stretching back at least thirty years. He had been at the Bruce castle at Turnberry in Ayrshire back in 1286 where he enlisted the support of the Bruces, Stewarts, and other Scots families for an offensive of his own in Ireland. A decade later his sister was given in marriage to the head of the Stewart family, Sir James, a leading ally of the future King Robert, and the dowry that went with her was a castle and estate at Roo, near Limavady in County Derry. Six years later, Robert Bruce married de Burgh's daughter, who was now, therefore, the queen of Scotland.[77] Well might Dubliners suspect that he was less than committed to the overthrow of his own son-in-law. And yet that seems more than likely to have been the case. When Robert Bruce married Elizabeth de Burgh it was a fairly conventional aristocratic alliance: Bruce and de Burgh, as earls of Carrick and Ulster respectively, were, for all intents and purposes, next-door neighbours separated only by a narrow channel thirty miles wide. Subsequent events, though, had driven a wedge between them. When Bruce seized the Scottish throne in 1306 he became a traitor to Edward I and any support that the earl of Ulster might have given him would leave him open to a charge of treason himself. Whatever else Richard de Burgh was, he was no fool, and neither

22. This is one of the few visible stretches of the medieval town walls of Dublin, which were said to be in a very bad state of disrepair when Robert Bruce approached the city in the early weeks of 1316, although however badly defended the town was, he chose not to attempt an assault

23. Nenagh Castle, County Tipperary: the town of Nenagh, a possession of the chief governor, Edmund Butler, was an inevitable target of Scottish attack in 1317 as they headed west towards Limerick

would Bruce have sought his assistance, because he would have known better than to expect any. That is why, when Robert was holed up in Rathlin island in the winter of 1306–07, and decided to send emissaries to the Irish mainland in pursuit of allies, it was to the native Irish he appealed – the only ones who could help him without being guilty of treason since they were by definition England's enemies, and outside the law.[78]

So it seems that de Burgh's arrest was just the consequence of the paranoia brought on by the approach of the Scots army ever closer to the outskirts of Dublin. From Slane, they had travelled via Skreen to Castleknock within sight of the city, where they set up camp on 23 February, capturing the lord of Castleknock, Hugh Tyrrell, and making use of his castle. The citizens of Dublin, in anticipation of an assault, had hurriedly tried to strengthen the defences by pulling down houses leaning against the walls and, since it was the north-west corner of the walled town, nearest the only bridge across the Liffey, that was most vulnerable, they decided in desperation to dismantle St Saviour's Dominican priory (on the north side of the river near the bridge) and use the stone to build up vulnerable stretches of the wall along the quay.[79] Now the only fear was that the Scots might nevertheless find vantage points in the suburbs to the west of the town, and quarter themselves there in advance of an assault or a siege, so the Dubliners took the drastic decision to fire the western suburbs along the old route that is now Thomas Street. This was the most effective way of denuding the area of enemy shelter but, of course, fire so started is difficult to stop and it was later claimed that up to four-fifths of the suburbs were destroyed on that critical night of 23 February 1317, although in view of the circumstances the citizens were later

24. Castleconnell, County Limerick: if proof was needed of the earl of Ulster's opposition to Bruce's plans for Ireland it was visible for all to see when the Scots burned Castleconnell in March 1317

pardoned for their actions and given a significant reduction lasting until 1323 on the annual rent (or 'farm') payable to the king.[80]

The tactic worked. King Robert, if indeed he had intended to take Dublin, thought the better of it (the last thing he needed was a siege that might pin his men down as long as that of Carrickfergus had), and marched south towards Leixlip, County Kildare, where he is said to have spent four days, burning and looting. Joined again by the de Lacys, the Bruces now headed towards Naas and then Castledermot where, as earlier at Dundalk, they acted with particular vengeance against the Franciscan friary, again destroying its books, vestments and altar ornament. From there they proceeded through Gowran, County Kilkenny, and had reached Callan by 12 March. By now the leading Anglo-Irish magnates were assembled in Kilkenny considering their options. They were led by the justiciar Edmund Butler, who had recently been given the title 'earl of Carrick' as a reward for his efforts, though it soon lapsed. Also there was John fitz Thomas's son; the latter had died in September 1316 soon after becoming the first earl of Kildare, and now his son, Thomas fitz John, was head of the family and the second earl of Kildare. Maurice fitz Thomas of Desmond and Richard de Clare of Thomond were there too, as were John le Poer of Dunoil and Arnold le Poer.[81] They dared not oppose the Bruce brothers in open battle, so the latter continued on their way into Munster, passing by Cashel and then Butler's own town of Nenagh, which they made sure to plunder. Their primary hope seems to have been that the O Briens of Thomond might join forces with them.[82]

Their expectation was not unreasonable. A jury of Anglo-Irishmen that met in 1316 had declared that the Skerries campaign of Edward Bruce had caused a

25. Although the capture of Limerick seems to have been their goal in early 1317, the Scots never did manage to cross the Shannon, and the defences of the city were not therefore put to the test

rebellion in Thomond by Brian Bán O Brien.[83] The great propagandist tract known as *Caithréim Thoirdhealbhaigh* ('The Battle-career of Turlough') preserves the information that Brian Bán's brother Donnchad then went north, met the Bruce brothers, and invited them to bring their campaign to Thomond, 'entreating them that they would come on this progress; as come they did'.[84] An annalist explains that it was their intention to join up 'with all the army of Ireland', near Singland in County Limerick,[85] and clearly their negotiations with the O Briens had led them to expect widespread backing for the offensive. But this was not to be; just as in Connacht where the O Conors were more concerned with internal contests, the Bruces found themselves embroiled in local rivalries between different contenders for the kingship which the Scots were powerless to surmount.[86] Another problem was that the Scots expeditionary force was all the time being shadowed by the government army.[87] The justiciar, Edmund Butler, had left Dublin before the Bruces arrived on the scene, intent upon raising an army in Munster to oppose them. Leaving his manor of Carrick-on-Suir, County Tipperary, on 24 February, he travelled by way of Dungarvan and Tallow in County Waterford until he reached Cork city on 27 February. Here he stayed for almost a week, bargaining with the Cork gentry about the terms under which they would serve against the Scots. On the day in which the Scots reached Castledermot, 5 March, he was in Affane, County Waterford, en route west to Ardmayle and Thurles, his own neck of the woods, where he recruited a force of nearly 300 men, hardly sufficient to tackle the Scots head on (although these are just paid troops, and would have been matched by equal or greater numbers of unpaid forces). But by the time the Bruces had reached Cashel, about 18 March, the justiciar's army had increased to about 200 horsemen and 300 foot, and this slightly larger force may just have been enough to cause the Scots to stop their southerly march and head west towards Nenagh, and from there to the earl of Ulster's unoccupied fortress at Castleconnell on the Shannon just above Limerick, at which point an attempt on that heavily fortified city, with the O Briens' support, may have been contemplated.

It would have now been clear to Butler that Limerick was the target, and so he headed for his own manors of Caherconlish and Ludden, just south of Limerick, by now commanding a force of about 1,000 men. There was some skirmishing – for example, the seneschal of Carlow, Adam Bretoun, was given £20 in return for 'fighting against the Scots in the district of Ludden, in the company of Thomas fitz John, earl of Kildare'[88] – but for a period of about ten days at the start of April there seems to have been something of a stand-off between both armies. The apparent inactivity on the part of the justiciar is easily explicable as caution: he had very little to gain from precipitating an open conflict with the enemy, and he was, after all, restricting their movement and delaying any possible advance by them. As for the Scots, they were presumably still seeking to assemble as wide as possible an alliance of Irish forces, but hunger was no doubt taking its toll since the famine of 1317 was worse than that of the year before. Then news reached them that Roger Mortimer of Wigmore, who had been appointed king's lieutenant in Ireland, had landed at Youghal on 7 April, bringing fresh troops, and was heading north to join Butler's force.[89] Robert Bruce knew the danger that this development spelt and so quietly but hurriedly set about a retreat back to Ulster. Butler followed him, attacking the Scots somewhere east of Thurles about 16 April, before disbanding. But the earl of Kildare, along with a reputedly undisciplined force of dispossessed Ulstermen, followed the Scots as far as Naas. Some days later, Bruce's hungry and exhausted troops were said to have been sheltering in a wood near Trim, where they stayed a week, before finally struggling back to Ulster about 1 May.

Soon afterwards, about 22 May, King Robert returned to Scotland and may not have reappeared in Ireland for the best part of a decade, leaving his brother Edward to salvage what he could there. Most modern accounts ignore the statement of Barbour that at this point another great gathering of the Irish kings took place at Carrickfergus, where all but one or two of them renewed their homage to him as king, and 'every one of the Irish kings went home to their own parts, undertaking to be obedient in all things to Sir Edward, whom they called their king'.[90] Yet there may be something to this. It was probably at this point that his leading Irish ally, Domnall Ó Néill, wrote to the pope, on his own behalf and that of 'the underkings and magnates of the same land and the Irish people', and styling himself 'king of Ulster and by hereditary right the true heir to the whole of Ireland', explaining why he had renounced the kingship in favour of Edward Bruce, and seeking papal approval.[91] Such an overture is likely to have been the product of a general assembly such as that mentioned by Barbour, and presumably therefore took place. Apart from that, though, the records are silent for a full year and a half, until he finally launched yet another march south in October 1318. We have, frankly, no idea what he was doing in the interval, short of biding his time until the famine conditions eased, which they finally did when the harvest of 1318 produced a bumper crop. As to why he moved south when he did, there may possibly be some clue in the fact of his association with the de Lacys.

The opening accusation facing the jury that met in 1317 to consider the role of the de Lacys in the invasion was that they had sent envoys and letters to Bruce inviting him to come and conquer Ireland from Edward II.[92] This may have been a lie, but is more likely to have been a gross exaggeration, with some basis in fact, however slight. After his arrival in Ireland in April 1317, Roger Mortimer concentrated on punishing the de Lacys, his tenants, for siding with the Scots. He was at Trim Castle by May 1317, but they remained recalcitrant, even executing the messenger he sent to negotiate with them, and he was forced into combat with them twice before they yielded, several members of the family, including Walter de Lacy, fleeing to Edward Bruce.[93] Undoubtedly the reason that the de Lacys were so obstinate in refusing to deal with Mortimer, and colluding with Bruce, was because they intended to recover for themselves what they considered to be their ancestral patrimony, all Meath. The other half of Meath, as we have seen, had gone to the de Verdons, but the de Lacys now had an added reason for wanting to campaign against the latter, since in the summer of 1316 the head of the de Verdons had died leaving four daughters as co-heiresses, among whose husbands this vast estate would subsequently be divided.[94]

Now, Roger Mortimer was recalled from Ireland in May 1318, which opened the way for a possible assault on his and the de Verdon lands. So, Edward Bruce marched south in October 1318, with the de Lacys in tow, only to meet his death at a battle fought on the hillside between Faughart and Dundalk on 14 October. The commander of the army that opposed him was John de Bermingham of Tethmoy on the Laois-Kildare border. Why him? It may not be a coincidence that there was a history of friction between John de Bermingham and the de Lacys: twice in 1310 the king had referred to 'divers controversies' and 'contentions' between de Bermingham on the one hand and Walter, Hugh and Richard de Lacy on the other, ordering them to appear before the king's council in order to solve the dispute.[95] When Roger Mortimer arrived in Ireland in 1317 the Kilkenny-based friar John Clyn describes what happened, as follows: 'being joined by Lord John de Bermingham and Lord Nicholas de Verdon, he [Mortimer] ejected all of the nation and surname of Lacy out of Ireland; and he forced them to flee to Scotland in the summer'.[96] An important and neglected set of Dublin Cistercian annals tells us that, after the flight of Walter and Hugh de Lacy 'and others of their surname', Mortimer took into his hands all their lands and goods, 'and he enfeoffed Lord Nicholas de Verdon of a certain part and Lord John de Bermingham of another'; the de Lacys, he tells us, remained among the Irish of Meath until Christmas 1317, 'and immediately afterwards retreated to the castle of Carrickfergus and remained there with Edward Bruce'.[97] Mortimer, as we have seen, returned to England in May 1318, and the same annalist has it that he appointed John de Bermingham as keeper of his lands and tenements in Meath.

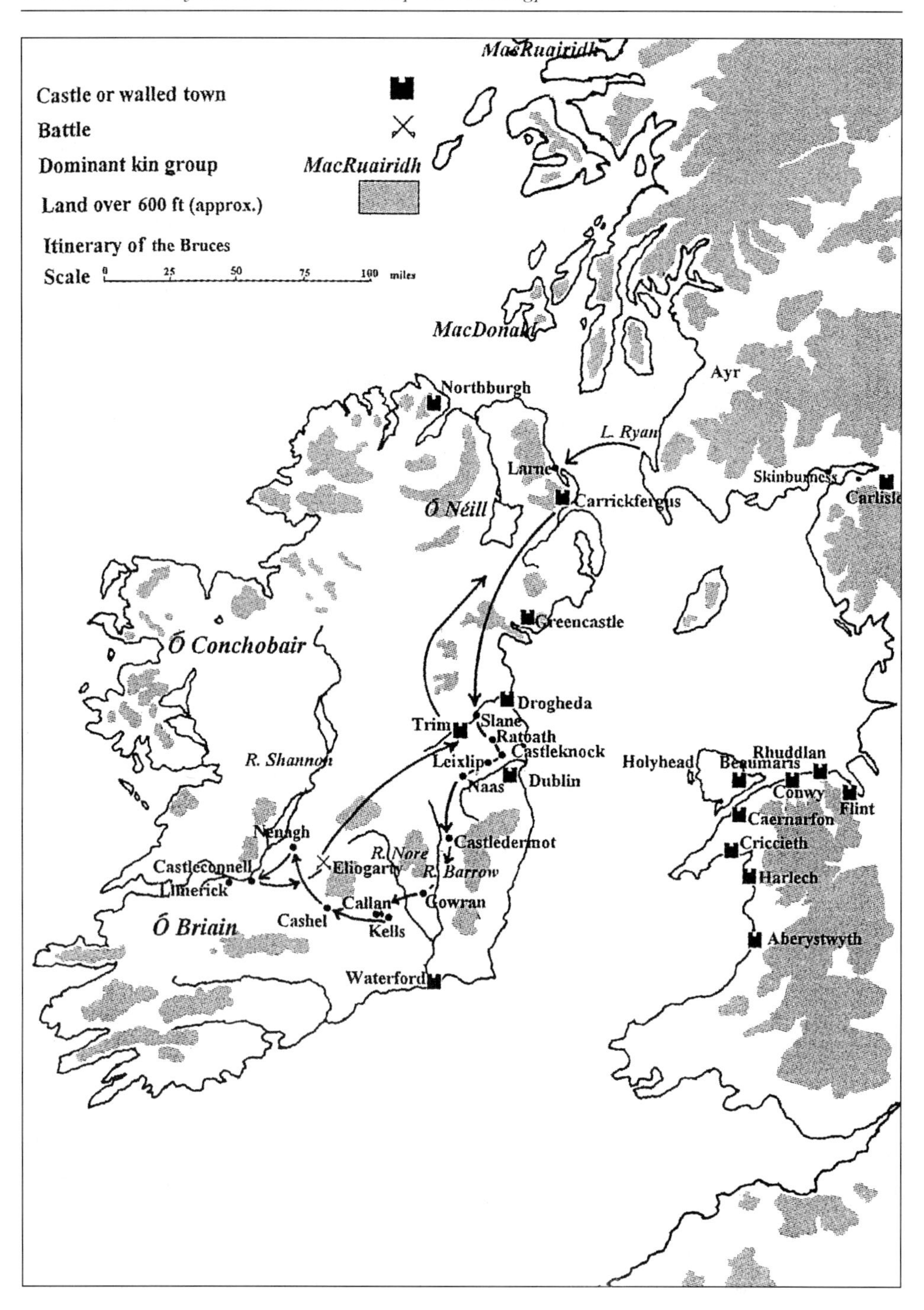

26. The Bruces in Ireland, 1317

Above *27. The local lords, the de Verdons, had earlier established a settlement at Faughart, as their motte still proves, and Bruce may have diverted his army to the location in order to plunder it*

Below *28. From the hilly ground at Faughart the town of Dundalk is visible below. It was a significant vantage point from which to fight against an army approaching from the town, and the defeat of the Scots must by any standard be deemed a shock result*

When, in October, Edward Bruce left Ulster on a new offensive for the first time in nearly a year and a half, the Dublin Cistercian annalist says that he, 'came with Lord Walter de Lacy and Lord Hugh de Lacy and with a multitude of Scots and Irish towards the town of Dundalk', a de Verdon town, of course, which Bruce had earlier burned. To let Friar Clyn finish the story: 'Lord Edward Bruce was killed with many Scots... at Dundalk, by John de Bermingham, and Milo de Verdon'. It seems from these accounts that at least part of the explanation for Bruce's last and fatal expedition was an attempt to assist the de Lacys to recover their Meath lands now that Mortimer was out of the way, or at least to wreak vengeance on those who had gained them, and that those 'loyalists' who ended the reign of King Edward Bruce were just as interested in driving away the de Lacys as in crushing the Scottish invader.

Whatever the reason, the battle of Faughart turned into a disaster.[98] According to Barbour, King Robert sent reinforcements to Ireland but Edward Bruce was too impatient for action and began his march south a day before they arrived. It is even possible that King Robert himself came to Ireland to help Edward – unusually, there is no record of any activity by him in Scotland for all of the period from August to November 1318 – but arrived too late to be of assistance.[99] Instead, his brother was accompanied by Sir John de Soules, younger brother of William de Soules, Sir Philip de Mowbray, several prominent members of the Stewart family, the de Lacys and their followers, and, commanding separate contingents of gallo-glass, the respective heads of the Clann Domnaill (Clandonald) and Clann Ruaidrí (Clanruari), none of whom survived the day. Opposing them were, as noted, John de Bermingham and Milo de Verdon, but also Richard Tuit and John Cusack, and even the archbishop of Armagh, Roland de Jorz. The date was 14 October, the location somewhere between Dundalk and Faughart, and the opposition were for the most the local gentry of Louth and Meath. Although we know that the fighting was intense and the outcome inevitably a close one to call, it was by no means a foregone conclusion that the Scots would lose. In fact, the great warrior and Scots nobleman Edward Bruce lost his life at the hands of an ordinary townsman of Drogheda, whose body was reputedly found after the battle covering that of the vanquished 'king of Ireland'. Contrary to the local tradition that Bruce was buried near the battle-site, he was decapitated after death, and his body quartered it seems; the leader of the victorious forces, John de Bermingham, brought Bruce's head to Edward II who rewarded him with a grant of the new earldom of Louth, while one of the four quarters, along with Bruce's heart and hand, was sent to Dublin, and the others to 'other places' to be gruesomely displayed, no doubt, hanging from the town walls.[100]

It was the end of a great experiment in Irish affairs, that would have seen the English regime overthrown and replaced by a Scottish one likely to receive more Irish support. Its collapse was greeted with joy by the English community in Ireland, and, if truth be told, Edward Bruce's death went unlamented by the Irish too. However, it is not true to say, as has frequently been asserted, that his death was 'universally' applauded by the Irish annalists: only one native obituarist condemns him, it is just that almost all surviving sets of Irish annals stem from this one source and therefore contain the entry. Nonetheless, it was the case that by the time of his death the Irish had had three years of war, famine, and misery and Bruce inevitably found himself being held responsible for events over which he had no control. And who could blame even his staunchest supporters if, as the inclement weather relented and the earth at last yielded forth a fruitful harvest, they breathed a silent sigh of relief that so too did the storm clouds of war finally lift with the death of Edward Bruce, the man who would be king.

2

The Bruce Brothers and the Irish Sea World, 1306–29

Seán Duffy

In the early summer of 1315, a fleet-load of Scots veterans of Bannockburn put ashore on the coast of what is now County Antrim. They were led by Edward Bruce, the only surviving brother of Robert I, and recently ratified as heir-presumptive to the Scottish throne. By any standards, it was a major expedition, apparently planned well in advance, to which a significant proportion of Scotland's hard-pressed resources was devoted. It amounted to a full-scale invasion: Edward Bruce adopted the title 'king of Ireland', set up his own administration (never really effective outside his powerbase in Ulster) to rival that of the Anglo-Irish colony based in Dublin, and, apart from occasional visits home to consult with his older brother, he was to spend the rest of his short life in Ireland, until his rather unexpected death in battle there in October 1318.

What the Bruce brothers hoped to achieve from their Irish venture is the subject of much debate.[1] At its core, argument centres on whether the Bruces ever really envisaged turning Edward Bruce's invasion into a permanent conquest, or whether they simply sought to exploit Irish dissidence as one of a number of levers likely to push Edward II into acknowledging Robert's claim to Scotland. Of course, the two theses are not mutually exclusive: Robert may have hoped for the former but been content with the latter.

It is not proposed here to seek to resolve the matter, merely to contribute to the debate in two ways. First, a degree of new light is thrown on the background to the invasion by two under-used texts discussed below, one an important chronicle account of the episode which has never previously been noted, the other a better-known letter of Robert I to the Irish kings, which I suggest redating. Second, the invasion will be discussed from a broader perspective than usual – broad, that is, both in a chronological sense, by treating of some of its precursors and parallels over the preceding two centuries or so, and also in a geographical sense, by opening up the discussion to include the 'Irish Sea province' (to borrow a phrase from the archaeologists and geographers). This refers here to the nexus of relationships and contacts between the native kingdoms and principalities of Wales, Ireland, Man and the Isles, and Scotland, and is an ever-present backdrop to the events of the period. Such relationships, needless to say, were of varying degrees of intensity. Within the Gaelic-speaking world they were particularly close, and I hope to show that the Bruce invasion is explicable – only, of course, in part, but to an extent generally underestimated – in the context of the long-term relations between Gaelic Ireland, Gaelic Scotland and the islands that lie between; much of what follows is an attempt to sketch in that background. But a still wider context should not be forgotten. Guided primarily by their common experience of English domination rather than by any sense of shared ancestry, the Welsh, Scots and Irish forged connections with each other (admittedly on quite rare occasions), and they were frequently perceived from without as a common threat to English royal policy in their own areas. This paper concludes with some discussion of this thorny subject, in particular whether there are grounds for believing that the Bruce brothers' invasion of Ireland was part of an attempt to form a broad-based league against England of this 'Irish Sea' world. This is what is intended by the 'Celtic alliance' of the final section of this paper, where 'Celtic' (as throughout) is merely a convenient shorthand for this four-sided set of relationships between the Celtic-speaking peoples of Wales, Ireland, the Isles and Scotland; it does not imply that they all shared a sense of common origin, let alone of 'Celticness'.

Historians treating the affairs of Ireland and Scotland in the Middle Ages rarely fail to note the existence of a single Gaelic world, extending in an arc from Mizen Head to the Moray Firth, and sharing a common language and culture and a broadly similar social order. The rigid division of historiography along national lines has, however, meant that until recently,[2] the theme has not been investigated much further, either with regard to the ways in which this shared 'Gaelicness' spilled over into the political arena, or, for that matter, with regard to the difficult question of its implications for the attitudes of Scots and Irish to each other. If this was indeed one 'world', it is perhaps a fair proposition that the bounds of political activity in it should to some degree have mirrored this sense of oneness: in other words, that an individual at one end of this common area should reasonably have contemplated, and have had little difficulty in justifying, political activity at the other end. It is perhaps the kind of problem that emerges when the bounds of what we would call statehood conflict with notions of nationhood: thus we regard *Alba* and *Éire* as separate countries, and the *Gaídil* as one people, but were the *Gaídil Alban* and the *Gaídil Érenn* one nation or two? Suffice it to say that throughout the Middle Ages, men

29. Robert Bruce's plans for an alliance of Scots, Irish and, if possible, the Welsh, have been the subject of much speculation over the years, but historians have recently come to view his plans as more than mere make believe; this stylised statue at the entrance to Edinburgh Castle is rather more fanciful

from one part of this Gaelic region involved themselves in the affairs of another part. It is an involvement better documented for some periods than for others and, if anything (perhaps only because of the wealth of source materials), seems to increase as the Middle Ages draw to a close. It is an involvement that is constant and, at times, particularly between Ulster and the highlands and islands of Scotland, all-pervading. And it is an involvement made with barely a nod in the direction of the nation-state boundaries to which we attach such importance. Somewhere into this pattern the Bruce invasion fits, at least in part.

Irish Links with the Isles

The islands that lie between Ireland and Scotland often provided the conduit through which this activity flowed. They were a no-man's-land, claimed for Norway in 1098 by the famous King Magnus Barelegs, and only ceded to Scotland in 1266. The Hebrides enjoyed a particularly close relationship with Ireland, beyond that dictated by mere geographical proximity. One of the legacies of the Vikings was the link they forged between Dublin and the Isles, so that under normal circumstances both shared the same ruler. When control over Dublin, often more nominal than real, passed to native Irish provincial kings from the mid-eleventh century onwards, so too did this link with and notional claim to the Irish Sea islands. Thus in 1060 Murchad, the eponymous ancestor of Diarmait Mac Murchada (the man who brought the Anglo-Normans to Ireland), took tribute from the Manx in his capacity as king of Dublin.[3] Two grandsons of the great Brian Bóruma were killed pursuing their family's dynastic interests in Man in 1073, another member of the same family (the Ó Briain royal house of Munster) perished there a generation later in 1096, and their influence remained real enough for a fourth scion of the dynasty actually to have himself installed some fifteen years later as 'king of the Isles'.[4] In or around 1153, three Dubliners who were nephews of a subsequent king of the Isles invaded Man from Dublin with an army of Manx refugees, and, at least temporarily, conquered the island for themselves.[5] The link outlasted the Anglo-Norman invasion of Ireland. According to Gerald of Wales, when the last native king of Ireland, Ruaidrí Ó Conchobair, besieged the new Anglo-Norman adventurers at Dublin in 1171, the men of the Isles came to his aid with a blockade of the harbour: they did so, he says, because of 'their [the Hebrideans'] fear of the threat of English domination, inspired by the successes of the English'.[6] It is an important statement. The English conquest of Ireland was, it seems, looked on as a threat to the whole Irish Sea polity.

The link with the Isles was also relevant in ecclesiastical matters. As late as 1219 the archbishop of Dublin was thought by the papacy to be metropolitan of the bishop of the Isles.[7] This has been assumed to be a momentary lapse of the otherwise precise papal memory,[8] since the Norwegian archbishop of Trondheim is later the undisputed claimant. But Trondheim's metropolitan claim may have been part of a renewed assertion of Norwegian supremacy in the Isles, a process which undoubtedly took place in the early thirteenth century, and especially after the accession of the powerful Haakon IV Haakonsson. In 1182 Pope Lucius III had confirmed to John Cumin, archbishop of Dublin, metropolitan status over the bishoprics of Wexford, Ossory, Leighlin, Kildare, and the bishopric of the Isles *(episcopatus Insularum)*.[9] And in the interval between the 1182 confirmation and the 1219 instance, two bishops of the Isles, Christian and Nicholas, neither of them Irish (both natives of Argyll, in fact), chose to be buried in Ireland at the monastery of Bangor, which suggests that they both did indeed acknowledge some Irish claim to superiority.[10] The papal chaplain, James, at the end of this period acted as legate not just for Ireland, but also for the Isles and Scotland, continuing a practice which had by then become regular.[11] Cardinal Vivian, in 1176, was appointed legate 'in Scotland, in the surrounding islands, in Ireland, and in Norway'; Peter of St Agatha, in 1178, was legate 'of Scotland, of Ireland, and the adjacent islands'.[12] It may be worth noting, by comparison, that the appointment in 1190 of William Longchamp, bishop of Ely, was as legate in England and Wales, and 'in those parts of Ireland in which the Lord John, earl of Mortain, the king's brother, has power and lordship';[13] John claimed to be lord of all of Ireland (and pre-invasion legates were indeed described as 'legate of all Ireland')[14] but the papacy here implicitly excludes the as yet unconquered parts of Gaelic Ireland from Longchamp's authority. One wonders whether this was not an acknowledgement that Gaelic Ireland was more appropriately dealt with in the context of its relationship with the Isles and Scotland. Whether this be so or not, some notion of Ireland's 'Irish Sea' hinterland remained current for a much longer period, for the university established in Dublin in the early years of the fourteenth century was intended to remedy the shortage of scholars not only in Ireland but also in a catchment area that included Man and the Hebrides, along the western mainland of Scotland, and on to Norway.[15]

It was commonplace for the Dublin government to be charged with the responsibility of keeping the peace in the Isles, at least at the southern end of the region. In 1212, for instance, King John commanded that if anyone should commit an act of forfeiture in the land of Ragnall (or Reginald), king of Man, his government in Ireland should aid in the destruction of such enemies.[16] In 1220, when the Manx king complained to Henry III that he feared a Norwegian invasion, it was the justiciar of Ireland who was again ordered to defend his kingdom for him.[17] Ragnall's brother, Amlaíb Dub (Olaf the Black), who succeeded him as king of the Isles, soon afterwards sought the assistance of Geoffrey de Marisco, justiciar of Ireland, in repelling attacks on Amlaíb and his merchants by pirates and by Alan, lord of Galloway.[18] When Amlaíb set out for Norway in 1237, the justiciar of Ireland was mandated 'to maintain and defend' him.[19] This remained standard procedure for as long as England was on friendly terms with the rulers of Man. After 1266 Man was legitimately held by the king of Scots, the heir to the throne bearing the title 'lord of Man' until his death in 1284.[20] The crisis following the death of Alexander III in 1286 gave Edward I his chance, and when a decision to annex the island was made, an Irish army undertook the task: in June 1290, Richard de Burgh, earl of Ulster, landed on the Isle of Man and oversaw its transference to Edward I's liege, Walter

30. Nothing brings home the closeness of the connection between Ireland and Scotland better the clear sight of one country visible from the other: the photograph, taken at the very castle in which Robert Bruce seems to have spent the winter of 1306–07, has Kintyre in the background

Huntercombe.[21] Even during the Bruce invasion of Ireland, when every penny was needed to stave off the Scots, Dublin was still expected to pay for measures to combat their activities as far north as the Hebrides.[22] It was fitting, therefore, that it was an Anglo-Irish sea captain, John of Athy, who, by capturing the Scots 'pirate' Thomas Dun in 1317, managed to overturn Scottish naval supremacy in the Irish Sea. His reward, and a way of compelling the Anglo-Irish to guard their back door, was a grant of custody of the Isle of Man, with instructions to provide from the issues thereof three ships for its defence.[23] There can be little doubt that, seen through Westminster eyes, both the intrusion of the Scots into Ireland and the rebellion of the Scots 'in maritime parts' were part of a single process.

The Irish Contribution to Scottish Wars

There were always men in Ireland ready and willing to throw their military muscle about in Scotland and in the islands. We tend to think of all the mercenary activity coming in the other direction, in the form of galloglasses. But it worked both ways. The underdog, the pretender and the malcontent in Scotland all found Irish support. Until well into the thirteenth century, the reigning Scottish dynasty continued to be vulnerable to the ambitions of rivals. On at least three occasions, in 1211, 1215 and 1235, Irish armies were the backbone of rebellions against royal

31. It is more than likely the case that Robert Bruce dispatched his now famous letter to the Irish, describing the Scots and Irish as 'our nation', from the Bisset castle on Rathlin island; little remains of it today, as this photograph shows

power in Scotland, on the latter two occasions being led by the sons of Irish kings.[24] When Man and the Isles acquired a new king in the year 1252, his backing too seems to have come from Ireland: late in the previous year the Irish justiciar had been warned by Henry III that Magnus, son of the former king Amlaíb Dub, proposed to raise an army in Ireland in order to invade the Isle of Man, and the justiciar was somehow expected to prevent such an army leaving Ireland.[25] And the Irish were not choosy about whom they helped. At the end of the thirteenth century pretensions to kingship in Scotland came from a much more dangerous source than the discarded scions of former royal stock, and there can be little doubt about the extent to which the Anglo-Irish and even the native Irish contributed, at a price, to Edward I's expeditions to conquer Scotland.[26] By now, though, one of history's most successful usurpers was waiting in the wings, and in his career too we can trace the ready recourse to Irish aid: one of Robert Bruce's first moves, having deposed the absentee reigning king John Balliol and set himself up in his stead, was to seek military assistance in Ireland.

In the autumn of 1306 Robert was forced to flee Scotland and took refuge, it appears, on Rathlin Island, off the north coast of Antrim. From there he despatched a diplomatic mission to the Irish mainland. In April 1307 four prominent individuals with strong Ulster links were paid ten pounds for 'their expenses in enquiring about enemies, rebels, and felons of Scotland who had come to Ireland and been received, together with religious persons and others, within the liberty of Ulster'.[27] Who were these 'felons of Scotland' and 'religious persons and others'? We are fortunate still to have a copy of Robert Bruce's now famous letter, addressed to 'all the kings of Ireland, to the prelates and clergy, and to the inhabitants of all Ireland', in which he talks about sharing the same ancestry, and being linked to the Irish by a common language and customs.[28] It was presented by deputies sent on Robert's behalf to negotiate some sort of alliance, and has generally been accepted as belonging to the period immediately prior to the Bruce invasion of 1315. Yet there are some strong clues in it to suggest an earlier date. To start with, the sender of the letter is styled 'king', so that, if Robert sent it (which is not entirely beyond doubt), it was written unquestionably after March 1306. He says that the purpose of the embassy is that 'our nation may be able to recover her ancient liberty' and, even though by this he means the Irish as well as the Scots nation, it sounds as if he is writing before his own reign began to be successful; certainly, after Bannockburn he would be less likely to talk about having yet to recover his nation's freedom. He then says that he is sending over to Ireland to negotiate in his name 'our beloved kinsmen' *(dilectos consanguineos nostros),* and, as the text survives only in a formulary, the scribe replaces the names that would have followed in the original with 'A, B, et C'. For some reason, though, when the document concludes by saying that Robert will ratify whatever the envoys conclude, they are named 'the aforesaid [envoys] T and A' *(predicti T et A).* The copyist appears to have neglected to alter the initials. Assuming this to be the case – and it must be emphasised that for as long as the formulary text remains our only copy of this document it can never be proven that the initials were not picked entirely at random – this means that the emissaries were kinsmen of Robert Bruce whose initials were T. and A. In the early spring of 1307, Thomas and Alexander Bruce, brothers of Robert, launched, almost certainly from Ireland, an invasion of Galloway comprising eighteen ships, a certain Irish king, and a large following. It was designed to coincide with Robert's own return from his Rathlin exile (in the company of a largely Irish host).[29] Alexander Bruce was at this point dean of Glasgow, and we may surmise that he was chief among the 'religious persons' mentioned above as having been received in Ulster at that time. The letter, therefore, is quite probably not the document which inspired the Bruce invasion of 1315 but a much earlier proposal sent by Robert Bruce in the winter of 1306–07.

The proposal was a failure, to the extent that the Irish army which responded to his call was wiped out upon landing, but it may have had longer-term implications. The value of Ireland as a source of supply to the English war effort has been demonstrated so forcibly[30] that we may be in danger of forgetting that the Scots too looked greedily upon Ireland for the same purpose. After the commencement of hostilities with England, the Scots could not continue to resist English pressure in the absence of supplies of horses, arms, foodstuffs and other provisions, and some at least of these came from Ireland. In 1295 writs were issued from the Irish chancery to prevent merchants taking out of Ireland 'any victuals etc. that might advantage anyone in Scotland', while attempts by the Scots to obtain assistance in Ireland were anticipated by the instruction to arrest anyone coming from Scotland to Ireland, 'clerics as well

32. There can hardly be a rock-sited castle in Ireland more majestic than Dunluce, County Antrim; although what survives is late, its origins lie in antiquity, and there was a castle here in the Anglo-Norman period, possibly constructed by or under the supervision of Richard de Burgh, Robert Bruce's father-in-law. Its location indicates the importance of the sea-route to Scotland

as laymen', something which closely parallels Robert's apparent embassy of 1306–07.[31] In January 1311, four years after this Ulster mission, Edward II ordered the chancellor and treasurer of Ireland to prohibit 'under the highest penalties' the exportation to 'the insurgent Scots' of victuals, horses, armour and other supplies which the king needed for himself and his forces in Scotland, but which he heard were being brought to the Scots by the merchants of Ireland: if a supply line of some sort was one of the products of Robert's Rathlin sojourn it may have proved pivotal in his independence struggle.[32] That the measures taken to disrupt it were less than effective is evident from the fact that the English government was now to attempt, at considerable expense, a permanent blockade of the Northern Channel to prevent supplies of men and goods reaching Scotland from Ireland.[33] For many years under the command of the Meic Dubgaill of Argyll and the Bissets of Antrim, these fleets were an attempt by the English to rule out Ireland as a source of supply to Scotland, and one may reasonably suggest that Edward Bruce's invasion of Ireland was partly an attempt to restore this source of supply, as much as to ruin Ireland as a source of supply for England. Certainly, that the need for supplies played some part in Edward's expedition is suggested by the fact that, immediately after defeating the earl of Ulster at Connor in September 1315, Thomas Randolph was sent back to Scotland with four ships 'laden with the goods of the land of Ireland'.[34]

ISLESMEN AND SCOTS IN IRELAND

The boundaries of Ireland may stop hard and fast at the island's coastline, but we have seen that the politico-military goals and activities of Irishmen did not. The reverse equally applies. To those beyond her shores there was nothing sacrosanct about Ireland's sea-board frontier. To some extent, it was merely one of the islands – admittedly the jewel in the crown – that lay to the west of Britain.

And throughout the Middle Ages any individual who came to control the other islands might reasonably seek to add Ireland to his domain. For the last quarter of the eleventh century, the Isles were dominated by Godred Crovan. The Manx *Chronicle* claims that he 'subjected to his rule Dublin and a great part of Leinster'.[35] Irish sources, calling him Gofraid Meránach, confirm that he ruled Dublin and had an active career in Irish power politics until his death from pestilence in 1095, and I think it not unreasonable to assume from what little we know of his actions that he did indeed extend into Leinster the boundaries of the Hiberno-Norse kingdom of Dublin, the *fine Gall*.[36] Others were quick to capitalise on his success. One of the few points on which most sources for the expeditions of Magnus, king of Norway, agree, is that between 1098 and 1103, having gained suzerainty over the Western Isles and having supplanted (temporarily) the Manx dynasty of Godred Crovan who ruled in the Isles and in Dublin, Magnus attempted in turn to subdue Ireland.[37] Irish Annals admit that the king of Ireland, Muirchertach Ó Briain, compromised with him, having hosted to Dublin to face him, and then consented to a marriage alliance and a year's peace; the *Saga of Magnus Barelegs* claims – not unreasonably – that he won 'Dublin and Dublinshire'.[38]

In or around 1156, Godred Crovan's grandson, Gofraid, king of Man and the Isles, tried to turn back the clock and make himself also king of Dublin; he appears to have been repulsed by Muirchertach Mac Lochlainn, king of Cenél nEógain in mid-Ulster, acting, however, in his capacity as king of Ireland.[39] Thirty years or so after the Anglo-Norman invasion of Ireland, a Gaelic poet urged this Gofraid's son, Ragnall, king of Man and the Isles, to attack Dublin and conquer Ireland.[40] The idea may be dismissed as a flourish of fanciful imagination; but then, if his dynasty had lost all chance of recovering Dublin, the poem's composition cannot long have preceded King John's grant to Ragnall of an alternative foothold in Ireland, which provided his galley fleet with a safe haven in the majestic harbour of Carlingford Lough.[41] By the same token, it is arguable that John de Courcy's decision to invade the kingdom of Ulaid or east Ulster was as much bound up with this involvement of the Isles in Irish affairs as it was a part of the Anglo-Norman occupation of Ireland. The Manx kings had a long history of mixed and often unfriendly relations with east Ulster, while at this time enjoying a friendly alliance with the Ulaid's natural enemy, the Meic Lochlainn of Cenél nEógain. Gofraid, the king of Man at the time, was married to Mac Lochlainn's daughter and he formed a similar alliance with de Courcy in giving him his own daughter, the famous Affreca.[42] Whatever de Courcy's own hopes and

33. Like most fortresses that cling to the north Irish Sea littoral and the Western Isles, Dunluce Castle was garrisoned and victualled by sea, probably by means of the extraordinary cave immediately below

34. The extant remnants of Castle Carra, near Cushendun, County Antrim, may now seem of little consequence, but the land was in the possession of the Bisset family from the mid-thirteenth century, who were presumably its builders (though perhaps at a later date); their transference from Scotland to Ulster at this point is an indication of the vitality of the links between the two countries

intentions, his intrusion into Ulaid was almost certainly used by the king of the Isles as a means of settling an old score.

The house of Somerled, ruler *(regulus)* of Argyll, was the main rival for power in the Irish Sea to the Manx kings descended from Godred Crovan. Somerled's descendants were no less active in Ireland. Domnall, his grandson, the eponymous ancestor of the Clann Domnaill (Clandonald), is said to have received messages from Ireland (indeed, from Tara!) to take 'the headship of the Western Isles and of the greater part of the Gaídil'.[43] The tradition is late and of negligible authority. Yet, in his youth, Domnall and one or more of his brothers allied themselves with the attempt by the Galloway adventurer, Thomas, earl of Atholl, to conquer a great swathe of territory in Ireland, from east of the river Bann to Lough Foyle, by attacking Derry and Inishowen in conjunction with the west Ulster kingdom of the Cenél Conaill;[44] and Domnall was probably the Mac Somurli *rí Airir Gaídil* ('king of Argyll') killed with the king of the Cenél Conaill at Ballyshannon in 1247.[45] It is perhaps to this latter event that the tradition of his summons to Ireland refers, for he did head the army of the Irish of north-west Ulster against Anglo-Norman intrusion into their kingdom.

Domnall's son and successor was Aengus Mór mac Domnaill, lord of Islay, and sometime about the middle of the thirteenth century a poet writing in Ireland composed a poem for him which not only recounts Aengus's many journeys around the west coast of Ireland, but also mentions three members of the former

Hiberno-Norse dynasty of Dublin – Thorkill, Ivar and Olaf – as being linked to Aengus (perhaps by marriage in an earlier generation). Significantly, too, he describes this Highland lord as *flaith Fáil,* prince of Ireland.[46] Fanciful? In one sense, yes. But forceful evidence links Aengus with the first stages of the Gaelic resurgence in Ireland. The famous revolt by Brian Ó Néill, king of Cenél nEógain, began in the early 1250s. In 1256, Henry III commanded his bailiffs and subjects in Ireland not to allow Aengus mac Domnaill, or other Scottish malefactors, to be received in Ireland, an instruction that was to remain in force for a period of seven years.[47] It is significant that the king of the Scots was to provide the names of Aengus's accomplices to royal officials in Ireland, suggesting that Henry III's action was taken at the Scots king's request. The evidence seems to suggest that Aengus or other men from Gaelic Scotland had entered into a two-way bond with Ó Néill. Perhaps they offered to help him out in Ulster, after which men from Ireland would be made available to resist the pressure which the Islesmen were clearly beginning to feel from the Scots king. This seems all the more likely in view of the fact that, just weeks before the infamous battle of Down in 1260, which cut short Brian Ó Néill's rising, and no doubt in connection with the preparations for it, the justiciar of Ireland was warned not to allow persons from Scotland to be received in Ireland; more importantly, he was to arrest any of them he found seeking confederacies with the Irish which might be *to the King of Scots' damage.*[48] This reference to the detriment that might ensue to the Scots king should anyone from Scotland succeed in forming a confederacy with the Irish is surely revealing. It points to the conclusion that the Irish campaign which began at Cael Uisce in 1258 and ended at Down in 1260 (considered critical to the 'Irish rally' since first highlighted by the great pioneer of the subject, Eoin Mac Néill)[49] was as much to do with undermining the expansionism of the house of Malcolm Canmore in Scotland as countering that of the Plantagenets in Ireland. If so, it is a helpful reminder of the danger of viewing events in the Gaelic world in too narrow a context.

But the Norwegians had not given up their hopes of making something of their western possessions. Norse activity in the Western Isles in the first half of the thirteenth century appears to have been more intensive than it had been for a long time. The Norse claim to overlordship, indeed their insistence on the personal performance of homage by the kings of the Isles, appears to have strengthened. With it came occasional, no doubt half-hearted, stirrings of interest in Ireland. In 1224, when Hugh de Lacy, Ulster's forfeited earl, was attempting to make a comeback there, it was secretly reported not merely that he sought to enlist both horse and foot in Scotland to accompany him (which in itself is an important indicator of transmarine activity), but also that the king of Norway would that summer go to Ireland to de Lacy's aid.[50] When King Haakon came west in 1263 it was partly to restore the Isles to Norwegian control, but his ambitions were not so limited. He had only three very enthusiastic allies in the Irish Sea region, all three of them deeply involved in Irish affairs. The first was Magnus, the king of Man who, as already noted, won his kingdom in 1252 with an army raised in Ireland. The second was Dubgall mac

Ruaidrí, who was father-in-law of the king of Connacht, Aed na nGall Ó Conchobair, and who was active off the west coast of Ireland in 1258, presumably helping his future son-in-law counteract English settlement of the area. The third was Dubgall's brother, Alain mac Ruaidrí, leader of the company of galloglasses whom Ó Conchobair obtained as his wife's dowry in the following year – an event usually, but no doubt erroneously, cited as the first instance of galloglass activity in Ireland.[51] It was Ó Conchobair who had been responsible for the above-mentioned Cael Uisce initiative of 1258, by which he aimed to secure a compromise candidate for a restored high kingship. He had offered the position to Brian Ó Néill, only to see him killed at Down within two years, and he is thought now to have offered that position to Haakon, as the saga says, 'if he would rid them of the trouble to which English men had subjected them, because they had occupied all the best lands by the sea'. Haakon sent a Hebridean embassy to Ireland, which reported that the Irish 'offered to maintain his whole army, until he freed them from the power of English men'. Though himself attracted to the idea, the Norse king was eventually dissuaded from sailing to Ireland in response.[52] Undoubtedly, the king of Scots had as much reason to fear a resumption of Norse activity in Ireland as the king of England had, and we may suspect that when the sheriff of Ayr accounted in 1265 for the expenses of Adam Bruning, sent at some point 'on a mission of the lord king [of Scotland] into Ireland', the embassy was part of an attempt to calm waters troubled by recent events.[53] In any event, Ó Conchobair's offer to the Norse king may have sprung from a belief (right or wrong) that, failing an Irish candidate, someone with the right power and connections in the Hebrides offered the best prospect of galvanising resistance in Ireland. But Haakon's whole expedition was disastrous. The Norse cut their losses and by the Treaty of Perth sold the Western Isles to the Scottish crown. As a result, far from the Hebrides wresting themselves free of Scots royal interference, from this point on the Isles were much more intimately entwined with mainland Scottish affairs. And if involvement in the west led almost inevitably, as it appears, to contact with Ireland, then the Scottish kings were heading rapidly in that direction.

The Bruces in the Gaelic World

An English chronicle, the 'Continuation of the Annals of Nicholas Trevet' (which has not previously been noted by writers on the Bruce invasion), contains an interesting account in which we are told that Edward Bruce's intention in 1315 was to make himself not just 'king of Ireland' but 'conqueror of the Isles'.[54] Edward, therefore, as Lord of Galloway and later earl of Carrick and, perhaps, as we shall see, prince of Wales, would rule over a kingdom that encompassed the entire Irish Sea world. If intended, it was a scheme that was breathtakingly innovative. However, it must be said that besides the 'Continuation' to Trevet, no other source as much as hints at such a prospect. At the very least, though, this account – which otherwise is very reliable, and particularly well versed in Scottish affairs – is

35. One of the most dramatically sited castles on the Irish coast, Kinbane in north Antrim, is all but cut off from the landward side and is testimony to the capacity of the sea to act as a means of communication, in this case between Somerled's MacDonnell descendants and their 'new' home in the Glens of Antrim

evidence that informed contemporaries could reasonably reach such a conclusion from recent events. In support, it is interesting to note that Robert Bruce's fourteenth-century biographer, Archdeacon Barbour, tells us that immediately after Edward Bruce's invasion-fleet set out for Ireland in the early summer of 1315, Robert himself sailed to the west, and had his ships carried over the isthmus at Tarbert; when the men of the Hebrides heard this they were utterly dismayed, Barbour says, for they knew by ancient prophecy that whoever should accomplish such a feat would have the dominion of the Isles, and no man's strength would stand against him, whereupon they all submitted to him.[55] One does not have to believe the full letter of the account to accept its spirit: that the attempt to subdue Ireland went hand in hand with an effort to conquer the Isles. Indeed, Edward Bruce's lieutenant in Ireland, Thomas Randolph, earl of Moray, was confirmed by King Robert as 'lord of Man' in 1316. The document securing his possession of it was almost certainly drawn up in Edward's presence, during one of his absences from Ireland; it is dated 30 September 1316, and was made 'by counsel and consent of Edward, by God's grace king of Ireland' and bears his seal.[56] This is perhaps an acknowledgement of Edward's position as Robert's heir-presumptive, but one wonders whether it does not reflect the fact that Man was within the sphere of influence of the new king of Ireland, Edward Bruce.

It is likely, indeed, that Edward only got the opportunity to attempt to make himself king in Ireland because he had already proved himself a figure to be reckoned with in the Irish Sea region. The Bruce family was popular there. One reason is that they appear to have been more fully integrated into Gaelic society than is generally allowed. There are a number of indications of this. Story has it that about the year 1140 one of the most illustrious of Irish saints, Malachy Ó Morgair, had cause to place a curse on an earlier Robert Bruce of Annandale and his successors. King Robert's grandfather sought to lift the imprecation on a visit to Saint Malachy's tomb at Clairvaux about 1272, by endowing the abbey with lands in Annandale to pay for lights to burn for ever at the Irish saint's shrine. Such reverence for the Irish holy man is surely revealing, and events, we may suspect, were to convince Robert I that the power of Malachy's malediction remained, because within weeks of the death of his last surviving brother, Edward, after a three-and-a-half-year reign as king of Ireland, Robert himself provided for a lamp and a candle to burn perpetually at the altar of Blessed Malachy in the Cistercian abbey of Coupar Angus.[57] Robert's mother was Marjorie, daughter of Neil, last in that line of native 'Celtic' earls of Carrick; Robert was therefore half 'Celtic', and we may see the family's interest in maintaining the link – or his mother's influence at work – in the decision to name one of Robert's brothers, Neil, after his grandfather. Robert's biographer, Barbour, who had no great affinity with the Celtic world, nevertheless recorded an episode in which 'Marthokys sone' (that is, Robert, a reference to his Celtic ancestry through his mother), survives a confrontation with Mac Dubgaill of Argyll at Dáil Rígh in 1306: Bruce's opponent compares his survival to the legendary escape of Goll mac Morna from Fionn mac Cumhaill;[58] Bruce, in other words, every bit as much as Mac Dubgaill, fitted into the mould of the hero/anti-hero of Ossianic tradition. The Bruce family practised fosterage: we know from Barbour that Robert Bruce had a foster-brother, and indeed one source, if accurate, seems to compel the conclusion that Edward Bruce himself was fostered in Ireland.[59] His brother Thomas, whom I mentioned earlier as probably having been sent to Ireland in 1306, was described by one writer who usually knew what he was talking about as having 'always hated the English'.[60] Among the Bruces' most constant allies were families much of whose recent wealth had been obtained by monopolising the mercenary trade with Ireland. For instance, Fordun credits Bruce's recovery in and after 1307 to the military help provided by Christina of the Isles; her father, Alain mac Ruaidrí, was, as already noted, one of the first galloglass captains that we know of to take service in Ireland. Edward Bruce's own Gaelic contacts are evident from the claim that the army involved in his Galloway campaign in the summer of 1308 was led by Edward and his lieutenants 'with the following which they had from the outer isles of Scotland', as the *Chronicle of Lanercost* has it[61] (and virtually the same phrase is used by Edward II to describe reports of a threatened assault by Robert Bruce on the Isle of Man in the winter of 1310–11).[62] Four years later, Moryauch Makenedy and twenty-two of his Scots accomplices were captured in the Isle of Man by opponents of the Bruces, and Professor Duncan is of the view that their 'activities may be part of an attempt by Edward Bruce, earl of Carrick, to hold the island as a logical extension of his conquest of Galloway in 1313'.[63]

All of this is, I think, a measure of the support upon which the Bruces could rely in the Gaelic world. In fact, only the Mac Dubgaill wing of the descendants of

Somerled supported Balliol in the struggle for the succession to the throne, and then the English cause during the war of independence after Balliol's rule collapsed. Leading members – probably the heads – of the two other branches, Mac Domnaill and Mac Ruaidrí, died with Edward Bruce trying to establish his new kingdom.[64] Why should they be willing to do so? They were surely not just mercenary recruits to the Bruce cause, but men with a political or dynastic axe to grind in their own right. One reason may be that opponents both of the Bruces and of their allies in the Hebrides were finding a convenient haven in Ireland that needed to be eliminated. It is perhaps not too much of a generalisation to suggest that while Islesmen friendly to Bruce may have been recruited to the army of Domnall Ó Néill and other Gaelic lords sympathetic to King Robert, men from Argyll and the Isles who were losing out with Robert Bruce on the throne found a refuge in Ireland among Ó Néill's enemies, with the ruling branch of the Cenél Conaill of north-west Ulster, with the Clann Aeda Buide to the east of Ó Néill, and with others of his natural enemies. A brief glance at the situation may illustrate the point. At the time of the Bruce invasion, the reigning king of the Cenél Conaill was Aed, son of Domnall Óg Ó Domnaill. Aed's mother was a MacSween of Knapdale in Kintyre, but he had a half-brother, Toirrdelbach, whose mother was of the Clann Domnaill of Islay.[65] The two half-brothers were inveterate opponents. Toirrdelbach had had himself proclaimed king in 1290, using the military might of his mother's family, the Clann Domnaill; both he and Domnall Ó Néill (later, of course, the Bruces' main ally in Ireland) were banished from their kingship within the year by the earl of Ulster, and we may take it that both, and ipso facto the Clann Domnaill, had made common cause.[66] When Toirrdelbach was banished again in 1295, the Four Masters, uniquely among the Gaelic annalists, tell us that he sought refuge among the Cenél nEógain (with Ó Néill) and the Clann Domnaill (presumably in the Isles). Toirrdelbach was killed in 1303 by his half-brother Aed,[67] who continued to rule after him, in opposition to Domnall Ó Néill and his Hebridean allies. Aed was anything but sympathetic to the Bruces when they invaded Ireland: when double tragedy struck Ó Néill in 1318, first with the death of King Edward Bruce at Fochart, and second with the death at Derry of his own eldest son and heir, Seoan (who may perhaps have been intended to succeed Edward Bruce as king of Ireland), it is worth noting that it was in a conflict with Aed Ó Domnaill, and that Seoan Ó Néill had by his side an unnamed 'Mac Domnaill' from Scotland.[68] The Clann Domnaill was, therefore, losing out while the unfriendly Aed Ó Domnaill was king of Cenél Conaill; it had much to gain by replacing him with a more accommodating relative. We can see just what could be gained by looking at the career of Aed Ó Domnaill's kinsman, John MacSween of Knapdale. He opposed Robert Bruce, and his family had lost their lands in Kintyre to John of Menteith, a man who backed Bruce. MacSween tried to persuade Edward II to restore his lands to him, showing his good faith by joining Hugh Bisset's galley-fleet in the Northern Channel. He failed, but at some point found compensation in Ireland: he came to north Donegal (doubtless with Aed Ó Domnaill's connivance), massacred the Uí Bresléin, and, as Eogan Mac Suibne, became the first in a long line of MacSweeney lords of Fanad.[69]

36. This O Conor tomb and effigy in the Dominican priory in Roscommon is ornamented with images of gallo-glass in full battle dress: they personified the military link between Ireland and western Scotland so prominent from the mid-thirteenth century onwards

Likewise, there were enemies of Bruce and his Highland supporters who not only harassed them with fleets operating out of bases in Ireland and financed by the English and Irish exchequers, but who also sought to obtain in return grants of land in Ireland. When Edward Bruce invaded Ireland, the head of the Meic Dubgaill, John of Argyll, having lost everything he possessed, was living the life of a refugee in Ireland, the Irish exchequer having been ordered 'to provide decent sustenance for him and his household'; when he retook the Isle of Man for the English in the winter of 1314–15, and installed therein a garrison of dispossessed Hebrideans – an expensive operation – the whole exercise was financed and supplied from Dublin.[70] In order 'to make good his losses from the Scots' the king ordered the (probably very reluctant) justiciar and treasurer of Ireland to make him a suitable grant.[71] Dungal Macdouall, the Galloway lord responsible for the capture and subsequent execution of Robert's brothers Thomas and Alexander in 1307, was vengefully ejected from his lands by Edward Bruce the next year, came to Ireland in the king's pay, and sought a grant of the land of Leixlip until he recovered his own estate.[72] Duncan Macgoffry, an adherent of Mac Dubgaill and the man responsible under him for the recapture of Man for the English, was in 1316 seeking a grant of the ward of the land of Nicholas Ledwich in Meath 'to maintain his wife and children till the latter are fit for the King's service'; soon afterwards the king granted him livery of lands in Meath held by the monks of Dundrennan in Galloway but forfeited for adherence to the Bruces, and Duncan, from having been a Hebridean sea captain, was to spend the next few years guarding the royal castles in the Wicklow mountains.[73] Rooting out these thorns in their side and putting a stop to their activities must have been a priority for Bruce and his allies. The Clann Domnaill, conversely, gained massively from their support of Bruce, obtaining lands forfeited by others who opposed him. They stood to gain further if Edward should prove successful in Ireland. Indeed, Aengus Óg Mac Domnaill (who obtained three very extensive grants of former Mac Dubgaill and Comyn lands from Robert Bruce) married into an Ulster dynasty which backed the invasion – the Uí Chatháin kings of Ciannachta in north-east Ulster.[74] The hope must have been that the outcome of Edward Bruce's campaign would provide rich pickings in Ireland similar to those coming their way at home.

All told, there is enough evidence to suggest more than a cynical interest in the Gaelic west on the part of the Bruces. It is normal to ascribe a certain cynicism on Robert's part in addressing his letter to the kings of Ireland, which I discussed earlier. Bruce was, after all, an unmistakably 'Norman' king – in the sense that, whatever his mixed ancestry, he fitted in comfortably (admittedly in the second rank) among the monarchs of western Christendom – and yet in this letter he speaks of himself and the Irish people 'stemming from the one seed of birth', and has the gall (as some would see it) to talk of the love he shares with the Irish by virtue of a common language and customs. The letter was brought to Ireland by an embassy at a critical point in his career, but such a mission, to have any credibility, since its *sole* appeal was this allusion to the shared Gaelic inheritance of both parties, would have to be composed of, let us say, Gaelic-speaking ambassadors, or, at the very least, individuals who could reasonably pass themselves off as reflecting that to which the letter appealed. Yet we have seen that the envoys who delivered it were very possibly his own brothers and one must assume that they were considered eminently qualified to make such an emotional appeal. The 'special friendship' which he proposes 'permanently strengthening and maintaining inviolate' may mean nothing more than Robert's attempt to obtain some military backing for his renewed offensive in Scotland, but this, we know, was something rather easily bought in Ireland. There was surely no need to make an appeal to a shared national ancestry in order to buy mercenary support. It would hardly have been necessary to pretend that his purpose was to restore her ancient liberty to 'our nation', the Irish and Scots nation, if he sought merely to enlist the backing of individual freebooters. Surely the image of a Gaelic league is only employed if such is what is sought. And, if it is correct to date this letter to the winter of 1306–07, the Bruces sought such an alliance long before, as the usual interpretation goes, the flush of victory at Bannockburn took them to Ireland. But they did not stop there: Wales also seems to have fitted into their plans.

Wales and the Irish Sea World

By the thirteenth century the most dominant Welsh lordship was that of the prince of north Wales or Gwynedd, whose stronghold was Anglesey. Anglesey, though, could be viewed traditionally as one half of a couplet of islands: together with the Isle of Man it formed the Menavians.[75] And there are some interesting parallels between Manx links with Anglesey and Manx links with Ulster. Just as John de Courcy crowned his conquest of Ulster by marrying the king of Man's daughter, so Llywelyn ap Iorwerth of Gwynedd sought to do the same about twenty years later.[76] When Llywelyn's uncle Rhodri tried to snatch Anglesey for himself in 1193, he called upon the aid of the Manx fleet, just as de Courcy was to do after being expelled by Hugh de Lacy in 1204.[77] When Dublin became, after the Anglo-Norman invasion, a less hospitable refuge for exiled Manxmen, they seem to have turned increasingly to Anglesey. Lochlainn, the keeper of Man *(custos Mannie)*, a relative of the ruling king of the Isles, Harald, son of Amlaíb Dub, was drowned off the Welsh coast in 1238 while fleeing his king's wrath.[78] In some cases these Manx refugees appear to have been trying to get the Welsh to back their re-instatement, and thus we find Llywelyn ap Gruffudd and his brother Owain being ordered in 1253 to prevent their men interfering in the lands of the king of Man and the Isles, Magnus son of Amlaíb Dub.[79] After the extinction of the Manx dynasty and a period of turbulent Scottish suzerainty, the Isle of Man came under English control. After a quarter of a century this was interrupted abruptly in the early summer of 1313, when Robert Bruce himself landed and took the island. As to the threat this posed, the English response speaks volumes: Edward II ordered his castles in north Wales to be provisioned with armour and victuals.[80] Hence the confession forced out of Thomas Dun, the Scottish privateer, after his capture in the summer of 1317: although the English had since retaken the island, the new Scottish 'lord of Man', Thomas Randolph, was about to attack it, and, with the aid of some English traitors, intended to attempt Anglesey.[81]

But much more than a shared interest in the Isle of Man went to form this Irish Sea partnership. Admittedly, where the Scots and Irish were brothers, the Welsh were only cousins. Even had they no notion of common origin, however, they shared a fate which was bound to turn their minds to thoughts of common action: all three viewed themselves as peoples suffering jointly at the hands of Anglo-Norman aggressors.[82] Thus, to go back no further than 1216, the Welsh and Scots backed the French invasion of England of this year.[83] Twenty years later the Scots king was attempting to annex Northumbria, 'given confidence by the shadowy and ever suspected friendship of Llywelyn', as Matthew Paris has it,[84] while, at the same time, Richard of Cornwall was refused permission to leave the country because 'the earl's presence is needed in connexion with important matters, to wit, the Welsh affairs, a solemn meeting with the king of Scotland, and the proposed visit of the king to Ireland'.[85] In the king's eyes there is clearly a confluence of concern with matters Celtic. The anxiety is clear from Henry III's response to the attempts of William Marshal (the younger), 'who is very powerful in England and Ireland', to find himself a new wife: about April 1224, Henry, explaining his reasons for choosing to give William his own sister in marriage, claimed it was done in case he should choose to marry the Scots king's daughter, 'where no small peril would have threatened King Henry, the closeness of Scotland to Ireland, and the land of the Marshal, making the alliance the more dangerous'.[86] Sometime later Henry is reputed to have refused to go on crusade, saying 'I suspect the king of France; I suspect more the king of Scots; clearly Prince David of Wales opposes me' – how closely he echoes the poet of the dying years of John's reign who wrote:[87]

> A fourfold rage had crept upon the English nation. The first rage was conceived by its own pride; the second drew hither the warlike legions of the French; the third conducted the black troops of the Scots; the fourth bent the inconstant Welsh under their light garment.

Part of the explanation lies in English paranoia at the thought of encirclement by enemies. But this was not unjustified.

In 1258 – and it is probably no coincidence that Henry III's baronial troubles broke out in the spring of the same year – at least some of the Irish agreed to swallow their differences and make common cause under the leadership of Brian Ó Néill, the Dublin government reporting that the latter had assumed the title of 'king of the kings of Ireland', the Gaelic annals noting that he was given 'the kingship of the Gaídil of Ireland'.[88] At precisely the same time, Llywelyn ap Gruffudd assembled nearly all the lesser Welsh princes, receiving their homage, and adopting the title 'prince of Wales'. Interestingly, as appears to have been the case with Ó Néill of Ulster, it was his peers and erstwhile rivals who voluntarily offered him their support, as the *Brut* records:[89]

> ... the princes of Wales came to complain to Llywelyn ap Gruffudd of their being expelled by the Saxons, and they told him that they preferred to die in battle than to suffer being trampled upon in bondage by foreigners.

Thereupon he made a curious alliance with a powerful group of Scottish magnates, by which they promised to give him aid against the king of England and never to make peace with the latter to the Welsh prince's disadvantage.[90] We have already seen that in the following year Henry III was anxious that no Scots should enter Ireland for mischievous ends; but he did give the steward of Scotland permission to purchase victuals there, provided security be given that they would not be carried to the King's enemies in Wales.[91] When Brian Ó Néill was killed at Down in the following year the unusual step was taken of despatching his head to London; just as the impaling of the head on the city gates was the direst of all warnings to potential friends of the deceased, so the removal of the head of the king of Ulster to London was seen, one suspects, as a warning to rebels everywhere, including those outside Ireland with whom he was possibly allied.[92]

It would be foolish to draw any firm conclusions from these and other events. Direct evidence of contact between the various participants is very slight. We have little more to work on than the fact of similar events occurring in different locations at the same time, motivated by similar impulses – anti-English bias, a growing sense of having been wronged, perhaps a greater unity of purpose. Nevertheless, one does get the impression that at least in the eyes of the English government – whether correctly or not is an entirely different matter – rebellions in the Celtic lands were viewed as in some sense interconnected. Thus, whereas Edward I refers, in a letter he wrote in November 1276 to Philip, king of France, to 'our wars of Ireland and Wales which have lately broken out', scholars today may reasonably doubt whether these events were linked; but one suspects that, rightly or wrongly, there were no such doubts in the mind of the man against whom the wars were ultimately directed, the king of England.[93] It was an attitude which justified Edward in bleeding the Irish exchequer dry to pay for his Scottish campaigns, in forcing Dublin to pay for peace-keeping in the Isles, and which allowed Edward II, during a later bout of Celtic rebelliousness, to order that the fines levied from those who took part in the Welsh rising of Llywelyn Bren, in 1316, were to be put aside for use in repelling the incursions of the Scots elsewhere.[94]

No doubt it took the Edwardian conquest of Wales firmly to fix upon the minds of men the full import of recent events. Thomas fitz Maurice, the Anglo-Irish lord of Kerry, a long way from Wales in the far south-western tip of Ireland, revealed, in a letter written about the time of what was to prove the final conquest of Wales in 1282–83, that:[95]

> because of the war of Wales the Irish in the parts of Ireland are more elated than is their custom, and some are stirred by the war, others are prompted to make war.

Within a few years Rhys ap Maredudd, lord of Dryslywn, rebelled, and when his efforts were thwarted he was reported in February 1289 to be intent upon crossing over to Ireland,[96] where the Welsh cause must at last have been acquiring friends. And, as if the Welsh experience at Edward's hands had indeed helped to crystallise opinion, it was reported in 1295 that the Irish, Scots and Welsh would all rise at one and the same time so that, with Edward I engaged on all sides, the king of France would invade England.[97] A popular English song of the period complains that:[98]

> Everywhere are preached the fraudulent actions of faithless men, who molest England by force of arms; the French, Scots, and Welsh, whose power may the Omnipotent, who holds the world, repress! ... In the wolves' jaws the English have been of late; for, when all the turbulent chiefs of Wales were reduced, the Scots raised their spears, armed in their rags.

And there can be no doubt that the impressive Welsh rising that broke out under the leadership of Madog ap Llywelyn of Merioneth in September 1294 was an enormous boost to the morale of the Scots; it came at precisely the juncture at which Anglo-Scottish relations were nearing breaking point, and must have been one of the factors that convinced them to push ahead with their opposition to the 'moral shabbiness' of King Edward's Scottish policy.[99] He, though, pretended to have no concern for any new alignments in the Celtic world, and is reputed to have said before the battle of Falkirk in July 1298, 'What matter if both Welsh and Scots are our foes? Let them join forces if they please. We shall beat them both in a day'.[100] Such public unconcern, however, was not matched in private. In a letter which Edward had despatched to the earl of Ulster some weeks earlier, on 30 March, he admitted that, being about to set out for Scotland, to repress the Scottish revolt, he 'very much wishes that peace and tranquility be maintained in Ireland, and chiefly while the king remains in Scotland, prays the earl so to exert himself that peace and tranquility will be firmly maintained in his lands', an important reminder of what must have been a constant fear of Scottish hostilities spilling over into Ulster.[101]

A reader of native Irish sources would not notice any empathy with their Celtic cousins across the water until after the Edwardian conquest. But the tone definitely changes at this point. When the Welsh revolted in the winter of 1294–95, the *Annals of Inisfallen,* for instance, reported it, adding that Edward I took many Welsh with him to oppose the French in Gascony: 'That, however, was a pity', we are told, 'for the English cared not whether [the Welsh] fell there or survived'. When Edward followed his subjection of the Welsh with defeat of the Scots in 1296, the *Inisfallen* chronicler seems quite taken aback by it. He says of the English that:

> ... the king of Scotland and Scotland herself were taken by them without opposition or strife, and that was a disappointment to the Gaídil, for the Scots had always had a great reputation for valour.

A very different view of this event is taken, needless to say, in the English chronicles, a few of which (and the point is perhaps revealing) make quite a fuss over the importance of the fact – more symbolic than anything else – that this conquest of Scotland was performed with the assistance of some of the Welsh and Irish. Peter of Langtoft perhaps best captures the mood:[102]

> Now King Edward possesses Scotland entirely,
> Like Albanach had it at the commencement.
> The Welsh, the Irish, to our English aid doughtily;
> Whereby, the Scots have through ours imprisonment,
> And that land by this war is lost forever.
> The Welsh are gone home, and the Irish returned
> With sail and with wind; you English remain there.

How ironic it must have seemed, and what a demonstration of Edward's domination it offered, for him to defeat the third of his Celtic enemies using the forces of the other two. The significance should not be underestimated. In 1324 the seneschal of Gascony recommended that Edward II bring there in his army 'some of the men-at-arms of Scotland and Ireland, and two commanders of the highest birth from each of the *pays* of Wales [as]... It would add to the king's prestige to lead men from all these lands'.[103] I suspect the point was not lost on the vanquished either. If one looks back at the *Annals of Inisfallen,* when Edward I dies in 1307, the same annalist, though praising his undoubted abilities, cannot refrain from pointing out that:

> ... he did much evil to the church and to the laity – for by him fell Llywelyn, king of Wales, and his brother, David. And by him the Welsh were subdued and are in servitude since, without a king of their own over them. By him also great oppression was inflicted on the Scots, after he had banished their king, for according to report he killed 50,000 of them in one day, and also a countless number of them on all sides on another occasion.

There seems, though, to be a deliberate feeling of consolation to be had from the very next entry for 1307, which bluntly remarks: 'Robert Bruce was defending the kingdom of Scotland, and expelling the English therefrom'.

THE BRUCES AND THE 'CELTIC ALLIANCE'

And, frankly, Robert would have been a fool had he not sought in his bid for the throne to make use of every weapon at his disposal. That included sending his embassy to the Irish kings which, as I suggest above, may have occurred in the winter of 1306–07, and it must certainly have involved trying to rouse the Welsh to simultaneous revolt. Thus, within a matter of weeks of Robert's return from Rathlin in the spring of 1307, we find that a report reached the ailing Edward I that there were 'false preachers' in Bruce's army, spreading rumour of a prophecy of Merlin that, after King Edward's death, the people of Scotland and the Welsh would 'band together and have full lordship and live in peace together to the end of the world'.[104] If I am correct, this was circulating at almost exactly the same moment as Robert's letter in similar vein had been despatched to the Irish, and strongly indicates that the Bruces were even at this early date flying the kite of a pan-Celtic alliance. That is, of course, precisely what Edward Bruce sought to do again in 1315.

If Robert's letter to the Irish was not written immediately before the invasion of 1315, a not dissimilar document must have been composed in advance of that event to try to win over Irish support, and one might expect that Robert addressed it too. This would conform with the view of those who see the invasion as little more than the opening of a new campaign, with Robert despatching one of his trusty lieutenants, in this case his younger brother Edward, to take charge. Inevitably, this interpretation has helped to perpetuate the belief that a permanent conquest of Ireland was not contemplated, at least in the initial decision to descend on Ulster. But there seems little reason to doubt that Edward Bruce's invasion was a real attempt to secure a permanent conquest of Ireland. The interesting chronicle account mentioned earlier, the 'Continuation' of Nicholas Trevet, throws important light upon this matter. It makes the remarkable claim that, before the launch of the invasion, Edward Bruce, and not Robert:

> ... sent ahead a letter to the inhabitants of Ireland, which proved a source of great mutual hatred [presumably between Irish and English], and firmly proposing himself as king of that land in the future, about to bear the crown, so that he and his successors should for all time be known throughout the world as king of Ireland and conqueror of the Isles.

Now this is only a chronicler's version of events, so one does have to be careful, but there are good grounds for accepting the accuracy of the statement. If Edward did pave the way for his descent upon Ireland by sending ahead such emotive propaganda, the vagaries of document preservation have meant, as one might expect, that none of these letters to the Irish have survived. But by a remarkable stroke of fortune, a copy of a letter sent to Wales by Edward Bruce has. There has always been a certain doubt about this document because it is extant only in a printed transcript of the seventeenth century.[105] However, if Trevet's 'continuator' is right in saying such letters were sent as well to the Irish, it adds some circumstantial support for this Welsh letter's authenticity. Not only that, but this letter sent to Wales does seem to have had precisely the function suggested by Trevet's 'continuator' for the Irish document. It sought to emphasise the common ancestry of the Welsh and Scots (in the letter to the Irish, if we had it, this would be the common ancestry of the Irish and Scots), and the continual oppression both had suffered at the hands of the English, who desired neither peace nor concord. Edward Bruce offers his help in order to relieve the Welsh from that distress which the Scots too had lately experienced. By combined effort they would remove the yoke of the English, and the Scots and Welsh peoples would be one for ever. Most important of all perhaps, he asks them to commit their cause to him and the lordship over them which their prince once had. All of this is fully consistent with the report of Trevet's 'continuator' that Edward sent a letter to the inhabitants of Ireland, even to the extent of proposing himself to be the future king (or prince in the Welsh case). Edward's Welsh letter was addressed not to any one individual but to 'all desiring to be liberated from servitude'. One would imagine a very similar letter, in which the Irish were substituted for the Welsh, having been sent to Ireland before Edward's mission there began; perhaps both were even issued at the same time.

Now, if we consider Edward Bruce's letter proposing an invasion of Wales, with himself being set up as prince, and the remark of Trevet's 'continuator' that he initiated his Irish conquest in similar fashion, it calls for a certain reassessment of the latter project. Robert's letter to the Irish kings, since its discovery, has been taken to be the overture to the invasion. If I am correct, that now appears to be of earlier date and we may have confirmation from Trevet's 'continuator' that it was Edward who was the instigator of the later scheme. Because it has been assumed to have been Robert's proposal alone (a means of ridding him of a troublesome younger brother), it has been easy to argue the case that Robert's preoccupation with the idea of an Irish conquest was but fleeting, that intervention in Ireland, therefore, was not a central plank of Scottish royal policy.[106] How much more difficult it has been to argue that a broader *Celtic* alliance was anything more than a passing fad or, as Professor Duncan recently put it, 'convenient rhetoric'.[107]

Yet, we have seen that the Bruce family at least toyed with the idea at the very beginning of Robert's reign in 1306–07, and acted upon it more decisively during the period of Edward's occupation of Ulster in 1315–18. If it was a momentary impulse, the collapse of Edward Bruce's kingdom should have put an end to the matter. But it did not. Edward II was, of course, the Scots' enemy at this point, but in 1326, facing invasion by Isabella and Mortimer and desperate for allies, he was inclined to look more favourably on their case. In the autumn of the year it was rumoured that his only hope lay in escape to Ireland, the raising of troops there and, in collaboration with the Scots, launching an invasion of England.[108] In the following year we find Donald, earl of Mar (admittedly one of Edward II's intimates, but nevertheless now reconciled with his uncle Robert Bruce), trying to incite Welsh and English to a revolt in favour of the deposed king; Robert Bruce came to Ireland again at this point and his visit was believed by the Dublin government to be an attempt to secure Irish co-operation for the landing of an army in Wales, and thence to invade England.[109]

Admittedly, of all of this it may be said that the Bruces merely used the Welsh and Irish when it suited their purpose. Indeed, when Isabella and Mortimer did finally agree by the Treaty of Edinburgh-Northampton that they would recognise his right to the Scottish throne – which may have been all that he had really sought throughout the war of independence – Robert I for his part agreed that the Scots would never again aid anyone waging war in Ireland against the king of England. But that is not the point. Of course the Scots only sought a Celtic league because there was something in it for them. It is time to forgive the Bruce brothers for being human in wanting something out of the arrangement, while admitting that they sought it wholeheartedly – to such an extent, indeed, that Robert lost all three of his surviving brothers in its pursuit. From the shaky beginnings of Robert's Irish embassy (apparently in the winter of 1306), to the 'breathtaking arrogance'[110] of Edward Bruce's plans for Ireland, the Isles and Wales in the aftermath of Bannockburn, and to the ultimately successful wielding of this Damoclean sword at the end of his life, efforts to form a confederacy of Scots, Welsh and Irish against England form a not inconsistent theme of Scottish royal policy throughout the reign of Robert I. The politics of the Irish Sea world and the pursuit of a 'Celtic alliance' claimed the attention of the Bruces; they deserve the attention of historians.[111]

3

The Bruce Invasion of Ireland: an Examination of Some Problems

James Lydon

Ye remembere and wyth all your myghte take hede
To kepen Yrelond that it be not loste,
For it is a boterasse and a poste
Undre England, and Wales is another.[1]

This well-known quatrain from the mid-fifteenth century is sometimes quoted as a public condemnation of English policy in Ireland, a policy which threatened the loss of the lordship and the possible creation of a new ally for France. But this is far from being the first occasion that Englishmen felt in danger of losing Ireland. Long before, in 1311, the Ordainers had complained that the king's land of Ireland was 'on the point of being lost, unless God improve the situation'.[2] There was every reason for apprehension with regard to Ireland in that year, for there a dangerous situation had developed which threatened to become worse unless strong action were taken. Edward II had already discovered that the Dublin Government faced a financial crisis which made it incapable of carrying on its work properly. And so he adopted a new measure of caution in dealing with his Irish lordship, reversing for a time the traditional colonial policy he had inherited from his father and making strenuous efforts to improve the financial position of his Dublin administration.[3] This was his answer to the crisis, and in a remarkable letter of 1311 he gives us his reasons for this change in policy: the great increase in civil disturbance and the growing threat from the native Irish, for which the lack of funds at the disposal of the Dublin administration was responsible, had demanded it.[4] This increase in lawlessness and disorder throughout Ireland is one of the outstanding features of the last years of Edward I's reign and is symptomatic of the gradual collapse of English authority in this country. Signs of this were already apparent in the thirteenth century; but it was during the following century, when the Government decided (in Curtis's phrase) to cut its losses in an attempt to hold on to the few loyal shires which eventually comprised the Pale, it was then that the full extent of the collapse became apparent, showing that much of Ireland had passed under the control of the 'wild Irish' or the 'rebel English'.

This extraordinary decline has been the subject of much speculation, and many causes for it have been suggested – the exclusion of Gaelic Ireland from the life and government of the colony, the so-called Gaelic Rally, the high incidence of absentee landlordism, the failure to maintain an adequate English population, the murder of the earl of Ulster in 1333 and the consequent loss of much of Ulster and Connaught, the neglect of Ireland by English kings, and many more besides. But almost invariably the Bruce invasion of Ireland has been given a prominent place in the list of such causes; it was an event described by one Irish writer shortly afterwards as:[5]

> [an] overwhelming wave, broken-topped, hoarsely rumbling, virulent in destructiveness, scorching terribly and giving off lively sparks; an earnest of enduring malice and ill will, breaking down all embankments, all hills and every hoary rock a black cloud with vaporous creeping offshoots and dark mist, hard to meet made up of close-packed Scots and, as a thick-bellowed deep-thundering flood, covered our Ireland's surface.

Even allowing for the flamboyance of the language, this passage gives us some idea of the terrific impact of the invasion, with its aftermath of famine and desolation, on Irish society in a period of transition. To contemporaries the invasion was a blight – for us it marks a turning point in Irish history, for it appears as a decisive year which points the contrast between the thirteenth century (a great age of development in Ireland, full of promise for the future), and the retrogression of the next age. It is this which gives it a prominent position in our view of Irish history, and whether or not we regard it as a primary cause of the collapse which followed, it will continue to hold its place as a great dividing line in our history.

The story of the invasion, of Edward Bruce's accession to the high-kingship of Ireland, of his early success but ultimate defeat and death at the battle of Faughart, is too well known to require retelling here.[6] There are, however, many problems connected with it which have received insufficient emphasis in the past, and while it would be impossible to consider most of them in the space available, we can with profit re-examine some of them.

First let us examine the motives which lay behind the invasion. Archdeacon Barbour, one of the primary authorities for the life of Robert Bruce, tells us that it was personal ambition which led Edward Bruce to attempt the conquest of Ireland. Scotland, according to Barbour, was too small to hold the two brothers; and so

37. The photograph illustrates the sad remains of the formerly impressive sea-girt castle on Rathlin Island, off the coast of County Antrim, probably built by the Bisset family in the thirteenth century

Edward was sent to Ireland to carve out a kingdom there for himself.[7] While there may be some truth in this assertion, it is difficult to believe that King Robert, still in need of every available man for the struggle against England, would send a large army of veteran troops to Ireland merely to gratify his brother's ambition.[8] We must look for some other motive and we don't need to go very far in order to find one.

During the Scottish war of independence, Ireland became one of the main sources of supply for the English army in Scotland; indeed, it became responsible for much of the western march of Scotland during the last few years of Edward I.[9] Not many years before this, Robert Bruce himself had fought side by side with the earl of Ulster and thousands of soldiers from Ireland against William Wallace. And on more than one occasion he had seen an English army rescued from starvation by the arrival of supplies from Ireland.[10] By assisting his brother invade Ireland in 1315 with a large army, he would be achieving two objects: a halt would be put to the exploitation of Ireland as a source of supply, at least in the immediate future, because the full resources of the Anglo-Norman colony would be needed to counter this invasion; and secondly, by opening up a second front in Ireland, not only would the energies of the Anglo-Irish be diverted from Scotland, but in all probability Edward II would have to switch some of the resources he had gathered for Scotland to meet the new crisis in Ireland.[11] In other words, Robert Bruce was carrying his war against England into Ireland. And if this was the primary purpose of the invasion, as I believe it was, then, contrary to the common view that the invasion was a failure, it must, in fact, be considered as in the main successful, despite the defeat and death of Edward Bruce; because for the moment Ireland was ruined as a source of supply, the Anglo-Irish *were* diverted from

Scotland, and Edward II had to divide his forces and switch his attention from Scotland to this country. This view of the invasion would also help to explain the appalling ravages committed by both Bruces throughout the Irish countryside, a policy of deliberate destruction reminiscent of William Wallace's scorched earth tactics in Scotland – and not a senseless activity as has so often been maintained.

On the Irish side there was, of course, a different motive for the invasion. Barbour tells us that once Edward received permission to undertake this expedition he entered into negotiations with the native Irish and found them willing to transfer their allegiance to him on condition that he expelled the English. It is a fact that nearly a year after his successful invasion of Ulster, Edward was awarded the high-kingship and was crowned, ironically, near Faughart, the scene of his ultimate failure and death. Eoin MacNeill has shown us that this must be connected with the resurgence of Gaelic Ireland in the thirteenth century and that it marks the last attempt to revive the high-kingship, in the hope that where a native king had failed, a foreigner coming from a country which was partly Gaelic and had long associations with Ireland, would be acceptable to the other Irish kings who were jealous of the ascendancy of one of themselves.[12] But we must treat with caution the subsequent claim of Donal O Neill, in the so-called Remonstrance addressed to Pope John XXII, that he spoke on behalf of the whole of Gaelic Ireland.[13] This is a plaintiff's case in what is explicitly termed by Fordun a Processus, a formal legal proceeding, and is therefore not to be taken as giving a true, or even unbiased, account of the events leading up to the invasion. Indeed, it can be demonstrated to be inaccurate, whether by omission or by misrepresentation of facts, on many counts, so that it cannot be introduced as evidence that Gaelic Ireland, for the most part, was willing to accept the sovereignty of Edward Bruce. Nowhere do the Gaelic sources suggest that anything more than a handful of chieftains was party to the invitation extended to Bruce. In fact, if the denunciations of Bruce by the annalists and other Irish writers represent in any way the true feelings of the Gaelic race, and not merely their disillusionment at his failure and their disgust at the destructive tactics he employed, then we can only suppose that most of Gaelic Ireland was in no way responsible for calling in Edward Bruce. The number of chieftains who actually fought against him is also indicative of the same thing.

On the other hand, there can be no doubt that O Neill and some others were party to a plot to overthrow English authority in Ireland, with the help of Bruce, and to re-establish an independent Gaelic kingdom. He himself admits as much in his appeal to the Pope and the famous O'Madden tract, edited by O'Donovan as *The Tribes and Customs of Hy-Many,* implies it.[14] Like the two earlier attempts to revive the high-kingship, this one, too, was centred on Ulster; and there is reason to suppose that for some years before 1315 the ground was being prepared for the invasion that was to come. We know, for example, that in 1310 the king ordered the arrest of 'those adhering to Robert Bruce' in Ireland.[15] But some years before this the Scots had been in contact with Ulster in an effort to procure help, and it is highly probable, though from the nature of the evidence we cannot be certain of this, that during the same period plans were made for a future invasion.

38. A view from within what remains of the Bisset castle on Rathlin in which Robert Bruce seems to have stayed, with or without its owners' consent, for at least part of the winter of 1306–07. Below is the landing-stage for sea-craft

39. What is commonly called 'Bruce's Castle' can be seen on this promontory, difficult to access by land; this is the view north-west to the Mull of Kintyre

In order to understand my reasons for suggesting this, it is necessary to go back to the year 1306. In the winter of that year, after his defeat by the earl of Pembroke at Methven and his pursuit, with a handful of followers, by the English, Robert Bruce found a safe refuge on the island of Rathlin, a few miles off the Antrim coast.[16] While King Edward sought him everywhere, knowing only that he was somewhere in the islands between Scotland and Ireland, Bruce was safe in his retreat on Rathlin. To procure food for himself and his people he had to make himself known to the inhabitants of the island, and there can be little doubt that Hugh Biset, lord of the island, was informed of his presence there. The obvious conclusion is that Biset turned a blind eye to his presence on the island, and this suggests some degree of collusion between the pair of them. If this conclusion appears somewhat extravagant, an examination of some aspects of Biset's career will, I think, support it. His family had originally come from Scotland, where they had been close adherents of the Bruces, then Earls of Carrick. In 1298 Hugh had been commissioned to 'harass the king's Scotch enemies by sea' and had set out at the head of a marine force, ostensibly to lead an offensive against the western isles.[17] The only English chronicler to report this incident, Walter of Guisborough, relates that it was commonly said at the time that Biset, in fact, had come to the assistance of the Scots, who handed over the island of Arran to him; but when he heard of Edward's great victory at Falkirk he immediately sent word to the king that he had conquered the island in his name and asked that it be confirmed to him and his heirs for ever.[18] The chronicler's interest in this incident is confined to its constitutional repercussions in England and he has nothing more to tell us about Biset's supposed duplicity. There is no way of checking the truth of his story; but when we remember that Biset's son John was one of the followers of Edward Bruce when he landed in Ireland, that Hugh himself sided with Bruce early on in the Irish war and that he was one of the few people who was refused pardon because, we are told, his 'crimes are too heinous', then the case against him becomes black indeed.[19] None of this is proof; but it does support the theory that Biset was acting in collusion with Bruce before the death of Edward I.

Unfortunately we know nothing definite about Bruce's activities while on Rathlin; but we may be sure that the famous episode of the spider, which, according to the story, Bruce took so much to heart, is an indication that he spent his time planning for his return to Scotland. Only a few miles off the Irish mainland, Rathlin was an ideal place whence Bruce could seek Irish aid. And there are signs that he made the most of his opportunity. That same winter Scottish agents were active in Ulster, where, we are told, 'they had been received by religious persons and others'.[20] Who these 'others' were is not, unfortunately, disclosed; Gaelic chieftains, almost certainly, and perhaps, too, Anglo-Irish magnates, must be numbered among the people contacted. The long-established connection of Scotland with Ulster, an association which had been greatly strengthened by the influx of Scottish mercenary soldiers (galloglasses) from the mid-thirteenth century onwards, had made the northern province sympathetic towards the Scots in their struggle with Edwardian England. Already, military supplies had been taken from Ireland to the Scots, in the main, though not exclusively, by racketeers who were willing to take their chance in running the blockade set up by Edward I.[21] Now, probably as a result of Bruce's negotiations in Ulster, the first military force to leave Ireland to help the Scots landed at Lochryan on 9 February. Two of Robert Bruce's brothers, Thomas and Alexander, were in command and with them, we are told, was a 'certain kinglet from Ireland'. They were met on disembarking by the men of Galloway, under their chieftain Dugald Macdowell, and cut to pieces; a few days later the Bruce brothers were handed over to the English and were executed at Carlisle.[22] It is interesting to note that this same Dugald Macdowell later came to Ireland to fight for the king against his Scottish enemies.[23] What happened to the 'certain Irish kinglet' we do not know – but the fact that some years later native Irishmen were taken prisoner on the Isle of Man, where they had been fighting with the Scots, suggests that either he escaped to fight another day or more likely (and more important) that other Irishmen had joined the Scottish army.[24]

The 'religious persons' contacted by the Scots in the winter of 1306–07 are also something of a mystery. What we do know is that subsequently many religious, particularly the Friars Minor, were very active in support of Bruce in Ireland, stirring the people in his favour by the power of their preaching and even giving him material assistance during his sojourn here.[25] Adam, Bishop of Ferns, was suspected by the king of adhering to the Scots in Ireland, 'counselling them and communicating with them, and aiding them with victuals and other necessaries, and sending armour and men-at-arms to them by his brother, by whom they were informed of the state of those parts'.[26] But Adam is only one of a large number of religious who were accused of helping Bruce in Ireland. Typical of them was Brother Robert, Prior of the Augustinian house of the Blessed Virgin Mary of Louth, who in February 1316 was accused (and later found guilty),[27]

> ... of receiving Edward le Bruys and his accomplices Scotch enemies of the king in his house at Louthe, and by himself and his fellow Canons of the said house, of warning the said Scotch at Iniskeen in the autumn last past that the Justiciar of Ireland and many more nobles and magnates of Ireland were coming, with a great army of the king and his banner displayed, to fight the Scots, by means of which warning the Scots who would have been slain, as it was hoped, if such warning had not been given, then retreated in flight through fear of the arrival of the army to the town of Coulrath in Ulster; and also being accused of buying various food from loyal Irish and afterwards sending it to the Scots for their sustenance in woody places and elsewhere.

All in all, then, there is some indication that even before 1315 the way was being prepared for an invasion of Ireland. From Rathlin, Robert Bruce began his remarkable recovery which was to lead to the great victory at Bannockburn in 1314. But in the interim he was in touch with Ulster again, in 1313 by licence of the earl of Ulster.[28] And fourteen years later he came for the last time, when he executed an agreement with Henry de Mandeville, seneschal of Ulster, by which King Robert granted a truce for one year to the people of Ulster, on condition of their delivering a certain quantity of wheat and barley to him in the harbour at Larne.[29] Of particular interest is the fact the 'Irish of Ulster who adhere to the Scottish king' are included in the truce.

The suggestion, made earlier, that some of the Anglo-Irish may also have been contacted by Bruce in 1307, is also worthy of some consideration. As we have seen, Hugh Biset and his son John were among those who fought with Bruce in Ireland. But they were only two of a great number of Anglo-Irish who took the Scottish side in 1315 and later. The number of pardons issued and the number of those who had their lands confiscated 'for adherence to the Scotch and Irish rebels of the king' is quite staggering. But there is no way of knowing if any of them had been contacted by Bruce at an earlier date: whether, for example, those Anglo-Irish from Ulster who were taken by John of Argyll in May 1315 on the Isle of Man 'in the company of the Scottish enemies of the king' are representative of anything other than a band of soldiers of fortune.[30] Attractive as is the thesis that some of the Anglo-Irish anticipated the arrival of Bruce, it cannot be supported for lack of evidence. Indeed, it is probable that those Anglo-Irish who did associate themselves with the invasion did so in much the same spirit as many of the native Irish, making use of a glorious opportunity to work off old scores, to claim rights which they felt had been denied them, or to better their position through the use of force.[31] The distinction between *fidelis Anglica* and English rebels was already an established one in Ireland and the Bruce war merely provided a further incentive to those who had a grudge against the Crown or against some of the great Anglo-Irish magnates. Certainly the king had no reason to trust his Irish vassals during this time of crisis: in February 1316 a number

40. This is the location of 'Bruce's Castle' with the mainland of Antrim in the distance

of the more important of them were brought to Dublin and there compelled to promise and swear:[32]

> ... to defend the king's rights in Ireland, certain traitors and the Scottish rebels having entered that land and having leagued with them all the Irish and a great part of the English. They agree that their bodies, their lands and chattels shall be forfeited if they fail in their loyalty, and to render hostages to the king for fulfilment thereof, who are to be put in Dublin Castle or elsewhere at the king's pleasure.

The hostages were delivered, some to Dublin Castle, some to other castles in Ireland and others to England, and for the next few years, until the danger in Ireland had been fully averted, payments for their upkeep figure on the issue rolls of the Irish exchequer and on the account books of the King's Wardrobe in England.[33]

During the war, rumours in Ireland suggested that some of the greatest men in the land were assisting the Scots. Even the justiciar of the time, Edmund Butler, did not escape this slander, though it was not until 1320 that the king issued a notification 'to clear the fair name of Edmund le Botiller, who has been accused of having assisted the Scots in Ireland, that he has borne himself well and faithfully towards the king'.[34] But the greatest name of all those with which rumour played was Richard de Burgh, the earl of Ulster; even today the suspicion which surrounds his name dies hard. Probably the full truth will never be known, though there is much to suggest that rumour in this instance was not without some foundation. It is significant that although the king, as we saw above, cleared Butler from the suspicion in which he was held, no such attempt was ever made to publicly clear the name of Richard de Burgh.

Even before the invasion occurred, de Burgh's close association with the king of Scotland was noted. As the father-in-law of Robert Bruce he had acted as mediator between the English and the Scots.[35] When the people of Ulster began to aid the Scots with supplies in around 1310, de Burgh was held responsible; and again in 1313 it was said that it was by his leave that Bruce had come to Ulster.[36] His refusal to join with Butler when the justiciar was on his way to Ulster to fight the Scots, his insistence that his own army was quite sufficient to drive Bruce back into the sea, his easy defeat at the mysterious battle of Connor, and then his diversion of supply ships which had been sent north from Dublin for Carrickfergus Castle, one of the few places in Ulster which was successfully resisting the invaders, with the result that the castle fell into the hands of Bruce and provided him with a strongly fortified base in the north – all of these things served to strengthen the suspicion that he was more than friendly disposed towards the Scots.[37] People recalled his close association with O Neill and the other Gaelic chieftains in Ulster who had been responsible for offering the high-kingship to Edward Bruce, with the de Lacys of Meath and with other English rebels in Ireland. Finally popular feeling against him ran so high that the citizens of Dublin took the law into their own hands and clapped him into prison, where, they felt, he could do no more harm.[38]

It is important that we understand why the citizens took this extreme measure, for more than anything else it was their action on this occasion and the fact that they were never brought to account for it subsequently, which has been responsible for keeping alive the suspicion which surrounds the Red Earl. The famous incident occurred on 21 February 1317, when the Bruce brothers were approaching Dublin with the obvious intention of laying siege to and taking the city. The defences of the city were in a hopeless state. Private dwelling-houses and even shops had been constructed along the walls, making their defence against attack difficult and dangerous. In some cases the weight of these buildings had caused the walls to collapse and had opened up great breaches, through which an enemy might enter.[39] The well-known list of grievances of the 'common folk' of Dublin, addressed to the mayor and bailiffs of the city just before this, had requested that 'under penalty of grievous amercement at least one man shall come to muster from every house at the tolling of the public bell by day or by night, while the land is troubled by the Scottish enemies and by hostile Irish, who daily threaten to burn the suburbs and do all possible damage to the city'. They requested that measures be taken in hand for the proper conduct of 'sallies from the city against the enemy', and that the Mayor, and no one else, should have the ordering of these surprise attacks, and that capable commanders be appointed to lead them.[40] On a previous occasion attention had been drawn to the perilous condition of the defences of the city, but no action was taken by the mayor or the officers of the Crown.[41] With the Scots approaching, panic mounted in Dublin. A petition from the mayor and citizens to the king requested that he order the justiciar to come to their assistance and stated that they 'are environed by Irish enemies who forcibly seize themselves and their goods when they go forth to purchase or traffic; that the Scots are about to make a

41. This is the only remnant of Olderfleet Castle, which guarded the harbour at Larne, where Robert Bruce was present in August 1328

descent on those parts, and that the city and its people are thus likely to be ruined'.[42] There is no exaggeration here, as we know from other sources.[43]

Indeed, the issue rolls of the exchequer record expenditure in putting the castle and the houses of the exchequer in a state of defence against the Scots and the Irish, and particular mention is made of 'those Irish who commence to invade and besiege the castle'.[44] Other payments record the employment of special night-watchmen in the exchequer 'to reprimand the malice of the Irish felons and enemies of the king in the parts of Leinster who seek to burn the houses of the exchequer'.[45] But despite all precautions the houses of the exchequer were eventually destroyed by fire, probably as a result of the burning of the suburbs by the citizens, for a later roll of payments records the cost of hiring two houses in the city 'pro scaccario in eisdem tenendo, post combustionem scaccarii in suburbio Dublinense'.[46]

In this situation, then, we can understand the panic which gripped Dublin in February 1317. Their despair of saving their city, the humiliations they had suffered at the hands of the Leinster Irish, and the failure of the government to take any proper precautions against attack – these were responsible for the outburst of the citizens at that time, for their arrest of de Burgh and for their desperate attempt to put their defences in order in the space of one night. The activities of that night, when the citizens burned the suburbs, destroyed Thomas Street, tore down the belfry of St Mary's to provide stone with which to repair breaches in the walls, and set fire to the bridges across the Liffey, were sufficient, we are told, to deter Bruce: Dublin, he thought, as he watched the burning suburbs from his camp at Castleknock, could only be taken with more time and at a greater cost than he could afford. And so he pressed forward on his circuit of Ireland, leaving Dublin for a later date.[47] This was a fatal mistake, for he was not given another opportunity to take the city, and without Dublin he could never call himself master of Ireland.

Panic, then, more than anything else was responsible for the arrest of de Burgh by the Dubliners. In that state of mind they were willing to believe the worst of the earl and were in no condition to listen to reason. But malice played its part as well, because there is no doubt that by now the citizens hated de Burgh and his Ulstermen. For if Dublin had suffered much from the Irish of Leinster, she also had to endure much from the armies of Ireland in the recent and more distant past. Again and again in accounts on the pipe rolls and elsewhere we read of the damage and destruction caused by Irish troops during this war. The Pipe roll 15 Edward II recites that Henry Kempe, who held ninety acres in the demesne lands of Newcastle in Wicklow, was 'injured by the Ulster army who came there with the king's banner to pursue Edward le Bruys and his men and who robbed Henry of divers goods to the value of £20'.[48] In the account of the temporalities of the Archbishopric of Dublin, on Pipe roll 9 Edward II, the allowances include various sums of money for 'damage to the meadows at Colonia and Fyneglas, to the woods of Clondalkin and Fyneglas, and to the gardens and orchards of St Sepulchre, Clondalkin and Fyneglas, all of which were injured by the king's army going towards Ulster to overcome the Scotch felons'.[49] Dublin city suffered in particular. In 1317, when Edward II allowed the citizens various sums in the farm of the city,

42. Carrickfergus Castle presented the greatest challenge to Bruce control over Ulster; the garrison's efforts to hold out against the Scots were not helped by the decision of the earl of Ulster, Richard de Burgh, who was Robert Bruce's father-in-law, to divert to his own use supplies intended for the castle's relief

to help them make good the losses they had sustained during February of that year, the large sum of £240 was allowed 'on account of the men at arms who came there, on their way to Ulster and other parts of Ireland, to repel the Scotch rebels'.[50] But such damage was a source of longstanding grievance with the Dubliners. During the wars of Edward I, when contingents of soldiers from Ireland were employed in Wales, Flanders and Scotland, Dublin was the principal port used as an embarkation centre for the troops and the great clearing centre for the great flood of supplies which flowed from Ireland to feed the king's armies overseas.[51] Dubliners found their ships being pressed into service, their supplies of food seized by the royal purveyors, and in general the commerce of their city disrupted and thrown into confusion by the activities of the king's agents, or those of the great magnates, during those war years. Even some of their houses were requisitioned to store the king's wine and victuals awaiting transportation overseas. But even worse than this, the armies *en route* to Scotland (or to Ulster during the Bruce war) were billeted on the city. It is easy to imagine the results of the influx of an army of 3,000 or more on a city the size of Dublin in those days. Medieval armies were undisciplined, with little respect for private property; certainly the Irish soldiery, if one is to judge by the damage they caused in Ghent, Carlisle, or elsewhere, was no exception and was given to looting whenever the opportunity to do so arose.[52] But there is no way of knowing precisely the amount of damage sustained by Dublin in this way; what we do know is that on a number of occasions the outraged citizens reacted in the most violent way possible – on one memorable night they

43. This is what survives of the ditch surrounding the archbishop of Dublin's castle at Castlekevin, County Wicklow, one of the targets of the resurgent Irish of the Wicklow mountains during the course of Bruce's occupation

attacked the soldiers billeted in the Coombe, killed a number of them and made off with many of their supplies.[53]

For the magnates of Ireland, then, and for the earl of Ulster in particular, who had been commander of some of the armies quartered on Dublin, the citizens had a natural dislike. In the summer of 1317, when a parliament was summoned to Dublin by the king, it was ordered that it be held outside the city, as Edward feared that 'damage may be done if the magnates of Ireland and their men enter the city on account of the disputes between them and the community of the city'.[54]

Against this background of suspicion and antagonism, and of panic caused by the attacks of the native Irish and the approach of the Scots, it is easy to understand why the Dubliners adopted such a drastic course of action against the person of Richard de Burgh. So that while this incident may serve as a particularly striking illustration of the high degree of suspicion in which the earl was held, it does nothing to help us in our attempt to arrive at the truth. The fact is, as I suggested earlier, that the truth eludes us in this instance. There is much to suggest that de Burgh remained loyal: his engagements with the Scots in Ulster (for which the king thanked him in September 1315),[55] the later requests by Edward II that the earl should come once more to Scotland, where he would be well paid for his service,[56] and above all the fact that never once was it officially stated, even by implication, that the earl was not to be trusted. On the other hand, there are the rumours, the suspicions of his loyalty (which incidentally were repeated in England),[57] his relationship with the king of Scotland and with many of the Irish who were responsible for offering the high-kingship to Edward Bruce, and the peculiar fact that once his son-in-law had become king of Scotland he refused to serve against him despite the highly extravagant terms of service offered him by the English king.[58] And if, as has been suggested, Hugh Biset and perhaps others in Ulster were working with the Scots before the invasion of 1315, it can hardly have been without the knowledge, if not with the connivance, of the earl of Ulster.

Whatever the truth of this matter, de Burgh has often been held responsible for the failure of the colony to counter the invasion successfully. But here the responsibility must lie squarely on the shoulders of the king. Edward I, through his over-exploitation of his Irish lordship in the last decade of his reign, had precipitated a financial crisis at the Dublin exchequer which resulted in its virtual bankruptcy.[59] Soon after his accession, his son made a determined effort to redress this situation by attempting to collect long-standing sums of money due to the Crown,[60] but more especially, as we saw before, by his avowal of a new policy in which no attempt would be made to draw on the revenues of Ireland for any expenditure outside the lordship. In his letter of 1311, to which I have already referred, the king makes it quite clear that he was now of the opinion that hitherto a wrong use had been made of the revenues of Ireland: for the most part, he said, they had been expended on his business outside Ireland, either on the wars in Scotland or else in England, with the result that what was left in Dublin was not sufficient for the conduct of good government there, or for the preservation of peace in Ireland. Because of this 'defectum pecunie' the Irish, day by day, burnt, killed, robbed and committed other transgressions in an intolerable manner. The king therefore decided that all the issues of Ireland should henceforth be spent in that country 'circa conservacionem pacis ejusdem terre' and on his other business there.

Unfortunately Edward did not continue with this new policy for very long; in fact, before a year had passed he had already begun to follow his father's policy of drawing on Ireland for money and military supplies whenever and wherever the need arose.[61] At the same time, while the Dublin exchequer lost much of its income in this way, the financial resources at the disposal of the government were further depleted by the steady decline in receipts at the exchequer.[62] The net result was that when Edward Bruce invaded Ireland, the government found itself without the money they needed to raise an army strong enough to resist the Scots. A letter issuing from the Irish chancery during the first weeks of the invasion makes this vividly clear.[63] It tells how the king had ordered supplies for Scotland, and goes on to say that these had been procured and were ready to be shipped to Scotland when Bruce and his army landed in Ulster; the council attempted to get an army together, but discovered that the money in the exchequer was less than was needed to pay the troops – only by selling these stores could some money be procured, and this, it was proposed, should be handed over to Nicholas Balscote, who was appointed paymaster to the troops. In fact, the army raised in this way was much too small to offer any effective resistance to the Scots, as John de Hothum, the special agent sent to report on the situation in Ireland, made clear when he wrote that the Scots 'with their allies puffed up with pride were doing all damage as they wished'.[64] Nor did the financial position of the Dublin administration show any marked improvement during the years which followed. The very small returns from the aid granted for the war against the Scots made little real difference, and were more than cancelled out by money which had to be found for meeting renewed demands from England for military supplies against Scotland.[65] In fact, a study of the critical months following the invasion makes one wonder if Edward II realised how serious the situation in Ireland really was. He still attempted to get supplies there for Scotland, ignoring the fact that every available penny was desperately needed in Ireland at that time.[66]

The shortage of ready cash, then, for which the king was almost entirely responsible, was the chief reason for the early failure against Bruce. It was this which allowed him such an easy success in 1315 and not, as has usually been suggested, the superior experience and fighting quality of the Scottish veterans in his army. Only after John de Hothum's second visit to Ireland, when he wrote to the king informing him of the state of the Dublin exchequer and asking for £500 to be sent to Ireland immediately, did Edward II realise the full extent of the crisis in Ireland.[67] Even then he remained unwilling to incur expenditure in Ireland, though it is highly significant that when Roger Mortimer was sent as Chief Governor to Dublin, with a small military force in attendance, it was agreed that the expenses incurred would be met by the King's Wardrobe and not, as had hitherto been the custom, by the Irish exchequer.[68] This was to be the practice in the future, when the Irish administration became financially dependent on England, so that expenditure on most of the military campaigns in Ireland was charged to the English exchequer.

There is one other aspect of the Bruce war in Ireland which also deserves greater emphasis than has usually been accorded it, and that is the war at sea. While it would be an exaggeration to say that it was here that the real issue of the war was decided, it is nevertheless true that once Bruce lost control of the sea the fate of his brother in Ireland was sealed. We sometimes tend to forget that even in the early fourteenth century naval forces were already well organised and had a useful, and sometimes necessary, part to play in the conduct of war. Even in Henry III's reign king's ships and galleys had been built in Ireland and were stationed at some of the ports on the east coast.[69] When merchant ships were used for war purposes they were converted into fighting ships beforehand.[70] Before Edward I died, a naval hierarchy had appeared in Ireland and commanded fleets on convoy duty to Scotland, in patrolling the Scottish coastline and on occasion helping with the victualling of castles on the coast.[71] Thus long before 1315 an Irish navy had played an important part in many of the wars of Edward I and his son.

During the period of the Bruce war in Ireland, the Scots for a time succeeded in winning control of part of the Irish sea, and this despite the fact that a combined fleet of English and Irish ships was based on Carrickfergus under the command of the king's Admiral of Ireland.[72] When Carrickfergus fell to the Scots, the navy lost its base in the north; but the capture of the Isle of Man had supplied a new one and it was from there that a naval recovery was effected.[73] With the capture of Thomas Dun, the 'scummar of the sea' as Barbour calls him, and the mainspring of the Scottish naval forces, Bruce lost whatever ascendancy he possessed in the Irish sea, with disastrous results for his brother in Ireland.[74] The main lines of communication between Ulster and Scotland were broken, Edward Bruce was cut off from his homeland and was left dependent on Irish allies, who were already refusing him material assistance. Worse still, he could no longer hope for reinforcements from Scotland or for any supplies in bulk, and so was forced to make the most of a situation of great peril in Ireland, where bad harvests and his own ruthless scorched-earth policy had already deprived him of the greater part of his food supplies. Perhaps worst of all he was removed from the restraining influence and wise counsel of his brother and left to pursue his own reckless way to his death at Faughart in October 1318.

It would perhaps be wrong to attribute all this to the English and Irish victory in the war at sea; but certainly that victory must be regarded as a major contribution to the ultimate defeat of Bruce. There is no doubt of the early success of the Scots in this phase of the war; when John de Hothum left Chester in November 1315 as the king's special emissary to Ireland, he was accompanied by eight heavily armed ships as a protection against Thomas Dun and his fleet.[75] It was this control of the sea which enabled Bruce to land a large army in Ulster and later enabled King Robert to cross to Ireland to offer help and advice. But once Thomas Dun was captured and control slipped from Robert Bruce's grasp, his brother was left to face the future virtually alone.

Before he died, however, Edward Bruce had shaken to its foundations the authority of the king's government in Ireland. The Irish annals call him the 'destroyer of all Erin',[76] and one contemporary writer described Ireland during his visitation as 'one trembling surface of commotion'.[77] Fire and destruction had been dealt out by the Bruces during their circuit of Ireland, so that much land fell back into waste and many died. Carlow, for example, suffered severely: in a petition to the king, the earl of Norfolk complained that his steward, treasurer and many free tenants were among the dead there.[78] The accounts of the escheators on the pipe rolls show a heavy fall in rents from much of the land in the king's hand, because of the damage caused by the Scots and the Irish. Even as late as 1327 it was proposed that Welsh or English colonists be introduced to reoccupy waste lands near Carrickfergus which had been unoccupied and uncultivated since 1315.[79] Such examples are rare, however, and at present we can do little more than guess at the extent of the destruction caused by the war. That it was extensive is hardly to be doubted; but my impression is that either the magnitude of the destruction has been greatly exaggerated in the past or else much of the area which suffered made a quick recovery.[80]

In other ways this invasion contributed to the gradual breakdown of the central authority in Ireland. Friar Clyn, the Kilkenny chronicler, in referring to the invasion says: 'There adhered to them [the Scots] while they were in Ireland almost all the Irish of the land, and few kept their faith and loyalty',[81] a sentiment expressed commonly at the time. This is an exaggerated estimate of the situation, but it does illustrate the common belief that most of Gaelic Ireland sided with Bruce. The fact is that very many did not; but a great number did and made good use of those years of disturbance to regain their lost lands. In the history of the Gaelic revival in Ireland, Scotland had an important part to play, mainly because of the contribution of the galloglasses to that recovery, but also because of the shock given to the king's administration in the localities by the Bruce invasion.

Perhaps the most important result of this war was its exposure of the essential weakness of the Dublin government. In itself the war was not a primary cause of that weakness. As I suggested earlier, the strain imposed by the over-exploitation of his Irish resources by Edward I was probably the principal factor in the undermining of the authority of his Dublin government. In its weakened state that government was no longer capable of maintaining the degree of control achieved in the thirteenth century. Its failure to cope adequately with the Bruce crisis and its gradual loss of control in the localities are signs of its insufficiency and of the decline of English power in Ireland. In the history of that decline the Bruce invasion has an important place, though not the first place. But because it did serve as the occasion which most effectively exposed the weakness of the king's government in Ireland, so that never afterwards in the Middle Ages was the authority of that government respected throughout the lordship, the Bruce invasion and 1315 may rightly be regarded as a great turning point in Irish history.

4

The Scottish Soldier Abroad: the Bruce Invasion and the Galloglass

James Lydon

In March 1474 a parliament meeting in Dublin elected representatives to travel to England and inform the king of the 'myserable state and desolacyon of his said land and his true subgettes of the same', asking for 'relief and socour' and telling him that if relief was not forthcoming, then they 'may not long endure under his obeysaunce or ligeaunce or by distress to depart out of the land'. When they came to list the causes of the 'pitiose decay of the said land and subgettes', they naturally began with the 'subduying and destrucyon' caused by the king's Irish enemies and English rebels, the cause of many a complaint over the years. But now, for the first time, the parliament included another element of destruction:[1]

> [The] Scottes which ben entred and dwellen in Ullester to the nomber of XM [10,000] and more which proposen and dayly conspiren to subdue all thys land to the obeysaunce of the Kyng of Scottes havyng in their mynd the grete conquest that Bruse some tyme seuer to the Kyng of Scottes made in the same land.

The parliament also said that it was impossible to resist their 'malycyous entent' because the king's subjects of Ireland 'be but pety nombre in comparyson of the grete multitude of her Iryssh ennemys, Englysh rebelez and Scottes'.

What is most remarkable about this message is not the threat posed by the supposed 10,000 Scots – King Edward IV in fact at that very time was negotiating with the Scots, which resulted in a marriage treaty and truce later in the year[2] – but the memory of the Bruce invasion of Ireland in 1315 and the 'grete conquest' he made. It is a measure of the impact of that great event on Anglo-Irish consciousness that more than 150 years later it should still be a vivid memory. It is particularly notable that parliament remembered it as a 'conquest', which in fact is true, if we confine ourselves to that part of the north of Ireland occupied by Edward Bruce for more than three years.

In the history of the English lordship of Ireland in the Middle Ages there is no single event more important than the invasion by Edward Bruce in 1315.[3] It not only marked an important stage in what historians have called the Gaelic resurgence, through which Gaelic lordships were re-established, lands re-conquered and anti-quarian institutions revived; it was also a landmark in the history of the decline of that English settlement established and augmented in the late twelfth and thirteenth centuries. Anglo-Irish relations were never the same again after the traumatic events of 1315–18. Needless to say it was also an event of the greatest importance in Hiberno-Scottish relations and, certainly of the Middle Ages, must rank as the greatest single occasion when Scottish soldiers were involved in the affairs of Ireland.

The question that immediately arises is: why did Bruce bother to involve himself with Ireland at all and on the massive scale he did? For, while we do not have the kind of precise information which the exchequer and other governmental records provide to calculate the size of English, and indeed Irish, armies in this period, there can be no doubt that the king of Scotland risked large forces and valuable resources on this enterprise in Ireland. What did he hope to achieve? Years ago I suggested that in simple military terms he was trying to open up a second front against England and thereby divert important English military and financial resources to the defence of the king's land of Ireland and his loyal subjects there.[4] The English king had an acknowledged duty to protect his subjects in Ireland and Edward II had explicitly recognised that duty in one of his first royal letters to Ireland in 1307.[5] Indeed, quite early in the course of the Bruce invasion, after his special envoy John de Hothum had reported on the dangerous situation in the lordship and asked for help, the king responded positively and even went so far as to recruit 1,000 Genoese mercenaries, under Antonio de Passagno, to serve in Ireland in the summer of 1317.[6] In addition, Robert Bruce had personal experience of the way in which Edward I and his son had used Irish resources in his war in Scotland and one effect of an invasion of Ireland would be to destroy it as a source of supply.[7]

But more recently it has been argued that Robert Bruce actually had a conquest of Ireland in mind, with the hope of a Welsh alliance, so that a great pan-Celtic invasion of England might result.[8] There is much to be said for this. King Robert himself in his famous letter to the Irish kings and 'the inhabitants of all Ireland, his friends', wrote that he and they had been 'free since ancient times' and that his special envoys would negotiate with them so that 'our nation [by which he meant the Irish and the Scots] may be able to recover her ancient liberty'.[9] His aim, therefore, was to free Ireland and it is a fact that when he himself came to join his brother in Ireland in the winter of 1316, the Annals of Connacht say that he came

44. Here, at Church Bay, on Rathlin Island, Robert Bruce would have disembarked in the winter of 1306–07, and no doubt from here he dispatched his letter to possible allies on the Irish mainland, visible in the background

'to expel the Gaill [the English] from Ireland'.[10] He came, then, as a liberator and to help his brother to conquer Ireland.

I have to add here that recently it has been argued that the bearers of this important letter, 'our beloved kinsmen', were in fact the two brothers of King Robert, Thomas and Alexander, and that the occasion was the winter of 1306–07 when Bruce was on Rathlin Island and trying to recruit help in Gaelic Ulster.[11] This certainly fits in with the invasion of Galloway from Ireland, in eighteen ships, led by the two Bruce brothers and including at least one Irish 'kinglet', in the spring of 1307.[12] The two brothers were captured by Dungal Macdouall and handed over to the young Prince of Wales, as were the heads of the leading Irishmen with the army. The two brothers were subsequently executed and their heads, together with that of the Irish king, were fixed over the gates into Carlisle.[13] So that was one enterprise which ended in disaster.

Even if King Robert's letter does belong to that earlier affair, it does not damage the argument that in 1315 the aim was to conquer Ireland. Not only do all the English chroniclers, with one exception, support this view of the invasion, leading Anglo-Irish magnates were also in agreement.[14] Milo de Verdon, Nicholas de Verdon and John fitz Thomas wrote separately to the king that, with the assistance of the Irish, the Scots intended a conquest of Ireland.[15] It has been argued that the Scottish assembly, which met at Ayr on 26 April 1315 and which made Edward Bruce heir presumptive to the Scottish throne, was also a muster for the expedition to Ireland.[16] It is also important that when the earl of Moray was sent from Ireland to Scotland late in 1315 to raise more troops, he returned with reinforcements in December.[17]

45. Castletown Mount, near Dundalk, was the caput of the de Verdon family, two members of which, Milo and Nicholas, wrote to Edward II in autumn 1315, stating their view that the Bruces intended the conquest of all Ireland, in alliance with the Irish

Finally, when King Robert himself arrived to join Edward in December 1316, he brought with him, according to Walter of Guisborough, 30,000 men to help in the conquest.[18] The number, of course, is an exaggeration, but it is the chronicler's way of telling us that the king brought substantial forces with him. The Lanercost chronicler, too, agrees and says that he came 'to conquer that country, or a large part of it, for his brother Edward'.[19] Indeed, such was the size of the army which the two brothers were able to lead out of Ulster in January 1317 that the Irish government was unable to muster a force large enough to challenge it openly. The justiciar was able to keep the best part of 1,000 men in pay, a substantial force by Irish standards, together with men supplied by the great Anglo-Irish lords of Leinster and Munster. But he chose to 'keep watch over and harry the Scots', as the journal of the clerk of the wages put it, implying that a head-on confrontation was impossible.[20]

An examination of the events of those years in Ireland also suggests that no army raised among the Anglo-Irish was capable of standing up to the Scots, even before King Robert arrived with reinforcements. The Anglo-Irish lost every pitched battle. The royal envoy, John de Hothum, described what happened at the battle of Ardscull in Kildare early in 1316. The Scots and their allies, he wrote to the king, who were full of pride, had penetrated deep into the heart of the lordship of Ireland and, were causing damage 'at their will and without arrest'. Most of the leading Anglo-Irish joined the justiciar with their retinues of men-at-arms, hobelars and foot – more than sufficient, he said, to have won the day. But 'by mischance' the enemy kept the field, even though they lost several of their best men and the Anglo-Irish 'by the mercy of

God' only lost one. Another letter, written by a royal clerk in Hothum's retinue, also told the king of this defeat and used the same excuse of 'mischance'.[21] Clearly they were trying to explain away to Edward II how it was that a numerically superior government force (the clerk actually admits that the assembled retinues under the different magnates were more than sufficient to win the battle), fighting in familiar territory, could be defeated by the Scots.

It seems, then, that right through the campaign, until the battle of Faughart in 1318, the armies of the Bruce brothers were always superior. When in February 1317 the Scots moved out of their base in Ulster and camped at Castleknock above Dublin on 23 February, the citizens in the exposed borough below panicked. Convinced that nothing could save the city from the Scots, they threw the father-in-law of King Robert into prison, accusing him of being a traitor. In desperation they fired the western suburbs, the side facing the Scots, threw down parts of churches and used the masonry to repair breaches in the walls, and accused the mayor and bailiffs of having left the city defenceless against the Scots.[22] Nothing more vividly illustrates the kind of panic which the Scottish army could generate.

It must be said that they were ruthless in this campaign, even more so than was normal in Irish warfare. In describing the taking of Dundalk, Barbour makes no attempt to hide the slaughter of the townsmen:[23]

> And in the town made such a slaughter,
> Such a shambles, that like water
> From lying bodies flowed the blood
> Through streets and gutters in a flood.

Friar Clyn of Kilkenny in his chronicle writes that –[24]

> ... they burnt Dundalk and the convent of the friars, they spoiled books, clothes, chalices, vestments and they killed many.

The Dublin chronicler also describes the 'spoiling and burning' and adds that they killed all the townsmen who resisted them. He then adds that having destroyed the greater part of Uriel, they burned 'the church of the Blessed Virgin Mary in Ardee, full of men and women and children'.[25] Friar Clyn later described the two Bruce brothers –[26]

> ... crossing Ireland through the whole land from Ulster where he [Robert] landed, almost right up to Limerick, burning, killing, destroying, spoiling vills, castles and also churches in going and returning.

There is lots more in the same vein. In a very significant passage in the Annals of Connacht – which is sometimes quoted to illustrate the fact that all armies in this campaign caused damage in the countryside through which they passed – there is a striking exception made in the case of the Scots. The annalist is describing the destruction caused by the Scots and the killings in Dundalk, and he adds:[27]

> Excepting homicide, however, deeds no less evil were done by an army drawn from different parts of Ireland to do battle with them, in the districts through which they passed.

The 'excepting homicides' is important: the Scots killed, the others simply caused damage. That is another reason why the Irish annals universally condemned Bruce after his defeat and death at Faughart. The Annals of Connacht said that:[28]

> ... never was a better deed done for the Irish than this, since the beginning of the world and the banishing of the Fomorians from Ireland. For in this Bruce's time, for three years and a half, falsehood and famine and homicide filled the country.

In the light of what was said earlier about the military superiority of the Scots, we might well wonder how it was that the battle of Faughart went against them in 1318. There were many reasons. There can be little doubt that the army had been weakened by the effects of the terrible famine which hit Ireland, like most of Europe, during those years.[29] Describing the arrival of the Scottish army at Geashill in Offaly on the feast of St Valentine (14 February) 1316, the Dublin annalist told 'how they suffered such great hunger that many of them died'.[30] Famine, then, depleted the forces at the disposal of Edward Bruce, once King Robert had returned to Scotland with his men in 1317. It seems, too, that Edward acted too hastily in facing the Anglo-Irish in battle, lacking reinforcements from Scotland. Nor was the shortfall made up by the Irish, most of whom held aloof and looked after their own interests, as they had done right through the campaign. Finally, it seems that a larger than usual Anglo-Irish army opposed Bruce on this occasion. It used to be thought that this army, under the leadership of John de Bermingham, was mainly composed of locals. Now we know, not least from the names of those who were subsequently rewarded for their part in the battle, that leaders of retinues came from far away, important magnates like Arnold le Poer, the seneschal of Kilkenny.[31]

Nevertheless, the great relief universally expressed in Anglo-Ireland at the victory suggests that many feared that it might well have gone the other way. A special messenger was sent from the battlefield to inform the king's ministers in the exchequer of what the record calls 'the great victory', and the news was recorded for posterity in the Red Book of the Exchequer, a sure indication of its importance. Even more telling is the comment of the scribe that thus 'by the hand of God was delivered the people of God from a foreseen and contrived slavery'.[32] The victor of Faughart, John de Bermingham, was rewarded with the earldom of Louth and many other participants were rewarded later. The head of the dead Edward Bruce was sent in triumph to the king in England, the rest of the body quartered, his heart, one hand and one quarter displayed in Dublin and the other three quarters sent to what the record simply calls 'other places'.[33] Both English and Irish narrative sources list some of those who fell on the Scottish side and it is plain that some of the great men who accompanied Edward Bruce to Ireland in the first place were with him to the

46. Ardscull 'motte': in these fields the battle of Skerries (Ardscull) was fought in January 1316; the army of the Anglo-Irish was very substantial but was forced to yield the field to the Scots 'by mischance', probably because of divisions amongst its leaders

end. But the Annals of Ulster also tell us that Mac Ruaidrí, king of Innse Gaill (the Hebrides), and Mac Domnaill, king of Argyll, also fell in battle with Bruce.[34]

So the great enterprise came to an end and the dream of an Irish conquest was shattered. But the story does not end there. Nine years later in what Ranald Nicholson called a sequel to the invasion, King Robert was back in Ulster, where he compelled the seneschal of the earldom, Henry de Mandeville, to recognise him as king of Scotland and to seal an indenture in which he promised to deliver specified quantities of wheat and barley to Bruce. In return, Bruce guaranteed the people of Ulster a truce from Scottish attack for one year from 1 August 1327. What is especially interesting about this indenture is that included in the truce are 'all those Irish of Ulster' who were the king of Scotland's adherents and who were to be free from attack by locals.[35] This suggests that Bruce had maintained some sort of continuous connection with Ulster and explains why he had a second purpose for his visit in 1327 – a plan to invade England with the help of Irish allies. Certainly the Dublin government was alarmed at his presence. The exchequer paid out money for the garrisoning of the royal castle of Leixlip against Scots rebels and enemies and the Irish chancellor was quickly 'to treat with the men of Ulster and examine their hearts regarding the resistance to the Scottish enemies and rebels'.[36]

But before long, on 4 May 1328, what was optimistically called 'the final peace' between Scotland and England was confirmed by the English parliament at Northampton. Amongst its terms was one by which the Scots agreed never again to support the enemies of the king of England in Ireland.[37] Later in that same year King

Robert was back in Ulster again, with the new earl of Ulster in tow. As sick as he was, the Dublin annalist tells us that he 'sent to the justiciar and council of Ireland that they should come to Greencastle to treat of the peace of Scotland and Ireland' – an invitation which the Dublin government ignored.[38] Whatever this 'peace' was, and it suggests that Bruce was still holding an Ulster card up his sleeve, it was his last act in Ireland. He died shortly afterwards, an event recorded by Friar Clyn of Kilkenny, who paid him a significant tribute:[39]

> ... vigorous in arms, learned and experienced in the business of war, by common consent in these matters he hardly had an equal in the whole world.

Never again in the Middle Ages did such large Scottish forces involve themselves in the affairs of Ireland. There were occasional flurries of activity. In 1385 great councils meeting at Dublin and Kilkenny complained of their weakness in the face of the great power of the Irish enemies and English rebels, confederated with other enemies of Scotland.[40] In 1404 another great council meeting at Castledermot granted a subsidy towards an army going to Ulster, destroyed, it was told, by the Irish and the Scots and other enemies of the 'out isles'.[41] In 1430 a Dublin great council discussed the conquests of the Irish enemies in many parts of Ireland, assisted by 'grete multitude of Scottes sende unto thaym oute of Scottelond'.[42] And in 1474, as we have seen, the Dublin parliament complained of 10,000 Scots in Ulster, conspiring 'to subdue al thys land to the obeysaunce of the Kyng of Scottes'. But none of these were serious threats which posed real danger outside of Ulster. Apart from the threat of an invasion from Scotland in support of the pretender Perkin Warbeck at the end of the fifteenth century, it was not until later in the sixteenth and seventeenth centuries that Scottish armies became once again a vital factor in the military history of Ireland.

That is not to say that there was no Scottish presence in Ireland during the fourteenth and fifteenth centuries. Argyll and the Hebrides were supporting Edward Bruce at the battle of Faughart. And earlier, when King Robert arrived in support of his brother and was greeted as a liberator by the annals, it was recorded by the Annals of Connacht that he brought 'many galloglass *(galloclaechaib)* to help his brother Edward'.[43] But earlier again the presence of galloglass in Ireland had been remarked on by annalists and chroniclers alike. These galloglass were mercenary soldiers from the western isles of Scotland, employed by Gaelic Irish chieftains to form the core of a professional army. Without them it would have been difficult, perhaps even impossible, for O Neills, O Conors, O Briens and many lesser Gaelic lords to overcome successfully that military superiority which the Anglo-Norman settlers had enjoyed since they came to Ireland in the twelfth century'.

The first mention of galloglass *(galloclaich)* by name comes from as late as 1290 in the Annals of Connacht. The entry describes how Aed O Donnell was deposed by his brother Turloch, who then 'assumed the kingship'. Turloch managed to do this, according to the annal, 'through the power of his mother's kin, the Clann Domnaill, and of many other galloglass'.[44] Quite plainly, the Clan Donald, as well as others,

47. The Franciscan friary, Dundalk: Friar Clyn says that in June 1315 the Scots 'burnt Dundalk and the convent of the Friars; they spoiled books, clothes, chalices and vestments, and they killed many'

48. Kilkenny Castle did not itself suffer at the hands of the Scots, but it had come into the king's hands following the death at Bannockburn of the last de Clare earl of Gloucester, and the steward (or 'seneschal') of the lordship of Kilkenny, Arnold le Poer, was to the fore in opposing Bruce

supplied galloglass and the context suggests that by 1290 galloglass were already an established feature of Donegal. More than that, they seem to have come with Turloch's mother of the Clan Donald, perhaps as a marriage dowry as happened in 1259 with Aed O Conor of Connacht. The Annals of Loch Cé record that Aed went to Derry to marry –[45]

> ... the daughter of Dubhgall Mac Somhairle; and he brought home eight score *óglaoch* (young warriors) with her, together with Ailin Mac Somhairle.

This Ailin was the uncle of the bride and the 160 *óglaoch* were under his command. It seems, then, that these were the first galloglass to come to Connacht and that they were imported as part of a marriage arrangement. It might be noted, too, that these same annals call this future king of Connacht Aed na-nGall (Aed of the Foreigners), almost certainly associating him with the importation of these foreign soldiers from Innse Gaill.[46] Earlier still, in 1247, on a famous occasion when O Donnell was attempting to halt Geraldine expansion northwards out of Connacht into Donegal, the Annals of Connacht record an affray at Ballyshannon where O Donnell himself was killed and add that 'Mac Somurli (Somhairle) king of Argyll was killed there'.[47] This seems to be the first recorded Scottish king to be killed while fighting for a Gaelic Irish king. Previous to that, it was the Norse of the Isles who were recruited, as Muirchertach Mac Lochlainn did in 1154, when he also hired the Norse of Dublin for his attack on Connacht.[48]

It was no coincidence that it was in the mid-thirteenth century that Scots were first employed as soldiers by Gaelic Irish kings. They were part of that militarisation of Irish society which also saw the emergence of kerne, professional native soldiers.[49] This process of militarisation had become necessary as the kings of post-Clontarf Ireland became increasingly ambitious and set about conquering land. They found their soldiers where they could – from the Norse of the Isles, as we saw, from Dublin, from Norman Wales (as O Brien did when he used Arnulf Montgomery early in the twelfth century).[50] The most famous example of all, of course, is Dermot Mac Murrough, who imported Anglo-Norman mercenaries in 1167 and after, and thus gave rise to the English conquest of Ireland. By the mid-thirteenth century the more important Gaelic kings were involved in attempts to check locally English expansion and the further loss of lands. To do this they needed to be able to win battles, take castles, garrison their own fortresses and generally rely on men permanently in arms, as distinct from those obliged through social contracts to serve on a seasonal basis. Even lesser lords, who could not afford to keep permanent armed retinues, needed mercenaries from time to time. The Scottish galloglass provided a ready source.

The galloglass were indispensable for another reason. Ireland, even then, had a reputation for producing fine horses of a particular kind, so much so that English kings regularly sought them. These were the hobbies, light and speedy, used by the hobelars who first appeared in Scotland from Ireland in 1296 and who were to help to revolutionise the art of warfare when from them came the mounted archer.[51] In Gaelic Ireland these hobbies carried lightly armed troops without armour, those whom Gerald of Wales described so vividly, if rather misleadingly, as riding naked into battle.[52] Effective as they were in harrying operations, especially in wooded or difficult terrain, they were not much good when it came to open battle against armoured men-at-arms of the kind the Anglo-Irish used. Nor were the lightly armed kerne very effective against such opponents. Here the galloglass came into their own, wearing armour and wielding the fearsome double-edged axe on its long shaft, deadly against cumbersome heavy horses when engaged at close quarters. No wonder they became so popular among the Irish.

The main elements in the story of galloglass expansion into Ireland are well known.[53] First the Mac Donalds and the Mac Sweeneys came in the thirteenth century and remained until the end of the Middle Ages as by far the greatest among the galloglass dynasties in Ireland. They were followed in the fourteenth century by the Mac Sheehys, Mac Dowells, Mac Cabes, Mac Rorys and others. All of these great names founded galloglass dynasties. They settled into the greater Gaelic lordships, where they were given hereditary office as captains or constables of gallo-glass, endowed with lands, and generally integrated into the structures of Gaelic society. For example, they were the subject of traditional bardic praise poetry just like the Gaelic lords, and indeed the gaelicised, Anglo-Irish lords. When Richard II was in Ireland in 1394–95 he treated some of these galloglass leaders on the same footing as great Gaelic lords like O Neill. On 16 March 1395, for example, John Mac Donald came to the king at the Dominican friary in Drogheda and did liege homage to the king in the old traditional way, using the Irish language which was rendered in English by Thomas Talbot the interpreter. Some weeks earlier Mac Donald had written to the king from Armagh, styling himself 'captain of his nation and constable of the Irish of Ulster'. Of particular interest is the request which he made to the king, 'much encouraged and comforted', he wrote, because 'your gracious fidelity is famed throughout the world as is just'. He asked that he might –[54]

> ... be your liegeman, captain, and constable throughout your whole land of Ireland with as many armed men as you wish me to have with your royal majesty.

This reads as if Mac Donald was suggesting that the king, too, should have his own company of galloglass in Ireland, anticipating what was to happen many years later. It certainly illustrates one characteristic of most of the galloglass, with the exception of the Mac Sweeneys and, later, the Mac Donalds, that they were always available to the highest bidder, even against their former employer.

On 19 March 1395, among those who did liege homage to the king in the Franciscan church in Dundalk was a man whom the record calls simply 'Mac Cabe of Clogher diocese'.[55] In the Annals of Ulster he is styled the 'constable of Oirgialla', who was the hereditary constable of galloglass in the service of the O Ruaircs, O Reillys and Mac Mahons of Cavan and Monaghan.[56]

By the end of the fourteenth century, then, the great galloglass families were already well integrated into Gaelic Ireland. But there is clear evidence that long before that, at least in Ulster, the galloglass had become so numerous that they were

49. There seems little to support the local tradition that the burial site of Edward Bruce, 'king of Ireland', lies in Faughart graveyard: in truth, there can have been little of his body to bury after his enemies had vented their revenge – a contemporary chronicler, based in Dublin, reports that after Edward Bruce was killed at Faughart in 1318, his head was sent to Edward II, his body quartered, his heart, hand and one quarter going to Dublin for public display, and the other quarters to 'other places'. It is, however, a firm conviction in local traditional memory, which asserts that he was buried in Faughart graveyard where this memorial was erected in the mid-nineteenth century. The formal marking out of the 'grave' seems to have been undertaken by local nationalist admirers of Bruce, led by the antiquarian Nicholas O'Kearney.

already a burden on the people and something of a problem. In 1297, O Neill of Tyrone, Mac Mahon of Uriel and Maguire of Fermanagh entered into an agreement with the archbishop of Armagh, the vigorous Nicholas Mac Maoilíosa, that in future they would restrict what they called 'our Scots and satellites' (in other words gallo-glass and kerne) from trespassing against the tenants on the lands of the archbishop.[57] In 1316 O Neill again issued letters patent to another archbishop of Armagh, again restricting the exactions demanded by his 'Scottish satellites' and others.[58]

The cause of the trouble was the Irish system of *buannacht* (bonnacht), the right of the Gaelic lord to quarter his soldiers on his subjects.[59] Inevitably this led to abuse and all attempts at control, as we might expect, ultimately failed. To the end of the Middle Ages the system of *buannacht*, and its expanded form of coyne and livery in the Anglo-Irish lordships, remained a constant source of bitter complaint. As the galloglass spread throughout the lordship so did these exactions. They became part of that complex system by which the magnates, Gaelic and Anglo-Irish alike, maintained their positions in their lordships. For, ever since the thirteenth century, when it became clear that the defence of the marches and the protection of what was called 'the land of peace' was a burden on the local magnate and community, successive parliaments gave legal sanction to the imposition of what amounted to local taxations in kind and the billeting of private armies on the population of the local communities. It provided one important element in the growth of what historians have called bastard feudalism, which developed along its own peculiar lines in Ireland, and in which the Scottish galloglass came to have a central role.

Exactly how and when the galloglass system spread is not very clear and so far has proved impossible to chart in detail.[60] From Ulster and Connacht the Scots moved south. The Dublin chronicler, for example, reported that on 12 November 1311 the lord Richard de Clare killed 600 galloglass in Thomond.[61] No details are given. But the slaughter was part of the O Brien civil war which dominated the politics of Thomond for years. In that year, 1311, the Anglo-Irish were ranged on opposing sides, with Richard de Burgh supporting one O Brien faction and the de Burghs of Connacht supporting the other. According to the Annals of Inisfallen it was William de Burgh who brought the galloglass with him from Connacht into Thomond and presumably it was these who were killed by de Clare.[62] It also means that in Connacht the de Burghs were already keeping galloglass, just as they maintained kerne and billetted them widely on their people. The Annals of Connacht, for example, record that in 1310 this same William de Burgh billeted 200 mercenaries *(sersenach)* on Síl Murray and 'there was not one of their townlands without its permanent quartering, nor a *tuath* free from exaction, nor a prince free from oppression, so long as William was in control of them'.[63]

From Thomond the galloglass, as might be expected, spread southwards into Desmond and into Munster, Maurice fitz Maurice, the 'rebellious first earl of Desmond', built up a formidable army which included large numbers of Irish kerne as well as Anglo-Irish outlaws and these came from Connacht, Thomond and Leinster as well as from Desmond itself.[64] Desmond was later accused of contacting the king of Scotland and inviting him to participate in his bizarre proposal to disengage the lordship of Ireland from the English crown and set up an independent kingdom with himself as ruler.[65] It is possible that such contact might have resulted in the importation of soldiers from Scotland, though hardly galloglass. What we do know is that on 23 July 1328 the earl's *rúta* (as his army was called) came to Youghal in county Cork, with Maurice himself at its head, and committed many felonies against the Barrys, Cogaris and other local Anglo-Irish families. Among the people named as joining the *rúta* on that occasion was Gregory Mac Ryry with his following, the same man who was constable of galloglass for Turloch O Conor of Connacht.[66]

It is not at all clear when the galloglass spread further in Munster or, more important, into Leinster. It may be significant that in 1361 and 1362 a 'Donaldus Gall' was serving with a retinue in the Wicklow area in the employment of the Dublin government. The name suggests that, whatever about the men he led, he himself was a galloglass.[67] But it is not until the early fifteenth century that we have proof positive of the widespread presence of galloglass in the great Butler lordship of Tipperary-

Kilkenny. In the well-known ordinances which were published in an assembly which met at Fethard, probably in 1432, it was enacted that 'none of our nation [i.e. the Butlers] shall billet kerne or galloglass on the *patria* of Tipperary and Kilkenny, unless they belong to the personal retinue of the earl and are led with the free consent of the community'.[68] Even earlier, in 1417, there were complaints of fifteen battles being billetted illegally on the *patria* and others in Cork and Limerick, and while galloglass are not specifically mentioned, the term 'battle' was the one normally used to describe a retinue of sixty to eighty galloglass.[69] It is plain that galloglass were by then an accepted part of the earl of Ormond's military establishment and so they remained. In 1517 the lordship accepted that the earl's 'horsemen, Scots or footmen who were called kernty' might be a burden on the country and that 'whenever any strangers shall attack, injure or prey' the country, 'then all the horsemen, Scots, footmen and all others, both gentry and husbandmen, shall rise in defence'.[70]

As for the other great earldom in late medieval Ireland, that of Kildare, galloglass were again a well-established feature by the fifteenth century. Indeed, in 1537, Justice Luttrell produced evidence that the first galloglass in Kildare were led by one Barret, 'being exyled oute of Conaght', who came to the eighth earl and offered his service. From then on the earl imposed coyne on his tenants.[71] The earl, too, was supplied with galloglass from elsewhere and just how effective they could be was seen from the battle of Knockdoe in 1504, when Kildare had with him, in addition to his own retainers from the earldom, Mayo Burkes, O Donnells, O Neills, Mac Mahons, Magennises, O Reillys, O Conors, Mac Dermots and others, both Gaelic and Anglo-Irish too, with contingents of galloglass. Kildare won the day and it was the galloglass who played a crucial role in defeating those galloglass who were no less prominent on the other side.[72]

It was Kildare, too, who more than anyone else was responsible for making galloglass a routine element in government armies. Serving under four kings – Edward IV, Richard III, Henry VII and Henry VIII – he showed that the only way in which the pale could be defended, given the limited resources available to the Dublin government, was by using galloglass and kerne as supplementary forces. In 1517 his son, the ninth earl, explained to the earl of Shrewsbury what the position was:

> Wherever the deputy goes for the common weal it is usual for his horsemen and galloglass to have their food in those parts, except at great hostings; otherwise he could not support them, were the king's revenue six times as large.

Three years later, on the occasion of the Surrey expedition to Ireland, an official memorandum explained the 'considerations why coign and livery may not be clearly and suddenly laid down'. Englishmen adjoining the Irish are compelled to keep galloglass and kerne to defend their land and coign and livery is necessary to support those troops. But in addition, 'without galloglass and kerne, the deputy cannot well defend the Englishry'.[73]

Galloglass under these circumstances necessarily began to infiltrate the pale, that small defended area around Dublin which was one part of Ireland where English

50. Nenagh Castle contains the finest of the round towers attached to medieval Irish castles (although the upper parts are modern); the property of the Butlers, their lordship of Tipperary was host to large contingents of galloglass certainly by the early fifteenth century, part of the personal retinue of the Butler earls of Ormond

institutions and customs were supposed to be preserved intact. Coign and livery, which had once been banned from the pale, now became normal, if not fully acceptable, to the inhabitants. Palesmen who valued their Englishness saw in the galloglass, as well as the Gaelic kerne who were so often associated with them, a symbol of Gaelicisation which should properly be resisted. A letter of Edmond Golding of Drogbeda, written in about 1487 to the earl of Ormond, complained that there was only one man he knew of in the shire (Uriel) 'that rydithe in a sadill dayly', that is, in the English as against the Irish fashion. In the shire of Meath there were only two 'that werithe gowne and dublet', again in the English fashion. He went on: 'And y my lord I ham an Englishe man. I pray you to defend... me or then shall cum a horse man and a galloglaghe in my stede [and settle in your lands] dowt ye hit not'.[74]

But by then the process of infiltration was unstoppable. When in 1494 Edward Poynings was sent to Ireland to prevent the Yorkist pretender Perkin Warbeck from repeating the military success of Lambert Simnel, he employed galloglass in a crucial military operation in the very heart of the pale in the Vale of Dublin. Significantly, too, with Kildare in disgrace – he had just been attainted of treason and was a prisoner on his way to England – Poynings found a ready supply of galloglass from the Butler lordship and they served him loyally under Sir James Ormond.[75] Later, the 1515 report on the state of Ireland summed it up:[76]

> ... howe garde of the Kinges Deputye is none other, but a multytude of Iryshe galloglagheis, and a multytude of Iryshe kernne and speres, with infynyt nombre of horsseladdes; and with the said garde, the Kinges Deputye is ever moveing and styreing from one place to another, and with extortion of coyne and lyverye consumeith and devowreith all the substaunce of the poore folke.

Later still, in 1537, Justice Luttrell condemned coyne and livery within the pale and the galloglass thus supported; but he had to admit that the common opinion was 'that the borders is best defendeid by kerne and galloglasheis'.[77]

So, despite all protests, galloglass remained in government pay. In August 1538 Peter O More elaborated the terms of his submission of the previous January. He agreed that 'the deputy may quarter 120 galloglass in Leix for 40 days each year', an interesting gloss on the ancient feudal service of the tenants-in-chief of the king. When 'treaties with Irishmen', as they were called, were extensively procured in 1540, the submitting Irishmen normally had to agree to provide galloglass for service with the government. Turloch Roe O Conor in January, for example, promised: 'that he shall pay yerelie to the King, or his Subthesaurer, £8 sterling at Mihilmas, and shall fynde yerelie during a moneth 80 galloglas'.

O Donnell promised 'to provide to go with the deputy, when needed, for one month, 60 horse, 120 kerne and 120 Scots alias galloglass'. In 1549 there are even references to what are specifically called 'the king's galloglass'.[78]

By then there were large numbers of galloglass all over Ireland. In 1539 the earl of Ormond was able to supply 800 galloglass to serve against the Geraldine league. In the same year a letter from Dublin to Thomas Cromwell told him that 'there is of

Scottes, now dwellying in Ireland, above two thowsand men of warre'. But a detailed description of 'the power of Irishmen', compiled about 1534, listed a total of forty-one battles of galloglass, together with 3,345 horse and 15,704 kerne and commented that 'a batayle of Galoglas be 60 or 80 men harneysed on foot with sparres, each with 1 knave to beare his harneys'.[79]

But in the second half of the sixteenth century a new era had begun. For various reasons, not least population pressure in the Hebrides, huge numbers of mercenary soldiers travelled to serve in Ireland. The name of galloglass virtually disappeared and that of redshank appeared in its place. In Ulster alone in the days of Turloch Luineach O Neill, who died in 1595, they came in their thousands. It has been estimated that not counting Turloch's own army of up to 8,000 and other Scots who had settled in the old galloglass fashion, about 35,000 came from Scotland as mercenaries.[80] The Scottish dimension was therefore maintained and Ireland became of vital importance in the complex history of Anglo-Scottish history, even well into the seventeenth century.[81]

We might ask one last question about the medieval galloglass. How good were they? The 1515 report was quite dismissive:[82]

> Nowe all the wylde Iryshe, with all ther galloglaheis, and Iryshe Scottes, called keteryns, have no more power, ne myght, to stande in the fylde, ne to mayntayne ther warres ageynst the Kinges subgettes then have the wolffe ageinste lyon, or the kyte ageynst the fawken.

But in 1543 the great St Leger gave a very different opinion to Henry VIII:

> And as to their footemen, they have one sorte, whiche be harnessed in mayle and bassenettes, having every of them his weapon, called a sparre, moche like the axe of the Towre, and they be named galloglasse... these sorte of men be those that doo not lightly abandon the fielde, but hyde the brunte to the deathe.

And he added that they and the kerne 'be of suche hardenes, that ther ys no man that ever I sawe, that will or can endure the paynes and evill fare that they will sustayne'.[83] Everything we know about the medieval galloglass would support St Leger. And even the 1515 report, in describing the more than sixty 'countryes' in Ireland, each with its own 'Chyef Captayne', admitted that no captain could succeed his father, or survive thereafter, 'withoute he be the strongeise of all his nation' and only by 'fort mayne'. The same was true of the 'more than 30 greate captaines of the Englyshe noble folke, that folowyth the same fryshe ordre, and kepeith the same rule'; only 'hym that is strongeyst' could survive, 'such that maye subdue them by the swerde'.[84] It was in these circumstances that the Scottish galloglass came into their own and provided the captains, Anglo-Irish as well as Gaelic, with the strongest, if not the most numerous, element in their rule by force.

5

The Battle of Faughart

G.O. Sayles

It is my privilege to speak to you about the battle of Faughart, or, as it sometimes called, Dundalk, a battle that brought to an end in 1318 the efforts, spread over three and a half years, of an army of Scots to conquer Ireland.[1] When we reflect that the consequences were so serious that the years 1315–18 are often held to form a turning point in Irish history, and when we remember that it was all so completely unexpected, a veritable bolt from the blue, we are at once confronted with that problem which always lies uncomfortably at the back of the serious historian's mind. It is this: how far is the course of history set and settled for us by long-term factors and deeply established traditions like geographical position and climate or the imponderable spirit of a people? Or, on the contrary, can its direction be changed by predictable accidents? Do we see in history not the causal but simply the casual, having no more value for us than a tale that is told? As it was once ironically expressed, if Cleopatra's nose had been just a little longer, would Antony have fallen in love with her, and, if he had not, then would the destinies of the countries bordering the Eastern Mediterranean have been vastly different? If there had been no Napoleon or no Hitler, would France or Germany be as they are today? And if an expeditionary force had not been sent from Scotland to England in the early fourteenth century, would we now be speaking of the 'Republic of Ireland'? In all this there lies hidden an endless controversy and a great mystery and happily it need not detain us. But my further remarks may be regarded as a commentary upon this theme.

On 26 May 1315 Edward Bruce, the brother of Robert Bruce, king of Scotland, crossed the narrow seas from Galloway with his troops and landed on the north-east coast of Ireland, not very far from Larne. So began a long series of campaigns to subjugate the whole of Ireland. Now, though we are first and foremost considering

51. Traditionally regarded as the birth-place of St Brigid, the shrine at Faughart is still a place of deep devotion to this day

the art and practice of warfare in the later Middle Ages – and Bruce's career in Ireland furnishes us with many apt illustrations – we can never arbitrarily place war and politics in as it were water-tight compartments and study them apart. Therefore, even though I have to speak briefly, I must for clarity's sake indicate why Edward Bruce should have thought of the conquest of Ireland at all, why that conquest was regarded as a quite practical proposition, and why it seemed not unlikely at one time that his high ambitions would be gratified.

Throughout the whole of the Middle Ages the North Channel between north-east Ireland and south-west Scotland had been in one respect like the English Channel between England and France: it was not in those days so much a barrier to communications as a means of contact, far easier than having to cross bogs or cut a way through forests. No Irishman needs to be reminded of this close connection when he remembers the Patrician Church and the missionary journey of St Columba of Donegal and Derry to Argyll. In a way, the plantation of Ulster by the Scots had begun as early as King John's reign, when men from Galloway settled on lands in and around Derry and Coleraine given to them by that king. The Scots apparently found no difficulty in establishing a *modus vivendi* with the native Irish. Indeed, they were too successful and, some fifty years later, the English government found it necessary to place an embargo upon any further immigration by Scots into Ireland. But the association was not broken, and not many more years went by before the liaison was demonstrated at the highest level when James, the Steward of Scotland, married the sister of the Red Earl of Ulster in 1296 and when the Red Earl's daughter in 1302 married Robert Bruce, earl of Carrick, who was four years later to be the crowned king of Scotland.

Still, there was nothing in all of this to foretell the whirlwind. The province of Ulster, though nominally a part of the dominions of the English crown, had been little drawn into the machinery of English government. Aided largely by its geography, Ulster remained separatist. It is true that coastal lands from Coleraine round to Carlingford Lough had been granted to Englishmen and that there was an enclave of them around Antrim. Nevertheless, the English government was very ready to leave the exercise of power with the Red Earl, Richard de Burgh. Though he owned much land in all the other provinces of Ireland, especially in Connacht, Ulster was the basis of his authority, and under him the native Irish and the English and Scots incomers seem to have achieved a state of relatively peaceful co-existence for well over a generation. Maybe this promise of stability was illusory. What did not appear open to doubt was the strength of the Red Earl, who was to all seeming a formidable man to overthrow. And yet in the event his power crumbled quickly at the onslaught of Edward Bruce, and it is not easy to find a satisfactory explanation why he should have proved so ineffective when put to the test.

Still, it was not the weakness of Ireland but the weakness of England that gave Edward Bruce his chance. I do not think that we need to search far for his motives. His expedition was very much a personal venture and it was a gamble, after the fashion of that of William the Conqueror in 1066. His brother, Robert, though himself an Anglo-Norman and Scottish only by his mother, had found himself led to make his

52. In Faughart graveyard, some way distant from the modern shrine to St Brigid, can be found this holy well dedicated to her

53. There was an Anglo-Norman manor established at Faughart in the thirteenth century, at the core of which stands the motte pictured here

choice between England and Scotland and, as it happened, he had won for himself a Scottish crown. Why should Edward Bruce not likewise take by the sword a kingdom in Ireland from the same inept and much harassed Edward II of England? As I already remarked, Ulster was not unknown or hard of access. Its political state was no secret and there was a chance that the native Irish might be induced to give their allegiance and support to the Norman Bruce rather than the Norman de Burgh. This perhaps above all: Robert Bruce knew how much he owed his brother for his active help in war right up to the battle of Bannockburn in 1314, and he knew also the restlessness, the feverish itch for action, that was Edward's dominant characteristic. It was commonly believed at the time that Scotland was too small to contain two such brothers. The fourteenth-century chronicler who wrote the *Scotichronicon* expressed it briefly when he said: 'Edward was a very mettlesome and high-spirited man and would not dwell together with his brother in peace unless he had half the kingdom to himself. And for this reason was stirred up in Ireland this war'.

So King Robert blessed the expedition: if it succeeded, it further weakened his enemy, England; even if it failed, it rid him of the embarrassment of his brother's presence in Scotland. Either way he profited.

It should be made quite clear at the outset that warfare in the later Middle Ages called for little military science in the sense of careful strategic planning beforehand and that big battles were very rare. Much that we dignify in our textbooks with the name of 'battle' implies no more than a skirmish, often of a most haphazard kind. When the opposing forces clashed, then the things that mattered were mainly two: tactics in the field, and – which was considered far more important – personal

54. This photograph, taken from the top of the de Verdon motte at Faughart, shows the medieval parish graveyard in the background

prowess. No matter how much ingenious skill was lavished on arms and armour, both for man and horse, it was still sheer physical strength and the aptitude for single combat that counted most. Warrior kings like Richard the Lion-Heart or Edward I or Henry V stood high for that reason in contemporary opinion: other rulers like John, who was contemptuously called 'Soft-Sword', or the completely uninterested Edward II, failed at once to act the part of a king. If, however, the forces of one side were obviously inferior, then it was their business to avoid pitched battles. Either they shut themselves up in a castle and stood a siege, during which it became the object of the besiegers to effect a breach and get to grips in hand-to-hand fighting; or else, if the terrain permitted it, those who were outnumbered took cover, not in castles but in forests, swamps or mountains, and thereby again created a position of stalemate until they thought the time opportune for emerging to give battle. All these general characteristics of medieval warfare are seen in Bruce's campaigns, and I shall simply seek to give illustrations of them from his activities without entering into tedious detail.

We who still remember the lengthy preparations that were needed for the Normandy landings in 1944 will be better able to realise that it required no slight effort on Scotland's part to raise, equip and transport across the sea in some 300 ships an army of 6,000 men with presumably a fair number of horses. How it was accomplished we do not know and we are not likely to know. It was certainly no rabble that came to Ireland but a force of professional soldiers who had learned their trade the hard way in the fierce conflict with England and who were led by soldiers of experience like Edward Bruce himself and the earl of Moray, who had each commanded a

55. What remains of the medieval parish church of Faughart, at the core of the de Verdon manor, and near the field of battle

division of the Scottish army at Bannockburn. Once ashore near Larne on 26 May 1315, the Scots were joined by a few, but not many, of the Irish chieftains in Ulster, the most important being Donnell O Neill of Tirowen, and they soon marched southwards without meeting any resistance even to bar their passage through the narrow Moiry Pass between Newry and Dundalk. Dundalk was itself captured, looted and burned on 29 June, little more than a month after they had landed.

The invaders had perforce to live always and everywhere on the country and the devastation of prosperous manors was harsh in the extreme; just as we can follow the course of William the Conqueror's march to London in 1066 by plotting the wasted lands set down in Domesday Book, so we can trace the route of the Scots in the Irish financial records which many years later were still reciting a total loss in revenue from estates harried by the Scots. When the Justiciar of Ireland and the earl of Ulster assembled their forces at Ardee, the Red Earl successfully insisted that with his own resources alone he could bring about Bruce's defeat. He might well have been correct in his contention if he could have forced a direct battle. But Bruce was over-persuaded by O Neill that it would be folly for his forces, consisting mainly of men on foot, to engage an enemy, superior in both cavalry and archers, in open land. Bruce therefore let his Irish allies guide him away through the bogs and fen-peats west of the river Bann and northwards on the far side of Lough Neagh up to the mouth of the Bann at Coleraine, where he broke down the bridge across the river. The Red Earl knew that pursuit was out of the question in such territory and he for his part took the rosier way east of Lough Neagh to Coleraine. The bridge being levelled, the Bann was at that point far too wide to be crossed otherwise and

56. This is the view south from the ancient shrine of St Brigid at Faughart and may be the battle-site

stalemate resulted. The earl, however, could not keep his forces at full strength indefinitely: family feuds and consequent disturbance in the south-west of Ireland drained away the Connacht contingent and, when the Scots had crossed the Bann on 10 September, they routed the much depleted forces of the over-confident earl of Ulster. That encounter ended the first episode of the war, leaving all Ulster in Bruce's control except at one point: the royal castle of Carrickfergus. What befell it will serve to illustrate the nature of siege warfare.

The castle was placed impregnably on a rocky headland overlooking Belfast Lough, and the stone keep and bailey, and the walls that defied all the assaults of Edward Bruce can still be seen today. After the battle of Connor, many of the Red Earl's supporters sought refuge within the castle, which was at once invested by the Scots. Bruce could hardly have relished venturing out of Ulster until it had capitulated, but defence was paramount and, as usual, the only means of triumphing over that defence was through famine or treachery within the walls, or both combined. The defenders of Carrickfergus could, of course, still get in touch with the outside world by way of the sea, and in spring 1316 they did receive reinforcements from Drogheda. But whilst food could not have been prevented from coming in, there was, as we shall see, little food to send, and in September 1316, after resisting a year, the starving garrison surrendered. The evidence in print of what actually happened is sparse, little more than the statement of an annalist that on Midsummer's Day 1316 the defenders had imprisoned thirty who had been sent to them by Bruce, under a guarantee of protection to receive the submission of the castle and in their extreme hunger they had later eaten eight such prisoners. The significant word is 'hunger': Carrickfergus did not fall to assault.

57. The approach to Faughart from Dundalk (in the distance): tactically, from the Scots' perspective, this would make the best vantage point from which to counter the approaching Anglo-Irish army

I can throw a little further light upon events from a record in the Four Courts in Dublin. On Saturday 23 July 1317, Henry of Thrapston was placed on trial at Drogheda on the charge that he had acted as a traitor in admitting Thomas Dun, a Scot and enemy to the king, to Carrickfergus Castle, giving him food and drink and some cloth for a cloak, and handing over three Scots prisoners to him at Edward Bruce's request. Furthermore, while he was Treasurer of Ulster and Keeper of Carrickfergus Castle and under no compulsion to leave the castle, he had gone outside the walls to meet Bruce in person and had acknowledged him as his lord, asserting that he wished to be his Treasurer in Ireland as he had been the Red Earl's Treasurer in Ulster. A further count against him was that he had sold so much corn and other foodstuffs after the Scots arrived that the castle was denuded of supplies and did not resist as long as it should have done. A jury was empanelled and declared that a truce had, indeed, been arranged between Bruce and the garrison to last for a month so that the two sides could communicate with each other at Carrickfergus and elsewhere. It was on account of this arrangement that Thrapston had allowed Dun into the castle, fed him and delivered two prisoners to him. Under interrogation, the jury agreed that the terms of the truce contained no definite provision permitting Scots to enter the castle itself and hold discussions with the garrison within its precincts, and for that reason Thrapston was committed to prison. But they did exonerate him from the charge of having done fealty to Bruce and from having negligently sold provisions. And when they were asked whether he had acted from good or evil motives, they had no hesitation in stating that what he had done had been done for the good and safety of the country and of the men of Ulster. In the following Michaelmas term the matter was discussed in council at Dublin, and Thrapston was granted a pardon on the ground that a praiseworthy report had been received upon his services in Carrickfergus Castle.

Whilst Carrickfergus was being besieged, Bruce began his bids for the conquest of Ireland. He put his trust in two campaigns in winter, knowing that this was the suitable time of year for the kind of forces under his command and hoping that rapid movement far and wide would bring him the widespread native Irish support he expected and without which he would sooner or later have to admit defeat. After mid-November 1315 he marched again to Dundalk, to Nobber in Meath, to Kells; then veered west to Granard in County Longford and spent Christmas at Ballymore Loughsewdy in West Meath before going south as far as Kildare and Castledermot. The results of this medieval blitzkrieg were clearly unsatisfactory, and Bruce returned to his base in Ulster at the end of January 1316 and remained there throughout the remainder of the year. At the end of 1316 he was joined at Carrickfergus by his brother, King Robert of Scotland. We may regard this rather surprising visit as a measure of how little Robert had to fear at home from the English government and how he still had faith in Edward's schemes. I would myself add the irresistible attraction that war and military exploits had for all men of their generation such as the Bruces. However that may be, the two brothers marched south again in February 1317, by-passed Drogheda and Dublin, advanced to Castledermot, to Gowran and Callan in Kilkenny, thence westwards through Cashel towards Limerick, which they did not reach, though they came to the Shannon at Castleconnell. In mid-April 1317 they made their return journey to Ulster. In May King Robert went back to Scotland.

In neither of these campaigns was there either time or specialised equipment or forces to spare to besiege castles like Kildare or walled towns like Dublin, where the citizens in February 1317 had looked to their own safety, repaired their walls and taken drastic measures to stand a siege, if that should prove necessary. The two campaigns should have shown Bruce that his ambitions were not going to be realised. It is true that in the first he met with concerted opposition from the Justiciar of Ireland and the great lords of Ireland only once, and that in the second the Justiciar was content to adopt shadow tactics and made no effort to intercept Bruce and cut off his retreat to the north. Still, the other side of the picture is that Bruce had not managed to engage and decisively destroy his enemies: their Fabian methods had at least kept their army in being, and, whilst they could afford to wait, he could not. Again, Bruce was unlucky in that in May 1315, the very month he landed in Ireland, a great famine descended upon the whole of Europe from Ireland to Russia. The interminable torrential floods made the spring and autumn sowings a complete failure, and the effects on an agricultural society, always living on the margin of existence, were horrible. Men died in their thousands and lay unburied in the streets and lanes, and reports of cannibalism came from every country, including Ireland. In this country the consequences were still felt until the summer of 1318. It is not therefore surprising that Bruce found it impossible to feed his troops on the march and that many died of hunger. We know that he raided and looted, harried and burnt, everywhere he went, and the native Irish, suffering along with everyone else, had little reason to rally to his support. Yet without them he would fail and the ceremony at Dundalk on 1 May 1316, when he had himself crowned king of Ireland, would remain empty bravado. He had twice marched his armies south and marched them back again, but he had no military advantages to show for it all. His campaigns had degenerated into mere plundering raids and as such they were a sheer waste of two armies and gave him but a Pyrrhic victory.

I have said little about the source of material on which the reconstruction of these events must rely. How sparse it is, how often we have to make bricks with hardly any straw, is sufficiently shown when I say that we have not the slightest information about Bruce's activities between May 1317 and October 1318. Then he made the last of his gambler's throws, took his way south through the Moiry Pass for the last time, and met his death at the battle of Faughart on 14 October. Of the battle itself we have a few, but very few, details from Scottish and Irish writers, but where they are not utterly incredible they are open to serious doubt. The Scottish account of Archdeacon Barbour relates that Bruce had given his coat-of-mail to his henchman, with the result that the head which was sent to the king of England was the henchman's and not that of Bruce himself. A Gaelic account, which alone purports to describe the tactics employed, spoils the effect by letting Bruce win the fight but be slain, as he sauntered round the battlefield, by one of his enemies who disguised himself as a juggler, put Bruce off his guard by one of his antics, and hit him on the head with a ball of iron attached to a chain. All this is part and parcel of the *chansons de geste,* the romances that served to while away the tedium of a winter night. Even when Barbour speaks of the unenthusiastic support Bruce got from his Irish allies – and we must remember that he wrote sixty years after the event – it is likely that as a good patriotic Scot he was intent on explaining away a Scottish defeat. Faughart can, however, illustrate what I have said before: that great battles were not common and that the prowess of individuals was the factor to which overriding importance was attached.

Bruce's army, even though augmented by the contingents furnished by the de Lacys, could not have been large: he could not have had at his disposal anything like the number of professional soldiery, the heavy-armed infantry, that followed him as its leader in earlier years, and contemporary estimates of up to 3,000 Scots alone should not be uncritically accepted. Since the attack came suddenly, the defence against it had to be quickly supplied by local landowners and townsmen who always maintained some kind of military organisation for their own protection: John de Cusack is singled out in the records as bringing with him sixty men-at-arms and the city of Drogheda as contributing twenty more. Such figures as these get us nearer to the realities. Bruce took up his position on rising ground at Faughart not far north of Dundalk, positioning the Irish at the top of the hill and the Scots in front of them lower down. Whether he had cavalry or archers and, if so, how he deployed them, we do not know. All we can be certain about is that the Anglo-Irish felt confident enough to make a head-on attack and that they engaged in hand-to-hand fighting and broke through the Scottish ranks. Their leader, John de Bermingham, slew Alan,

Steward of Scotland, in single fight. Bruce himself was apparently killed by John Maupas, one of the Drogheda contingent, who was himself slain in the fight. So died one on whom the Irish compiler of the Annals of Loch Cé passed this judgement:

> Edward Bruce, the destroyer of all Erin in general, both English and Gael... no better deed for the men of all Erin was performed since the beginning of the world... for theft and famine destruction of men occurred throughout Erin during his time.

Indeed, the prosperity of many of the English districts never came back and both English and Irish were the losers thereby. Economic was inseparable from a moral collapse and the thirteenth century promise that English and Irish might manage to live together as English and Welsh contrived to do was belied. For that Edward Bruce was greatly, if not wholly, responsible. I end where I began: would the tale have been different if the Bruces had not come to Ireland?

6

THE IMPACT OF THE BRUCE INVASION, 1315–27

JAMES LYDON

When Edward I died in 1307, he was leading yet another army against the Scots, now led by Robert Bruce. As always, the Dublin government was involved in this expedition. It was the murder of John Comyn by Bruce in February 1306 that forced Edward to begin preparing yet again for another intervention in Scotland, and it is a measure of the shock that the murder caused that the news was immediately sent to Ireland as a matter of great urgency. Almost immediately the king began looking for victuals in Ireland and a stream of writs followed, urging haste in gathering supplies.[1] But it soon became apparent that there was no money available in Dublin to meet the royal demands, unless payment of arrears of wages owing to the earl of Ulster and others was postponed.[2] Shortage of ready cash was becoming a problem. In late April the king ordered that wool custom receipts should be recovered from the Frescobaldi because, he said, 'the exchequer stands very much in need of money'.[3]

There were other signs that the Irish exchequer was finding it increasingly difficult, if not impossible, to meet the demands now being placed on limited resources. At a time when the treasurer was paying out nearly £2,500 to royal purveyors for supplies for Scotland, he was trying to find well over £2,500 for the clerk of the wages appointed for Wogan's 1306 expedition to the Leinster mountains.[4] Together these two sums ate up most of the receipts of the exchequer and left little over for the ordinary expenses of government. Something had to be skimped. The escalation of war in the colony, the contraction of the land of peace and the economic decline that necessarily resulted, meant that even less money flowed into the Dublin exchequer. A financial crisis resulted. Figures for the last years of the reign of Edward I show a fall

58. The familiar Sugarloaf Mountain is located in what was the royal manor of Obrun (from Uí Briúin Chualainn) in the northern foothills of the Wicklow mountains. The justiciar, John Wogan, campaigned here in 1306, but the area continued to present the government with problems and was a cause of concern especially during the Bruce wars

from £6,112 in 1302 to as little as £3,641 in 1305–06. There was a brief recovery to £5,893 in 1306–07 and £5,237 in 1307–08. But thereafter the decline continued year by year: £3,477, £2,586, £3,003, £2,865.[5]

Shortage of cash meant an increase in assignment (that is, the exchequer began to operate a system of credit based on anticipated receipts from specified sources of income) which almost inevitably meant that debts began to pile up. It is noticeable, for example, that even the fees of officials (many in arrears) were being paid by assignment.[6] With the fees of constables in arrears, even the royal castles began seriously to deteriorate. In the summer of 1313 the earl of Ulster complained that the walls and houses of the castles of Roscommon, Athlone and Rindown were 'mostly ruined for want of repair'.[7] A year later Wogan informed the council in England that Limerick castle, 'situated in the dangerous march between the Irish and English', was 'threatened with ruin and fallen down and broken on all sides'.[8] This kind of deterioration was alarming and demanded some attempt at reform that would improve the flow of revenue into the exchequer and increase the ready cash available to the government. But the best it seemed to be able to do was to initiate an inquiry into old debts that were still being recorded on the pipe rolls, and to try to flush out debtors through intensive local investigations, such as were conducted by the chancellor, Walter of Thornbury, during tours that he made in 1308 and 1309.[9]

It was not local Irish needs, however, that immediately prompted this attempt to increase revenues but rather the great need of Edward II to meet the demands of the renewed war in Scotland. In 1320 he explained to Wogan how urgently he needed

59. Limerick Castle, described in 1314, on the eve of the Bruce invasion, as being 'situated in the dangerous march between the English and the Irish', and 'threatened with ruin and fallen down and broken on all sides'

money, and soon the English council, weary of the failure of the Irish administration to collect debts, took the unprecedented step of sending its own agents over to urge on the work. But it was all to no avail. The disturbed condition of the country and the continuing wars there were all in favour of the debtors. The Irish council, too, was increasingly worried about the problem of defence. In August 1311 it decided that all revenue from customs, which again had been assigned to the Frescobaldi, should be paid instead into the Dublin exchequer and be applied 'to the safety of Ireland'.[10] The last phrase was not lightly used. A letter from the king to Wogan and Bicknor, the treasurer of Ireland, ordered all revenues to be applied 'in reforming the state of Ireland and towards the safety of the same'. Once more the English council took a hand and devised an ordinance for imposing an extraordinary procedure for levying debts in Ireland. It is clear that the ordinary machinery for levying through local government officials had altogether broken down, which is a good indication of the erosion of central control of the localities. But not even the extraordinary procedures devised in England were sufficient to overcome the delinquency of Irish sheriffs, and there seems to have been little to show by way of increased revenue for all the effort.

In 1311, too, the famous ordinances initiated a programme of reform in England which also had repercussions in Ireland. It was almost certainly the ordainers who were responsible for the remarkable letter that came to Ireland in the name of the king and that announced a revolutionary change in policy, whereby in future all Irish revenues were to be spent in Ireland on maintaining the peace. But all too soon the king reverted to his customary policy of exploitation. In 1312 and again in 1313 huge quantities of supplies were sent to castles threatened by Bruce.[11] In 1314, when preparing for the campaign which preceded Bannockburn, the king ordered the Irish treasurer to hand over all the money then in the exchequer and all the issues of Ireland during the next four months to the agent sent to raise troops for Scotland.[12] But already the Irish exchequer was so short of money that it could only find a few hundred pounds to meet the king's wishes. By now Edward was aware of this and seems to have taken steps to subsidise the war effort in Ireland: in 1314 we hear that a 'great sum of money' which he was sending to Ireland was stolen on its way through Wales.[13] This marked the beginning of a momentous change in Anglo-Irish relations whereby Ireland, no longer capable of paying her own way, gradually became a charge on the English exchequer. In February 1315, when the Irish justiciar was ordered to raise troops for Scotland, the king made the unprecedented promise that he would send sufficient money to pay their wages.[14] The invasion of Edward Bruce soon made it impossible for Irish troops to go to Scotland, even though the king had sent money for their wages, and eventually an appeal had to be sent to England for £500 to help fight the Scots in Ireland.

For some years after the havoc of the Bruce wars, Ireland was in no condition to help the king. By 1322, however, the lordship had recovered sufficiently to send large quantities of food to Scotland.[15] But the difficulties the administration encountered in finding the necessary supplies, and the impossibility of paying for them from an impoverished exchequer, forced the king to call a halt and no further demands were made on Ireland to the end of the reign. The disturbed condition of Ireland would in any case have made it impossible to raise armies for Scotland, even though a small army did serve there in 1322.[16]

Quarrelling factions gave plenty of scope to those who wanted an outlet for martial spirit. The increase in the number of 'rebel English' and the continuing wars with Gaelic lords maintained a steady demand for troops at home. Lawlessness was on the increase, and when the Kilkenny parliament of 1310 heard the report of a special commission appointed to investigate the recent steep rise in prices, it laid the blame squarely on 'those of great lineage' who regularly robbed merchants of their goods as they travelled through the country or held them to ransom, and who also were in the habit of taking 'bread, wine, beer, flesh, and other victuals and things saleable, wherever they be, without making reasonable payment'.[17] The failure of the central government to maintain the rule of law was exposed even more in the decision of the parliament that each magnate ('chieftain of great lineage') should be responsible for the punishment of errant members of his family. This was a notable extension of an Irish statute of 1278 which made the heads of Gaelic lineages responsible for bringing lawbreakers to justice.[18] Before the end of the reign of Edward I this practice had spread to the Anglo-Irish lineages. In 1290 one of the most important magnates, Eustace le Poer, assembled his lineage before the sheriff of Waterford and swore that they would bring his cousin Robert le Poer to justice[19]. It seems that the justiciar formally licensed some heads of lineages to arrest those of their families found breaking the law. In 1306, when Philip Christopher was accused of wrongfully imprisoning Geoffrey Christopher, he defended himself by appealing

60. The site of Carrickmines Castle, in south County Dublin; here the government came face to face with the Irish of the Wicklow mountains, and the rebellious Harold and Archbold families. Only the remains of one wall survive, incorporated into a barn, but recent archaeological excavations have revealed a series of ditches revetted in stone which may have served a defensive purpose

to a licence from the justiciar 'to arrest those of his race whom he should find malefactors'.[20] So the 1310 parliament was giving statutory force to what had become an established practice. It also invoked the sanction of excommunication against defaulters, which seems to have been effective, since the magnates at the 1324 parliament requested absolution from the sentence.[21]

The 1310 parliament was notable for the large number of magnates (eighty-seven) individually summoned and for the procedure adopted.[22] Its legislation, too, was extensive, concentrating on what by then had become endemic problems in the colony. The defence of the marches was highlighted and the quartering of private armies on local communities was forbidden. It is significant, too, that the four counties of Leinster were treated as a single unit, which mirrors the growing concentration of the government on this important and most densely settled part of the colony. Perhaps most important of all, the parliament enacted a statute that provided that if 'any man enfeoff another of his land, with the intent of going to war or commit any other felony', the enfeoffment was to be invalid and the land was to become an escheat.[23] Clearly this practice, which was to become so notorious an abuse in the later Middle Ages, was already widespread and indicates the serious nature of the problem facing the government.

Altogether, the legislation of 1310, and the huge number of people summoned to the parliament, are a measure of the determination of the government to deal vigorously with the more acute threats to the rule of law in the lordship. But making the

61. Castleroche, County Louth, one of the principal lines of defence of the English of County Louth, who remained loyal throughout the Bruce invasion even though the family who built Roche, the de Verdons, were themselves in rebellion against the crown as recently as 1312

statutes was easy enough: enforcing them was seemingly beyond the capacity of any administration. As the Dublin chronicler put it: 'many provisions were made as statutes, of much use to the land of Ireland if they had been observed'.[24] The cynicism was justified and the writer recounts that even at that Kilkenny parliament itself 'great discords arose between certain magnates of Ireland'. By now the warlike state of Ireland encouraged dissidents among the settlers to rise in rebellion in pursuit of illegal gain. These 'rebel English', who appear in increasing numbers from the early fourteenth century on, not only aggravated the government's problem of enforcing the law but confused relations with Gaelic Ireland as well. In the Wicklow mountains, for example, Harolds and Archbolds allied with O Byrnes and O Tooles; further south de Cauntetons not only joined forces with O Byrnes and other Irish from the mountains, but were willing to help a harper gain his revenge upon men who had refused him traditional hospitality;[25] in the south Maurice fitz Thomas, later first earl of Desmond, was allied with Ó Briain and MacCarthaig. In Meath the de Lacys went into open rebellion, and in Munster Barrys, Cogans and Roches were only some of the great names listed as rebels.

Such rebels were motivated in many different ways, though personal gain was always the main driving force. Mainly they seem to have been people who had little or no hope of fortune, being younger brothers or from cadet branches of lineages. One of the most notorious examples is the rebellion of Maurice de Caunteton in south Leinster. It started with the murder of Richard Talon on 17 June 1309.[26] It soon escalated and de Caunteton, in alliance with 'Dulyng Obryn and other Irishmen from the mountains of Leinster, openly put themselves at war with the king with standards displayed, doing many murders, robberies and other evils'.[27] The government had to mount a major campaign in September, when the clerk of the wages received a total of £440 for those serving for pay.[28] The huge number pardoned for service in this campaign is also impressive, not least for showing the large number of Irish who served in the royal army.[29] De Caunteton was killed, but the remnants of his force continued to roam the countryside as a danger to law and order.[30] The rebel's lands were naturally confiscated, though the government was unable to prevent the manor of Glascarraig in Wexford from being devastated by the MacMurroughs.[31] In the end, therefore, it was the Leinster Irish who benefited.

Surprisingly, the king had been willing to take de Caunteton into his peace, but he was killed long before the royal command reached the justiciar.[32] His son, however, regained the royal favour and served the king in Scotland in 1312.[33] This is a useful reminder that nowhere, least of all in Ireland, could the king afford to alienate magnates, a fact that is well illustrated in another great rebellion in Ireland at this time.[34] It began in 1312 when, on 21 February, Robert de Verdon, the younger brother of Theobald de Verdon, and some others began what the Dublin chronicle calls 'the riot of Uriel'.[35] Soon they were openly at war with the king, 'appropriating to themselves as if by conquest the demesne land of the king, administering the oath of fealty as well to free tenants and betaghs of the king as to other inhabitants of the said country, and taking homage'.[36] The justiciar, John Wogan, had to send an army against them. At this point the community of Louth made a signif-

62. Trim Castle: the so-called 'de Verdon Rebellion' was only brought to an end by the intervention of the lord of Trim, Roger Mortimer (the photograph shows the barbican gate under excavation)

icant request of the justiciar: because they feared the damage that would be caused by the royal army, they asked to be let protect the country themselves with a force to be led by two brothers of Robert de Verdon, Nicholas and Milo. Wogan must have been convinced by the argument of their appeal (which amounted to an extraordinary indictment of the conduct of royal armies), for he disbanded his army. But the two de Verdons joined their rebel brother, and Wogan had to send another royal army against them from Ardee. This, according to the Dublin annalist, was 'miserably destroyed' by the rebels, a sore blow to the fast-diminishing prestige of the government.[37] Eventually, through the strong action of Roger Mortimer, whose interests were involved, Robert de Verdon and the others made peace on good conditions (they were guaranteed safety of life and limb) and the community of Louth was forced to pay a fine of 500 marks.

The failure of the government was never more cruelly exposed than in this defeat of a royal army in the spring of 1312, and with a reforming baronial party in control in England some attempt had to be made to provide better government in Ireland. On 7 August 1312 Edmund Butler was installed as acting justiciar,[38] and according to the Dublin chronicle he quickly enjoyed a spectacular success against the Irish in Glenmalure.[39] His achievement subsequently in making Ireland quiet was such that he was supposedly able to progress from one side of the island to the other with only three mounted men as escort.[40]

But already there were signs of the disaster which was to come. At the end of May 1313 King Robert Bruce landed in Ulster, and although he was put to flight by the Ulstermen, according to the Dublin chronicle, it was said at the time that he had come ashore by licence of the earl of Ulster in order to take tribute.[41] However unlikely that may seem, there is no denying that rumour regularly linked the names of the two men. Bruce's subsequent achievements were reported by the same chronicle, especially the success at Bannockburn, the attack on Northumbria and the siege of Carlisle. Then, according to the same source, 'not content with their own land and swollen with pride', the Scots under Edward Bruce landed near Carrickfergus on 26 May 1315.[42] With Bruce was a substantial army: the best tradition says he had 6,000 men, which is undoubtedly a great exaggeration. But the number of important men who came with him suggests that he did have adequate military backing: men such as Sir Philip Mowbray, Sir John de Soulis, Sir John Stewart (whose mother was sister to the earl of Ulster), Sir Alan Stewart, Sir Gilbert Boyd, Fergus of Ardrossan and Ramsay of Auchterhouse. This was clearly no mere exploratory mission, but a full-scale invasion designed to conquer and hold land. It immediately raises the important question of the reason behind this Scottish presence in Ireland at this time. There are a number of different traditions which naturally stress different reasons for the invasion, and it is impossible to be absolutely certain of the exact circumstances that involved the Scots in Ireland. The Scottish tradition, as reflected in Barbour's *The Bruce,* is not entirely reliable since Barbour wrote his poem at least sixty years after the event and in any case was prone to exaggerate and distort so as to emphasise the epic stature of his hero King Robert. His suggestion that Edward was sent to Ireland to get him out of the way seems hardly likely. The parliament that met at Ayr in April 1315, and which must have sanctioned the proposed invasion of Ireland, recognised Edward as heir to his brother King Robert should he die without having a son.[43] It would not come amiss if Edward were to find a kingdom for himself in Ireland, but his hard-pressed brother was not likely to divert badly needed resources to Ireland merely for that. It makes much more sense to see Robert Bruce using the opportunity to open up a second front against England in Ireland. It would at least prevent Ireland from being used as a source of supply for future campaigns in Scotland, and with a bit of luck might even cause English resources to be diverted from Scotland to meet a perilous situation in Ireland.

It is quite likely that Bruce himself had made the first diplomatic contacts with Gaelic Ireland. He was, after all, the son-in-law of the earl of Ulster; he had been in Ulster twice before 1315; some of his agents had been captured in Ulster years before; one of the Bissets of the Glens of Antrim accompanied Edward Bruce to Ireland in 1315. Apart from that, there was continuous traffic between Ulster and Scotland, and ever since the first galloglass had been imported in the thirteenth century there had been a continuous Scottish military presence in Ireland. One English chronicler, who had a special interest in Scotland, records that Edward Bruce was invited to Ireland by 'a certain magnate of Ireland with whom he had been educated in his youth'.[44] This suggests close contact, though not necessarily with Gaelic Ireland. There is the evidence, too, of the letter written by King Robert 'to all the kings of Ireland, the prelates and clergy, and to the inhabitants of all Ireland, our friends'.[45] It was sent at some date prior to Edward's expedition, perhaps in the early part of 1315, when seven Scots, as well as a certain Henry, 'messenger of Robert le Bruys', were taken prisoner

63. Roscrea Castle: the Tipperary-based magnate, Edmund Butler, can hardly have anticipated the arduous appointment he accepted when he agreed to become justiciar in August 1313, a position he held for the next six years. The king's grant to him of Roscrea Castle in 1315 was in part compensation for losses sustained as chief governor

and held captive in Dublin castle, and its clear purpose was to make diplomatic contact easier by appealing to Gaelic national sentiment.[46] 'Whereas we and you, and our people and your people, free in times past, share the same national ancestry and are urged to come together more eagerly and joyfully in friendship by a common language and common custom', the king says that his agents bearing these letters will treat on his behalf 'about permanently strengthening and maintaining inviolate the union of special friendship between us and you, so that, God willing, our nation may be restored to her former liberty'. Bruce obviously did not lightly use phrases of this kind. He was appealing to sentiments that he knew existed in Ireland and posing as a possible deliverer. It is in this guise that he is depicted in the annals: in 1317 he is recorded as coming to 'expel the Galls from Ireland'.[47] The deliberate linking of Scots and Irish into one people (which is what he meant by *nostra natio*, our nation) was calculated to appeal to Gaelic sensibilities, and especially to such anti-English sentiments as might be aroused.

The Irish tradition places the initiative firmly in the hands of Domnall Ó Néill of Ulster, who invited King Robert to Ireland. His hope, apparently, was to revive the high-kingship of Ireland in the person of Bruce and later, in the address to Pope John XXII, where he claims to be speaking on behalf of Gaelic Ireland, he grandly renounces his own supposed claims to the title. His address, too, lays great stress on the common language and common ancestry that binds both peoples: 'besides the kings of lesser Scotia, who all drew the source of their blood from our greater Scotia, retaining to some extent our language and habits, 197 kings of our blood have reigned over the whole island of Ireland'.[48] In due course Edward Bruce was inaugurated king of Ireland in the traditional manner and he certainly began to king it in Ulster at least.

But one can hardly suppose that Domnall Ó Néill, like a latter-day patriot, was willing to sacrifice all for Ireland. He, too, was to benefit from the invasion. As we have already seen, his own situation was becoming increasingly precarious in the north, with pressure from Ó Domnaill from the west and the earl of Ulster favouring his rival Énrí and and threatening Domnall to the north and east. By 1315 the situation was desperate, and it was this that forced Ó Néill to appeal to Bruce. What he was doing, in fact, was continuing the well-established policy of importing Scottish galloglass, only now on a gigantic scale.[49] Handing a supposed kingship of Ireland to Edward Bruce was a small price to pay for his own security in the north.

Both sides, then, had much to gain. Robert Bruce would have a friendly Ireland at least, and possibly a useful ally as well; Ó Néill would have his enemies toppled and possibly the enlargement of his kingdom too. But if anything lasting was to be achieved, the support of Gaelic Ireland was necessary and, if possible, the defection of some of the Anglo-Irish as well. Even though a substantial force accompanied Edward Bruce, it can hardly have been intended to achieve more than the acquisition of a permanent foothold in Ulster. A real conquest would demand much larger forces, and this, of necessity, meant that other Gaelic lords would have to rise in support of the invader. Domnall Ó Néill said as much in his letter to Mac Carthaig:

64. Castlekevin, County Wicklow: the latest in a long succession of campaigns against the Irish of Glenmalure took place in 1312. Led by the justiciar, Edmund Butler, as was frequent practice, the base-camp was the archiepis copal manor at Castlekevin, of which only fragmentary remains of the gate house survive

> When we were about to shake off the heavy yoke and tyranny of the English, we took counsel with you and with many other magnates in Ireland... as to how far you would assist our efforts in that matter with active assistance and help, nor was the hope thereof vain, seeing that by offering your forces you are bearing part in the undertaking.

He then describes how Bruce is to be king of Ireland, and he sends letters from Bruce confirming that he will drive the English from Ireland, and reminds Mac Carthaig of the damage that has been caused by Gaelic lords fighting among themselves, 'so that we owe to ourselves the miseries with which we are afflicted, degenerate and manifestly unworthy of our ancestors, by whose valour and splendid deeds the Irish race in all the past ages has retained its liberty'. They must now stop fighting each other: 'it is necessary for us to be at harmony at home and to prosecute the war with our united forces, if we would regain our liberty'.[50] But whatever promises Ó Néill or Bruce had managed to procure from Gaelic lords such as Mac Carthaig, it is apparent that very many of the Irish refused to have anything to do with the Scots, and Bruce's plans were therefore completely frustrated. Even in Ulster the Gaelic lords were divided, and if the likes of Ó Catháin, Ó hAnluain, Mac Giolla Mhuire, Mac Artáin and Ó hÁgáin (each of them an *uirrí* of Ó Néill) sided with the Scots, others held aloof. In descending from Ulster to the plains of Louth and Meath, Bruce and his army were attacked by the local Irish as he tried to get through the Moiry Pass near Newry. One of these seems to have been that same Mac Artáin who had pledged support to Bruce soon after he had landed. The only Irish to remain true to Bruce were Ó Néill and his immediate supporters.

The other circumstance that ruined Bruce in Ireland was that his invasion coincided with the worst famine of the Middle Ages. Very wet weather meant a series of bad harvests, and famine inevitably followed in a society where so many people lived at a bare subsistence level. Ireland suffered as much as any other part of western Europe, and Gaelic Ireland suffered more than most. What the annals call 'intolerable, destructive bad weather' had made the harvest a complete failure and soon even reports of cannibalism were recorded.[51] Sober official records confirm the effect of the bad weather. In his account of the temporalities of the archbishopric of Dublin, the escheator was allowed for 'loss because of meadows that could not be mown on account of the rainy season and of turf that could not be cut... for the same reason'.[52] The Irish annals record the famine and deaths in 1315, 1316, 1317 and 1318, when one annalist wrote of 'snow the like of which had not been seen for many a long year'.[53] A stark entry for 1315 sums it up: 'Many afflictions in all parts of Ireland: very many deaths, famine and many strange diseases, murders, and intolerable storms as well'.[54] This meant that at no time was Bruce able to live off the country through which he passed, but was dependent on what he could procure from Gaelic allies, and that was little. More than anything else it was starvation that caused him to retreat. He ravaged widely, but it was houses and property (as well as people, of course) which suffered most from the Scots. Conditions grew so bad in 1317 that the Ulster army 'were so destroyed with hunger that they raised the bodies of the dead from the cemeteries' and ate them, 'and women ate their children from hunger'.[55]

After he landed in Larne, Bruce sent his ships back to Scotland and pressed on for Carrickfergus.[56] He was immediately opposed by the local magnates, with Mandeville, Savage, Logan and a loyal Bisset prominent. The Scots won an easy victory, giving a frightening sign of their power. A quick surrender of the town of Carrickfergus gave Bruce a secure base; the castle held out for a year. It was there that he established his court. In a matter of days he had secured an important section of the earldom of Ulster. Now he began to engulf the rich settlement stretching away towards Lough Neagh. Next he attacked the settlements further south, in the modern County Down, which made his base in Ulster more secure, as well as providing him with badly needed victuals. There was no compromise with those who refused to accept the new order. The bishop of Down was subsequently granted a pension by the Irish council because he refused to accept Edward Bruce, but fled to Dublin 'leaving his men, lands, goods, rents, and all his possessions in his bishopric of Down'.[57] With a safe retreat Bruce could now afford to move out of Ulster. The difficult Moiry Pass was successfully negotiated, despite local Gaelic opposition, and Dundalk was taken on 29 June. All of the extant sources record the ruthless slaughter and destruction: Barbour says that the streets ran with blood, and Clyn recounts the burning of the town and the looting of the Franciscan friary.[58] So terrible was the destruction that the Dublin government took the unprecedented step of awarding nearly £50 to the community to help repair the vill 'recently robbed and burned by the Scots'.[59] This pattern of destruction and death was to be repeated wherever the

65. Dublin Castle: among the prisoners in Dublin Castle at the onset of the Bruce invasion were seven Scots, including a certain Henry, 'messenger of Robert le Bruys'

Scots went. It was probably now, too, that Brace was formally inaugurated high-king of Ireland near Faughart. Then the surrounding countryside was ravaged. Louth and Ardee were burned and many were killed. The destruction was such that even a generation later many parts of the area had not recovered. The worst atrocity reported was the burning of a church in Ardee that was full of men, women and children seeking sanctuary.

These early weeks of the war had shown the Scots to be ruthless, destroying everything in their path, and seemingly invincible. The Dublin government was not slow to react, even if the only opposition was local. By 22 July, according to the Dublin chronicler, the justiciar 'collected a great army from Munster and Leinster and other parts, and the earl of Ulster, as if in opposition, came from Connacht with an innumerable army and they both came to Dundalk and consulted together so as to kill the Scots'.[60] The chief governor's intention was to pursue the Scots into Ulster. A royal service had been proclaimed for Greencastle and in official records the force raised by the government is called the army of Ulster. But de Burgh refused to allow a royal army into the earldom. For one thing he felt that Ulster was his responsibility and he was confident of his capacity to defeat the Scots on his own. But a more convincing reason for his refusal is offered by an Irish annalist who said that it was 'because he feared the ruin of his lands' by a government army. This was a reasonable fear. The same annals, after recounting the damage sustained by Dundalk at the hands of the Scots, adds that 'excepting homicide, however, deeds not less evil were done by the army drawn from different parts of Ireland to do battle with them, in the districts through which they passed'.[61] There is plenty of evidence in official records to support this. Dublin was granted £240 by the king, 'on account of the damage caused by the men at arms who came there, on their way to Ulster and other parts of Ireland, to repel the Scots rebels'.[62] Damage at Finglas, Clondalkin, and other places is also recorded. So the earl seems to have had plenty of justification for his stand. But the result was disaster. Bruce made a tactical retreat northwards, drawing the earl after him. Feidlim Ó Conchobair and the Connachtmen were lured away, thus greatly weakening de Burgh's army. When the two forces finally met at Connor in Antrim, on 10 September, the earl's army was no match for the Scots and he suffered a heavy defeat. This important victory secured Ulster for the Scots, and Bruce was now able to turn his attention to the siege of Carrickfergus castle.

By now the English government had taken note of the serious situation in Ireland. As early as 21 June 1315, the king ordered the Welsh coast to be defended and the castles to be provisioned because of the arrival of the Scots in Ireland.[63] And on 10 July letters were sent to the leading Anglo-Irish magnates requesting information about the Scots and commanding them to resist the invasion with all their power.[64] Edward II was clearly worried. He told the king of France on 28 September that he could not help him because 'of his late troubles with the Scots, who have since entered Ireland plundering and burning', so that he has sent his ships there 'to harass them'.[65] On 1 September the council met at Lincoln and after discussing the invasion of Ireland, decided to send John de Hothum, the chancellor of the exchequer, as a special envoy to Dublin.[66] He was given wide powers, was particularly to investigate the revenues of the lordship, and was to convey a special message from the king to an assembly of the magnates. The English government can hardly have been reassured by the news sent by de Hothum in February of the following year and by the urgent appeal for money that came shortly afterwards. According to de Hothum the Scots seemed to be irresistible: he said that they and their allies 'had passed far into your country doing damage at their will without being arrested'.[67]

Things had indeed taken a turn for the worse in Ireland. In the weeks following Bruce's landing the Dublin government had done its best to bring together an army against him. Nicholas de Balscot was appointed clerk of the wages and was paid just short of £2,000 in Trinity term 1315.[68] The victuals supplied by the royal purveyors for Scotland were used for the castles of Dublin, Carrickfergus and Northburgh, and the vill of Dundalk, as well as to help pay the wages of the army.[69] But this expenditure achieved nothing, since the army raised by the government never encountered Bruce. He was allowed to consolidate his position in Ulster and then to move south in winter, reinforced by new men from Scotland. His success, and the discomfiture of de Burgh, had encouraged risings in Connacht and Meath which further endangered the position of the settiers and increased the problem that the already hard-pressed government had to face. It was Roger Mortimer, the lord of Trim, who had to oppose the Scots when they advanced on Kells. He was quickly defeated and forced to flee to Dublin. The way was now left open to the Scots to advance further into the old lordship of Meath, and having burned Kells they pressed on westwards as far as Granard. This, too, was burned, as was Finnea and Loughsewdy, where Bruce spent Christmas. These were all important English centres, and their delib-

66. In the distance stands Moyry Castle, a later tower house guarding the pass of that name, through which Edward Bruce's army made their southerly march in June 1315

erate destruction was a deadly blow to the feudal settlement. By now the de Lacys of Meath had joined the Scots, and it was they who led Bruce through hostile Irish territories into Tethmoy and Kildare.

The progress of destruction continued, the Scots never bothering to waste time besieging well-garrisoned castles. The aim was to move rapidly, destroy as much as possible, and probably try to rouse Gaelic Ireland into rebellion. So far the resistance encountered had easily been swept aside. But by the time the Scots had ravaged through Castledermot, Athy and Reban, another royal army was waiting to oppose them. By this time Bruce's men must have been tired and hungry. The army which they met was not only larger, but fresher. By all accounts the Scots should have been beaten when battle was joined at Skerries, near Ardscull. De Hothum in his report to England admitted as much and said that 'by bad luck they kept the field'. The Scots won an important victory. The impact on Gaelic Ireland was immediate. Far away in Desmond, when the Irish heard of the victory they rose in rebellion. Maurice fitz Maurice had to rush from Dungarvan to protect Limerick and Kerry. He found settlers in flight for fear of the Irish and a jury told the justiciar in 1318 that but for his prompt action the whole of Kerry and Limerick, up to the gate of the city, would have been destroyed.[70] The Dublin chronicler, however, says that the leaders on the government side quarrelled and allowed the Scots to win.[71] Butler, the justiciar, seems to have been unable to hold the Angio-Irish in check. He had failed with de Burgh and now he failed again with fitz Thomas and Power. So when the disconsolate leaders reached Dublin they had to put their seals to a solemn declaration in which they swore:[72]

67. Gatehouse of Limerick Castle: a jury in 1318 found that Maurice fitz Thomas of Desmond had been in Dungarvan at the time of the Scots' arrival in Ireland in 1315 but rushed to protect Kerry and Limerick from the Irish who were rising up in revolt in support of Bruce; had he not done so, they agreed that the whole of Kerry and Limerick 'up to the gate of the city' would have been destroyed

> ... to defend the king's rights in Ireland, certain traitors and the Scottish rebels having entered that land and having leagued with them all the Irish and a great part of the English. They agree that their bodies, their lands and chattels shall be forfeited if they fail in their loyalty, and to render hostages to the king for the fulfilment thereof, who are to be put in Dublin castle or elsewhere at the king's pleasure.

We can hardly take at its face value this horrific picture of wholesale Irish and English defection to the Scottish side. But it does emphasise how serious the situation was in the eyes of the magnates. The hostages were delivered, some to Dublin castle and others to castles in other parts of Ireland and England, and for the next few years, until the danger in Ireland was averted, payments for their upkeep figure on the issue rolls of the Irish exchequer and in the records of the king's wardrobe. Some never returned. In 1324 the eldest son of John fitz Thomas died in England, still a hostage.[73]

Meanwhile Bruce continued on his campaign of destruction. He destroyed the important Geraldine Castle of Lea. But by now the scarcity of food in the famine-stricken countryside was beginning to take its toll and the Scots retreated to Ulster in mid-February 1316. Bruce had successfully probed deep into feudal Ireland, had tested the government and magnates and had found them wanting, and had wreaked havoc over a wide area. He had also experienced the inadequacy of his army for conquest and the failure of support from Gaelic Ireland. Reinforcements from Scotland and positive help from the Gaelic lords of the south were necessary if a campaign or conquest were to be attempted in the future. It was probably now that Ó Néill began to negotiate with the Gaelic lords, urging them to unite and to join Bruce against the English, while the earl of Moray was sent back to Scotland to find the necessary reinforcements.

Bruce in the interim was kept busy in Ulster, taking the great castles which had held out against him (such as Greencastle and Northburgh) and establishing his own administration there. But the most important fortress in the north, Carrickfergus Castle, defied all his efforts. It was victualled successfully by sea in April 1316 and again in July eight ships were loaded with supplies in Drogheda and set out for the castle. But they were diverted by the earl of Ulster to Scotland in exchange for the release of his cousin, William de Burgh. The situation in Carrickfergus then became so desperate that it was reported that the garrison was reduced to eating some Scots they had held prisoner! There was little they could do except surrender, which they did in September 1316.[74] This really made Bruce master of Ulster.

By this time the position of the Dublin government was extremely precarious. Rebellions in Gaelic Leinster and elsewhere had added to the confusion, and the acute shortage of money made it difficult to plan a successful resistance to the Scots. De Hothum in his report had informed the king that the financial situation was desperate, mainly because the army that had been mustered in 1315 had cost so much.[75] An ominous sign was not only that receipts began to fall and that the government was overspending, but that assignments began to increase. Even so the amount of money available for the war against the Scots was pitifully small. The council decided in 1316,

68. Part of Dublin's medieval quay wall with signs of re-facing that can be dated to the fourteenth century; we know that the walls in this area of the city were deemed vulnerable when Edward and Robert Bruce approached Dublin in February 1317 and that buildings were demolished to strengthen the walls

for example, that £4,000 should be made available to de Balscot, clerk of the wages in the justiciar's army; all he got was £578. For putting Dublin castle in a state of defence £400 was allowed; but only £145 was provided by the treasurer.[76] Much attention was devoted to preparing defences in the area around Dublin, where the administration largely fell back on the popular obligation to defend.[77] Despite this some of the Leinster Irish managed to penetrate right into the city and, as events were to show, even the defences of Dublin itself were hopelessly inadequate. Altogether the government was failing miserably in its fitful preparations to meet the next Scottish onslaught out of Ulster, being perhaps misled into complacency by the long sojourn of Edward Bruce there from February 1316 to February 1317.

But Bruce was making careful preparations. He went to Scotland himself to confer with his brother. He succeeded in persuading him to come to Ireland, and by February 1317 King Robert was in Ireland. He must have considered a heavy investment in the Irish enterprise worthwhile, and this can only be as a result of the success of Edward up to this, particularly the exploratory campaign of 1315–16. Scottish control of the sea between Ulster and Scotland made this intervention possible. Thomas Dun was the man who was responsible. He had kept an open passage available to the Scots, so that the necessary reinforcements could be shipped to Carrickfergus. At one time he controlled the sea right down as far as Holyhead, so that the main sea route between Ireland and England became dangerous. When John de Hothum came on his mission to Ireland he was protected by no less than eight ships and eighty *satellites* and crossbowmen 'to have a safe passage because Thomas

Dun and divers other enemy robbers daily perpetrate and commit many and divers injuries on the sea between the lands of England, Wales and Ireland'.[78]

Confident of success, the Scots moved out of Ulster early in February 1317. According to Barbour they were determined to march throughout Ireland from one end to the other. It is significant that they made their way towards Dublin for the first time. Once again the army ravaged the rich country of Meath as it moved south. There is one dubious tradition that says that the earl of Ulster ambushed the rear of the army at Ratoath before he fled to Dublin. But there is no doubt about what happened next. The mayor of Dublin arrested the earl on February and imprisoned him in Dublin castle. What provoked such an action was the suspicion that de Burgh had acted in collusion with the Scots, coupled with the fear that he might yet betray Dublin. He was, after all, the father-in-law of King Robert, and had been closely associated with him in the past, as far back as 1286, when, as a young man, the earl had been party to a remarkable alliance involving Bruce, his father and a number of leading Scots.[79] Rumour had linked the two men in 1310 and again in 1313. In England it was said that Bruce had made himself king of Ireland 'with the connivance of the earl of Ulster'.[80] It was remembered, too, that it was his diversion of the relief ships which had brought about the fall of Carrickfergus Castle. It is hard to believe that de Burgh was in any way involved with Bruce, but he was kept a prisoner a long time before he was allowed to go to England.

Meanwhile Dublin was in a panic, and with good reason. The defences were in a hopeless state, with great breaches in the walls in places. That they could be penetrated by the Leinster Irish did nothing to reassure the apprehensive citizens. Shortly before this complaints had been made by the 'common folk' about the inadequacies of the defensive system, suggesting measures to be taken to provide armed men to protect the city.[81] But the mayor and bailiffs had done nothing. Now, with the Scots approaching from Meath and with no one to bar their way, the men of Dublin faced the prospect of capitulation. So they took measures into their own hands. A number of buildings, including churches, were torn down and the masonry used to construct a new wall facing the river. Then when Bruce arrived at Castleknock on the other side of the river on 23 February, the Dubliners set fire to the suburbs facing him, so that they could not be used to provide shelter during an assault on the city from that side. The fire got out of hand and a huge area (including the houses of the exchequer) was destroyed.[82] As it happened, this may have been a fortunate accident, causing Bruce to turn away from Dublin in the belief that a siege would be long and costly.

We can only speculate on the motives of Bruce in passing Dublin by in this way. It is noteworthy that, with the exception of Carrickfergus, the Scots never involved themselves in long sieges. On this occasion they had made no attempt to take Drogheda as they moved south and now they were to leave more walled towns behind them as they progressed through the country. Naas, Castledermot, Gowran, Callan and Kells were all plundered: but Kilkenny was left alone as the army moved on through Cashel and Nenagh towards the Shannon, causing terrible destruction in Butler's lands on the way. It was now clear that Bruce was hoping to link up with

69. The remains of Isolde's Tower, Dublin, under excavation. A thirteenth-century circular tower at the north-east corner of the medieval town, it was Dublin's bulwark against a sea-borne assault

the Irish of Thomond and possibly Desmond as well. He had no time to spare for lengthy sieges and so ignored the walled towns he could not take by storm.

It seems, too, that the government for once had anticipated what Bruce was trying to do and tried to prevent or at least meet it. The fortunate survival of a view of the account of John of Patrickschurch, clerk of the wages in the army of the justiciar, enables us to follow Butler as he moved rapidly through Munster raising men.[83] From 24 February, when he went to Cork for this purpose, to 17 April when his retinue 'assaulted the Scots as they were crossing the bog of Ely', Butler remained in touch with the Scots without actually bringing them to battle. For a time he had as many as 920 paid troops with him: 220 men at arms, 300 hobelars and 400 foot. The Scottish army must have been formidable if Butler hesitated to meet it in the open. Had Bruce succeeded in his plan to link up with Donnchad Ó Briain, he would have been able to press on with the business of conquest. But instead he found Donnchad's great rival, Muirchertach Ó Briain, waiting for him across the Shannon, ready to give battle. Now it was Butler who suddenly held the advantage and there was little the Scots could do except retreat. From Castleconnell on the Shannon, not far from Limerick, they moved through Kildare and into Meath, reaching Ulster on 1 May. Later that month King Robert returned to Scotland. The hope of winning Ireland for his brother was now ruined, and when control of the sea was lost in July, with the capture of Thomas Dun by the Irish admiral John of Athy, there was the added problem of getting help to Edward in the future.

Robert Bruce was probably helped in his decision to retreat from the Shannon by the news that Roger Mortimer had landed in Ireland. Backed by powerful interests in

70. Leaving Dublin unmolested, the Scots army moved west where, on their way to their next target at Leixlip, they would have passed the modest castle at Ballowen, near Lucan, the earlier phase of which is here shown under excavation

England, Mortimer had been appointed lieutenant of Ireland and brought a small military force with him. It is significant that for the first time the king agreed that his expenses would be met by the wardrobe and not, as hitherto had been the case, out of the Irish exchequer. In addition the government contracted with a certain Antonio de Passagno for the provision of 1,000 Genoese mercenaries who were to be in Ireland by July 1317. The Genoese certainly received money, but there is no evidence that any of the mercenaries ever arrived in Ireland. Nevertheless the English government was finally taking the Irish problem seriously. Absentees were ordered to return to defend their lands. But by now, in fact, the crisis had broken in Ireland. Edward Bruce remained in Ulster for the next year and a half, and the Dublin government was able to devote its energies to the restoration of order in the rest of the country. The release of the earl of Ulster was procured; the de Lacys were put to flight; and the problem of the Leinster Irish was tackled with some measure of success.

At the same time attention switched to Avignon, where a new pope, John XXII, had been elected in August 1316. A diplomatic war followed.[84] Edward II had complained that some of the Irish prelates were 'countenancing and resetting the Scots and preaching against him and his realm'.[85] The Franciscans, in particular, had been active promoters of Bruce, and in August 1316 the minister of the Irish province was sent to Avignon to complain of this to the minister general of the order. At the same time Edward II kept the pressure on the pope, who issued a general condemnation of the supporters of Bruce. The Irish reply was the famous remonstrance from Domnall Ó Néill.[86] This, inevitably, failed to provide papal recognition of Bruce as king of Ireland, though the pope did tell Edward II to act justly and instructed his legates in England to keep urging the Irish case of injustice on the king.

What exactly Bruce had been doing in Ulster since May 1317 is a mystery. Perhaps he was hoping to get more help from Scotland. But the long silence was broken at last when on 14 October 1318, according to the Dublin chronicler, 'war commenced between the Scots and the English of Ireland two leagues from the vill of Dundalk'.[87] There is nothing to suggest what Bruce's motives were in thus moving south again. But the evidence indicates that he may have had some reinforcements from Scotland: the annals mention that 'Mac Ruaidri, king of the Hebrides, and Mac Domnaill, king of Argyle, and their Scots were killed with him'.[88] All the evidence, too, suggests that his army was considerable, with de Lacys prominent amongst the leaders. An army, led by John de Bermingham, and including Milo de Verdon, together with the archbishop of Armagh and many local magnates, as well as the men of Drogheda, opposed the Scots near Faughart. There was a major battle between the two armies and Bruce was killed, 'by dint of fierce fighting'.[89] Many Scots died with him.

A special messenger was immediately dispatched to inform the Dublin exchequer of the 'great victory' and the death of Bruce.[90] His head was sent to the king by de Bermingham, who was rewarded with a grant of the new earldom of Louth. The rest of Bruce's body was quartered. His heart, hand and one quarter were brought to Dublin and the other quarters were sent 'to other places'.[91] Thus, ignominiously, did the great Bruce enterprise come to an end.

Bruce's death was greeted with remarkably unanimous approval in nearly all the Gaelic sources. He was 'the common ruin of the Galls and Gaels of Ireland' and 'never was there a better deed done for the Irish than this, since the beginning of the world and the banishing of the Fomorians from Ireland'.[92] Those who supported him were roundly condemned and he was blamed for the famine, death and destruction which gripped the whole of Ireland during those years. He reduced Ireland to 'one trembling surface of commotion'.[93] Another near-contemporary writer graphically compared the Scots to an 'overwhelming wave, broken-topped, hoarsely rumbling, virulent in destructiveness, scorching terribly and giving off lively sparks; an earnest of enduring malice and ill-will, breaking down all embankments, all hills and every hoary rock'; they were like a 'black cloud with vaporous-creeping offshoots and dark mist... [which] covered our Ireland's surface'.[94]

It is true that the Scots left a trail of destruction and desolation behind them whenever they moved through the country. All the sources support that. For example, the earl of Norfolk later complained of the losses suffered in his liberty of Carlow, where stewards, treasurers and many free tenants had been killed in successive raids.[95] There was, too, a significant fall in rents from many of the royal manors for which the escheator later accounted, because of damage caused by the Scots and the Irish. Hugh Lawless, who farmed the royal manor of Bray, received only £85 in rents during five and a half years after 1314 because the lands were devastated after the Scots arrived and, he claimed in 1320, were now lying waste and uncultivated.[96] This is matched by a fall in the value of many ecclesiastical benefices for the same reason. The valuations for the purpose of ecclesiastical taxation make this clear. For example, the archdiocese of Dublin shows a fall from £2,800 in the late thirteenth century to £800 after the invasion. In the diocese of Ossory, ten prebends fell from £56 to £28 and fifteen others from £58 to £27.[97] So severely had the area around Carrickfergus suffered that as late as 1327 it was proposed that the lands which had been lying waste since 1315 should be colonised from Wales and England.[98] But if the Scots were destructive, so too were the armies of the lordship, especially the men of Ulster, who seem to have caused havoc wherever they went. There are many entries of allowances for such damage in different accounts on the pipe rolls: for example, to Henry Kempe, who 'was injured by the Ulster army who came there with the king's banner to pursue Edward de Bruys and his men and who robbed Henry of divers goods to the value of £20'.[99]

The devastation of the armies, coupled with the terrible famine and associated deaths, must have left much of Ireland in a frightful state. It is easy, therefore, to understand the universal condemnation of Bruce, though it is ironic that he should have been held responsible for the famine which played havoc with his own plans for a conquest of Ireland. The general attitude of condemnation suggests, too, that Gaelic Ireland in general did not support Bruce, despite the assertion of the usually reliable Friar Clyn that there adhered to the Scots 'all the time they were in Ireland almost all the Irish of the land, with very few keeping their faith and fealty'.[100] Outside of Ulster the Scots failed to find the Gaelic support which was vital to success. The Gaelic lords used the occasion to secure advantages for themselves.

71. Heading south, the Bruces came to Callan, County Kilkenny, which they proceeded to assault. The motte castle, shown here, about a century old at the time of this assault, would have been an easy target; it was the property of the de Clare family, who had held the earldom of Gloucester until the last earl was killed by the Scots at Bannockburn two and a half years earlier

Whatever hopes Bruce had of securing support from Connacht were dashed by the Anglo-Irish triumph at Athenry, and the great design for an alliance with Donnchad Ó Briain was ruined by the ascendancy of his arch-rival Muirchertach. Bruce, in fact, fell victim to the ambitions and rivalties of the Gaelic lords, and so in retrospect we can see that his attempt to revive a kingdom of Ireland was doomed to failure.

This is not to say that the Scots did not for a time pose the greatest of threats to Anglo-Ireland. Until the end at Faughart they were never defeated in battle. They secured the sympathy, at least for a time, of many churchmen, and no small number of the settlers joined them, especially in Ulster, of course, where many of them had little choice. Such were the defections that nervous suspicions of the loyalty of many leading magnates were generated, and this atmosphere of distrust was not conducive to efficient resistance to the Scots. We have already seen that it led to the imprisonment of the earl of Ulster. Many leading magnates had to leave hostages with the government. Rumour played with the good name of even the greatest. Edmund Butler was one who suffered, so that in 1320 the king had to publish a formal declaration 'to clear the fair name of Edmund le Botiller, who has been accused of having assisted the Scots in Ireland, that he has borne himself well and faithfully towards the king'.[101] During the war a petition asked for the removal of Richard d' Exeter, chief justice of the common bench, who was suspect because of his association with the rebel Walter de Lacy, who had married his daughter, and with many others who were hostile to the king.[102]

The disturbed state of the country was very evident and resulted in a collapse of the rule of law in some localities. The courts became less active. The Dublin bench adjourned cases in 1316 because it was impossible for parties to get to the city without peril to their lives on account of the dangerous conditions on the roads to the city and the continuous presence of enemies. It is noteworthy that the very size of the plea rolls reflects a fall in the volume of business before the courts, since there was a dramatic reduction in the number of membranes required to preserve the record: in Hilary term 1316 there were only fourteen, compared with forty-three for the preceding Michaelmas term. Though there was some recovery after the wars, it was only marginal, and the business of the court continued to be very much less than it had been in the first decade of the century. This evidence of a contraction in the land of peace, where the royal justices were active, is matched by the evidence of the number of Irish cases that appeared in the king's bench in England, for they almost disappear from now on. The emergency powers granted by the government to the Lawless family who lived 'in a narrow part of the country between Newcastle McKynegan and Wicklow' show the same failure to impose the common law: they were empowered to deal with the Irish who harassed them 'in the manner of the marchers'.[103] Nor could the government afford to take too strict a view of infringements of the law during the period of invasion. In 1319 no less a person than the treasurer, Walter of Islip, thought it prudent to obtain a royal indemnity for misdemeanours during the war; and when the citizens of Dublin were similarly indemnified for burning their suburbs, it was because the 'urgent necessity of war' excused infringement of the common law.[104]

The years of the Bruce invasion, then, were traumatic in the life of the island. The destruction of the armies, coupled with the great famine and followed by devastating epidemics among livestock which were shattering in their effect on an economy in which the pastoral element was so pronounced, resulted in sore loss of life. The hardship was worsened by calamitous outbreaks of smallpox and influenza in the 1320s. There was crop failure again, too, in 1321, and in 1328 when there was 'much thunder and lightning, whereby much of the fruit and produce of all Ireland was ruined and the corn grew up white and blind'. During the summer there was a 'great intolerable wind... with scarcity of food and clothing'.[105] These calamities naturally had a devastating effect on the population, which seems not only to have been seriously dislocated in places, but to have declined as well. An economic recession was the inevitable result.

It is impossible now to be sure of the extent of this decline, for it seems to have got worse as new calamities such as the Black Death hit the lordship later in the century. Some facts gave the impression of a recovery. For example, the enormous quantities of grain shipped to Scotland for the campaign of 1322 suggest that tillage was again flourishing in some parts at least. The building of new stone bridges across the Liffey at Kilcullen in 1319 and across the Barrow at Leighlin in 1320 implies that traffic was once more heavy on the highway from Dublin to Carlow and Kilkenny.[106] The general mood of optimism that prevailed is indicated by the foundation of a university in Dublin in 1320, the realisation of a plan first mooted in 1311 when the

72. Built in the mid-thirteenth century, St Mary's parish church in Callan, County Kilkenny, may also have fallen prey to the Scots' attack

73. Next in line for a Scots raid was the town of Kells-in-Ossory, County Kilkenny, and although the castle may have been the prime target, the Augustinian canons (whose house appears in the photograph) hardly managed to avoid the enemies' attention, especially as their prior was a spiritual peer of the Irish parliament

archbishop of Dublin procured a bull from Pope Clement V. But its lack of success for want of adequate endowment suggests that the optimism was misguided and that Dublin was not capable of supporting a *studium generale.*[107]

A less favourable view of Ireland after Bruce is given by the statutes of the Dublin parliament of 1320. We see a people 'greatly distressed and well nigh destroyed' by the magnates and their armies, suffering from corrupt officials, and at the mercy of the many 'idle men' who enjoyed the protection of magnates so that it was impossible to bring them to justice.[108] This picture of a society where the rule of law is beginning to break down is reinforced by the ominous decision of the parliament of 1324 that the 'grandees of great lineage' should, as far as lay in their power, 'take and cause to be taken the felons, robbers, and thieves of their own family and surname, and their adherents'.[109] This virtual repetition of an earlier statute of 1320, with its emphasis on the importance of blood relationship, highlights the loosening of the feudal bond which was evident all over the lordship. Even in the thirteenth century something like a clan system was emerging in feudal Ireland. But it was the confusion of unending raids and wars and the lack of adequate governance that made the family bond important again. With it went 'bastard feudalism', which produced a new family based not on the ties of blood, but on service and fees. No wonder society groaned under the oppression of private armies and the magnates who employed them.

The best example of such a magnate is Maurice fitz Thomas, created earl of Desmond in 1329, whose notorious career of crime and rebellion spanned the years from 1319 to 1346.[110] In the former year, perhaps encouraged by the failure of the government to cope adequately with the disorders of the period of the Bruce war and its aftermath, he raised a small army which grievously oppressed not only his own tenants in his vast lordship, but those of other lordships as well. According to later indictments of Maurice, this had the effect of attracting to him dissidents, English as well as Irish, 'from Connacht and Thomond, from Leinster and Desmond. And Maurice received them and avowed them'.[111] Such avowries were one of the most pernicious causes of public disorder in Ireland, since they gave the protection of a powerful magnate and all the influence that he could control to the man avowed, so that he was hardly amenable to the ordinary processes of the law. This was certainly true in the case of fitz Thomas. As the number of his armed retainers increased they became well known as 'mac Thomas's rout' and they ravaged widely. Soon other magnates joined with him and the scale of destruction increased. On 16 May 1321, for example, they came into the district around Pomeroy in County Cork and burned the vills and houses they found, including a church which they had robbed of goods to the value of 100 marks, and they forced David Roche to hand over two members of his family as hostages. Some atrocious crimes were committed. In 1325, for example, the constable of Bunratty Castle, Richard of Harmston, was taken by some of the 'rout', who cut out his tongue and put out his eyes. They seized the vill and castle of Bunratty and killed two men in the castle. On another occasion Maurice seized William fitz Nicholas and put out his eyes because he had killed Mac Carthaig, and then he took William's men who had been party to the killing and 'some he beheaded, others he hanged, and more he tore apart with horses'.[112] The catalogue of crime was endless.

But matters did not end there, for Maurice became ambitious and according to those who later indicted them he 'had filled his heart with such pride and ambition that he thought to obtain the whole of Ireland for his own and to crown himself as a false king'.[113] There seems to be some substance to this fantastic accusation. In July 1326 a meeting was held in Kilkenny, at which the earl of Kildare, the earl of Louth, the future earls of Ormond and Desmond, together with the bishop of Ossory and a number of lesser magnates, and Brian Ó Briain, were present. They agreed to rebel against the king, assume control of Ireland, elect and crown Maurice fitz Thomas king, and share Ireland among themselves in proportion to the contribution each man made to the conquest.[114] It is very likely that events in England, which were to lead to the deposition of Edward II, prompted this plot in Ireland. In any event it came to nothing. But there were to be later plots to make fitz Thomas king of Ireland, involving powerful Gaelic as well as Anglo-Irish lords and even a restoration of some of the old provincial kingdoms.

The story of Maurice's high ambitions belongs to a later period for the most part. But the development of his 'rout', the illegal burdens placed on his tenants and then on other communities, the crime and civil disturbance, are all typical of what was happening in many parts of Ireland during this period of change. The feudal structure of society, which in any event had never been really suited to Irish conditions, was beginning to change, and already the new lordships, based on family, personal loyalty, and service, were appearing. The social map of Ireland as it was to be in the later Middle Ages was being drawn. Naturally the upheaval was hard. The illegal impositions of the likes of fitz Thomas were bound to engender quarrels with his neighbours. His forays into east Cork and Waterford were more than simple raids, they were more in the nature of military campaigns: we read of his army moving forward with standards raised and flags flying. They brought him into violent conflict with Barrys, Cogans and Roches, and ultimately with the Powers. Maurice had allies from those parts, too, and doubtless they were using him to work off old scores against local rivals. And it seems, too, that high politics were not without effect. Events in England were helping new alignments to take place in Ireland, and these were another potent factor in the creation of civil disturbance. There seems to be little doubt, for example, that the Despensers had an Irish ally in Arnold le Poer, seneschal of Kilkenny, and that his war, for such it was, with fitz Thomas in summer 1325 was to some extent a reflection of the great Mortimer-Despenser quarrel in England. It is even possible that the vicious attack on le Poer by the bishop of Ossory, who involved him in the notorious charges of witchcraft made against the wealthy Kilkenny woman, Alice Kyteler, may have had a similar political motive. But the root cause of the quarrels was in Ireland, where local rivalties had long histories and were always liable to erupt into violence.[115]

After the successful Mortimer coup in England in the autumn of 1326, the political alignments in Ireland became less clear-cut.[116] fitz Thomas, and the Butlers, de Berminghams, le Poers and de Burghs were involved in factions. Civil war followed in 1327, causing widespread devastation of lands and castles. If we are to believe the Dublin chronicler, the Dublin government was rendered so powerless by all this that at one stage fitz Thomas, Butler and de Bermingham 'ordered the council of the king to come to Kilkenny and there they would clear themselves that they had plotted no evil against the king's lands, but only to avenge themselves on their enemies'.[117] It is hard to imagine such an open declaration of the right to make private war being made in a period of strong rule.

The popular belief at the time, as reported in Dublin, was that this war had been caused by personal animosity between fitz Thomas and le Poer. We are told that late in September 1327, 'because the Lord Arnold [le Poer] came to the aid of the de Burghs [*des Bourkeym*], and because of the monstrous words used by Arnold in calling him [fitz Thomas] a rhymer [*rymoure*], fitz Thomas went to war against him.[118] And certainly we cannot rule out the personal element. But it is noticeable that it was fitz Thomas and his allies who were later rewarded by the triumphant Mortimer faction in England, anxious to win new allies in Ireland, while le Poer was imprisoned in Dublin castle and left to die there. In October 1328 Butler was made earl of Ormond and in the following August fitz Thomas was created earl of Desmond.

Nothing better illustrates the failure of the government to maintain its control in the localities than the massacre that occurred at Braganstown in County Louth in June 1329.[119] John de Bermingham, earl of Louth, his brother Peter, many close relatives, some friends (including Richard Talbot of Malahide) and more than 160 others were killed by a mob which attacked his manor. The incident was sparked off by the murder of an inhabitant of Ardee by de Bermingham's kern on 9 June 1329. The incensed

74. Castleconnell, County Limerick, belonging to Richard de Burgh, earl of Ulster, represented the most southerly point reached by the Scots under Robert Bruce in winter 1316–17

townsmen turned on the kern, killed fifteen of them on the spot, and pursued the remaining twenty-two as far as the local Carmelite church where they sought sanctuary. But the mob broke the sanctuary and slaughtered nineteen of the kern in the church. The three who escaped, together with other de Bermingham kern who were in the area and were now terrified of the mob, fled to the earl in his manor. Then hue and cry was raised in the county and an even larger mob (which technically was the *posse comitatus*) pursued the kern, stormed the manor, and slaughtered the inhabitants. Only a few, including the wife of the earl and some children, escaped.

It is clear that while resentment against the kern boiled over, there were deeper reasons for this attack by the Louth tenants. Clyn says simply that 'all of his county conspired against him, not wishing that he should rule over them'.[120] This may well be the truth. De Bermingham was an outsider, imposed on them by the king after the trauma of the Bruce invasion. He may well have imported into Louth customs and habits that sustained him in Tethmoy but that were alien to the less tolerant Anglo-Irish of his new earldom. But whatever the reason for the hatred, the savagery of the attack by townsmen and local gentry well illustrates the extent to which the forces of disorder could get out of control.

Many stories later grew up around the massacre, including one that told of the earl taking a daughter of one of the de Verdons against her will and thus sparking off the whole affair. There was a woman involved, too, in another famous and much more disastrous murder in 1333, that of the young earl of Ulster.[121] He had imprisoned and starved to death his cousin Walter de Burgh in 1332 and it was Walter's sister, Gyle, married to Richard de Mandeville, who instigated the murder in revenge. The

75. The royal castle at Newcastle McKynegan, County Wicklow, was vital to the government's attempts to maintain control over the Leinster Irish. The area between it and Wicklow town was inhabited by the Anglo-Norman family of Lawless, but because of the endemic warfare in the area they were given government authority to deal with the Irish 'in the manner of the marchers' and they themselves were treated as if an Irish sept, so that they were ordered that, 'if any of their name offend against the peace, they may take and imprison them'. The photograph shows the gatehouse on the motte

consequences were momentous in Irish history, leading ultimately to the collapse of the great de Burgh lordship in Ulster and Connacht. But these two murders, and many less important ones, show how fragile the feudal bond had become by now. Fealty had little place in the new world of the fourteenth century. Men were bought, and not even the royal officials were above corruption. When it was proposed to John Darcy in summer 1328 that he should go as chief governor to Ireland, he replied by stating a number of conditions, among them that his own nominees should fill the more important offices in the Irish administration; he clearly placed no faith in the existing holders of these offices.

Even more important, however, was another demand made by Darcy that he should be paid more than the normal fee which the chief governor received ('for he cannot live on his fee in the state in which the land is now'), money for his expenses, money in advance, and 'because there is nothing in the treasury, according to what he has heard', he must have £1,000 for an army.[122] A new era in Anglo-Irish relations had been inaugurated. Chief governors could bargain before taking up office, control from England was weakened, and most important of all the English taxpayer was beginning to accept responsibility for the cost of maintaining the king's peace in Ireland. A new pattern was emerging in Ireland, too, in which the Dublin government counted for less than the powerful local lord in many parts of the lordship. Already the tendency to focus governmental attention on what later became known as the four loyal counties in the east was manifest. And as the process of assimilation to the Gaelic way of life continued, many of the Anglo-Irish lordships were becoming hardly distinguishable from those ruled by Gaelic lords. The settlers in many places had already been swallowed up or displaced. In the west, especially, gaelicisation was widespread. There is a remarkable statement by the court poet of the O'Maddens in a passage on Bruce, where writing of 'our own foreigners' he says that:[123]

> the old chieftains of Erin prospered under those princely English lords who were our chief rulers, and who gave up their foreignness for a pure mind, their surliness for good manners, and their stubbornness for sweet mildness, and who had given up their perverseness for hospitality.

This is a far cry from the attitude displayed in the Ó Néill remonstrance of *c.*1317.

The success of the Gaelic revival was evident on many levels. It had gained a momentum of its own now and was impossible to check in the old way by employing brute force, treachery and exclusion. Even John Darcy realised this when he demanded as one of his conditions of service in Ireland that all Irishmen who wished to live under English law should be permitted by statute of an Irish parliament to do so: there should be one and the same law for all Ireland. But it was too late. The Irish had their own laws and were not now interested in the benefits of English law. It was no longer a disadvantage to most of them to be outside the law, since the land of peace had contracted so much that the king's justice could be available in only a small part of the island. The change could be violent and even sudden. In 1342, according to Clyn, Laoighseach Ó Mórdha 'violently ejected almost all the English from their lands and inheritance' and in one night burned eight of their castles, as well as destroying Roger Mortimer's 'noble castle' of Dunamase. 'He usurped to himself the dominion of that country, from a serf becoming a lord, from a subject a prince'.[124]

There is one event which perhaps can be taken to symbolise the success of the Gaelic revival and which shows how much Ireland had changed in a couple of generations. In 1327,[125]

> the Irish of Leinster came together and made a certain king, that is Domnall son of Art MacMurrough. Who, when he had been made king, ordered that his banner should be placed within two miles of Dublin and afterwards to travel throughout all the lands of Ireland.

This was the first inauguration of its kind in Leinster since the twelfth century and it marks a significant advance in the revival of old Irish institutions. It is important not only because it was done in a formal and public way, but because the leading lords of Gaelic Leinster seem to have been party to it and to have acquiesced in the choice of Domnall as king. And he for his part immediately declared his intention of marching on Dublin itself and then leading a conquest of Ireland. That he did not succeed, and indeed was ignominiously captured and imprisoned in Dublin castle, hardly matters, though the fact that his captor was rewarded with the huge payment of £100 is a sure indication of the fright he had given the government.[126] The alarm in Dublin was worsened by the news that Robert Bruce had landed in Ulster and had forced the seneschal to accept a truce for one year and recognise him as king of Scotland.[127] There were also rumours that Bruce intended to invade England via Ulster with Irish help. But the Dublin government believed that the real danger lay in a possible rising in Ulster and sent the chancellor northwards to persuade the Anglo-Irish to resist the Scots, should they land in the future.[128]

But in Leinster, the important thing was that the Irish had a king who was ready to challenge the English. From now on the Leinster Irish were to be more of a problem than ever to the government. They could not be suppressed. They grew more menacing all the time. Like the other great Gaelic lords of Ireland, the MacMurroughs were part of the new pattern that had emerged from the breakup of the old feudal structure which the settlers had imposed. The Dublin government, the English king, and the *Gaill* and *Gaedhil* alike now had to find a way of living within the new structure that was shaping Ireland.

7

A Sequel to Edward Bruce's Invasion of Ireland[1]

Ranald Nicholson

The years between 1315 and 1318, when the Anglo-Scottish conflict transferred itself to Irish soil, have rightly engaged the attention of historians. To most of them it has seemed that the Bruce invasion of Ireland ended once and for all with the defeat and death of Edward Bruce at the battle of Faughart. But that striking event is perhaps misleading: if Edward Bruce's career in Ireland had obviously come to an end, that of Robert Bruce had not.[2]

Before the death of his brother, Robert Bruce had withdrawn from Ireland; and a decade was to pass before he had returned. In the meanwhile he concentrated upon the recapture of Berwick and the harrying of the northern shires of England. In contrast to the disaster at Faughart this policy was highly successful. On the other hand, the removal of the Scottish pressure upon Ireland enabled Edward II once more to draw upon its resources. Thus in 1323 contingents levied in Ireland were to have joined the English king for a campaign against the Scots.[3] But these preparations were cancelled after the shock of Sir Andrew Harclay's treason had forced Edward II to call a halt to Anglo-Scottish hostilities. At Bishopthorpe, Scots and English concluded a truce that was designed to last for thirteen years and lead to a final peace.[4]

For a few years the truce of 1323 was uneasily kept. What ended it and inaugurated a new period of instability was the crisis in English domestic politics that brought the reign of Edward II to a close. In the autumn of 1326, when Edward was fleeing westward before the invading forces of Mortimer and Isabella, he was credited with a scheme for overawing his rebellious English subjects. According to the Lanercost chronicler, Edward hoped to escape to Ireland and there to raise troops

76. The remains of Olderfleet Castle, the 'Wolrynfurth' visited by Robert Bruce at Easter 1327

who would descend upon England in collaboration with the Scots. In return for this intervention on behalf of Edward II, the Scots would be well rewarded: Robert Bruce, we are told, would be recognised as king of an independent Scotland and much of the north of England would be ceded to him.[5]

Whether or not Edward II meditated such projects he himself was soon unable to pursue them: he was imprisoned in Kenilworth while Mortimer and Isabella ruled in the name of the young Edward III. But this was not the end of plans for a Scoto-Irish descent upon England, though now those plans were to be of a somewhat different character. English dissensions provided the Scots with a favourable occasion for the renewal of the war. In the altered circumstances Bruce would accept no truce or peace without recognition as king of an independent Scotland. To achieve this, he planned to wage war simultaneously on two or more fronts. It was natural that the Scots should again fan the smouldering animosities of Ireland.

Scottish propaganda had once assured the native Irish that the Scots were sprung of the same racial stock as they, that both peoples shared the same language and customs, and that an enduring league between them would restore the ancient liberty of their race.[6] Whilst the course of Edward Bruce's invasion had shown that not all of the native Irish had been convinced by this propaganda, it had also shown that it was in Ulster that the Scots might most readily establish a base and find sympathisers.[7] Ireland, or Ulster at least, was to be one of the fronts in the renewed Anglo-Scottish war of 1327. The Irish *Annals of the Four Masters* mention the bald fact that the king of Scotland came to Ireland in that year.[8] Although few Scottish sources even hint at such an expedition,[9] it seems clear that sometime around Easter 1327 King Robert disembarked in Ireland at the haven of 'Wolrynfurth' near Larne.[10]

It was not, perhaps, in Ireland itself that Bruce's ambitions lay. It was reported that he had come to secure Irish co-operation for a further landing of an army in Wales and an invasion of England from that quarter.[11] The strategy behind this plan was not new,[12] but it was impressive. England would be faced by a grand alliance of Scots, Irish and Welsh, united, if not by common sentiments of racial kinship, then at least by common antipathies towards English rule. To increase the chance of success it was doubtless pre-arranged that the earl of Moray and Sir James Douglas would invade England from across the Scottish border. In addition, Donald, earl of Mar, now reconciled to King Robert, was soon busy inciting both English and Welsh to rise in favour of the imprisoned Edward II.[13]

It was an obscure Irishman who claimed to have delivered England from the perils consequent upon Bruce's arrival in Ireland. John, son of William Jordan, had been despatched by the earl of Kildare, then justiciar of Ireland, to deflect Bruce from his purpose.[14] Whether or not John's mission was decisive, the Scottish king certainly did abandon any intention of a landing in Wales and sailed back to Scotland.

But Bruce's intervention in northern Ireland had not been unprofitable. Under the threat of Scottish raids, Henry Mandeville, the Ulster seneschal,[15] recognised Bruce as king of Scotland and concluded with him a humiliating indenture, sealed *alternatim* and dated at Glendun (Antrim) on 12 July 1327.[16]

Although less open to the charge of treason than the abortive treaty between Bruce and Sir Andrew Harclay in 1323, the indenture of 1327 was equally symptomatic of the decay of royal control in the areas most harassed by Scottish attacks. The result of Mandeville's negotiations was that the people of Ulster bought a truce to last a full year from 1 August 1327. The inequality of the two parties to the indenture was underlined by the absence of any clause binding Bruce to its observance, and an acknowledgment by Mandeville that for his part he would see to its observance on pain of full forfeiture. In return for the truce the Ulstermen would deliver to the Scots in the haven of 'Wlingfrith' (Larne) 100 'cendres'[17] of wheat and 100 'cendres' of barley, half at Martinmas and half at Whitsunday. The landing in Ulster had apparently shown that Bruce might still rely upon support in the region, and in the terms of the truce he took care to provide for his own adherents: they were to enjoy the terms of the truce and were not to be attacked by their local opponents.[18]

Whatever the strength of Bruce's Irish adherents, there were other factors that made it difficult for Henry Mandeville to resist the renewal of Scots influence. In 1327 there was a faction fight throughout all Ireland.[19] The north and west in particular were more than usually troubled by reason of the death of the Red Earl

77. The havens of the Antrim coast were familiar ground to Robert I, whose family, as earls of Carrick, inherited a claim to all of the modern barony of Upper Glenarm, stretching from Larne Harbour to the village of Glenarm

of Ulster in 1326. Even for the crown to take seisin of the dead earl's lands and castles required a military expedition under John Darcy the justiciar.[20] Despite this, any other measures recorded in the Irish close and patent rolls, little had been done to restore order in the vast de Burgh lordship before Bruce arrived.[21] It was an official of the late earl who sent to England a copy of Bruce's indenture with Mandeville as a warning of what might happen if Ulster were neglected. In a covering letter,[22] he described the prevailing confusion: if the earl's heir did not soon arrive with a strong company to assert his rights, the Ulstermen might choose another lord 'pur meyntenaunce avoir'.[23] Moreover, if the war with the Scots should outlast the local truce between Bruce and Mandeville, measures would have to be taken for the defence of Ulster.

Fortunately, in the writer's view, there were hopes that Bruce himself would not outlive the truce: 'Sire Robert de Brus est si feble et si defait qe il ne durra mie tanqe a cel oure oue laide de Dieu, car il ne poait guere mover, forsqe la lange'.[24] The claim that Bruce was so weak that he could move only his tongue was probably wishful thinking, but it could scarcely have been advanced unless the king were already gravely ill.

Nonetheless, when Bruce sailed back to Scotland after the conclusion of the truce with Mandeville, Ulster had not seen the last of him. For the moment, however, his concern was England itself. The campaign led by Moray and Douglas ended brilliantly on 7 August 1327. Soon afterwards the Scottish king was besieging Norham and threatening to annex Northumberland.[25] Faced with such a prospect Mortimer and Isabella wavered. The ensuing 'final peace' between England and Scotland was

78. Lea Castle: one of the principal residences of the earl of Kildare, Thomas fitz John. As justiciar of Ireland, he was the man responsible for its defence when Robert Bruce unexpectedly descended on Ulster in 1327, with the rumoured intention of organising an army for a descent via Wales on England

one that in its essentials had been dictated by Bruce.[26] Henceforward Scots and English were to be allies: the English would not help Bruce's enemies in the Western Isles; and the Scots renounced any future intervention in Ireland in support of the foes of the English king.[27] By another clause in the treaty it had been agreed that Joan, younger sister of Edward III, should be given in marriage to David Bruce, King Robert's son and heir. On 17 July 1328 the ceremony duly took place.

It was not a good augury for the future relations of Scotland and England that Edward III absented himself from his sister's wedding. Although Bruce must have looked upon the marriage as the ultimate symbol of his triumph, he too was absent. According to the Scottish chronicler Barbour, 'ane male ess tuk hym so sare that he on na viss mycht be thar... at Cardross all that tym he lay'.[28] While Bruce was undoubtedly a stricken man, it seems more likely that it was a point of honour that kept him from the nuptials at Berwick: the insult of Edward III's absence could be mitigated only by his own. For if Bruce was too ill to attend his son's wedding it seems strange that within a month he was able to give strenuous personal attention to the problems of one of the wedding guests.

Among the magnates who had attended Joan on her way to Berwick was William de Burgh, grandson and heir of the deceased Red Earl of Ulster. Though only fifteen years of age, William had been knighted at Whitsuntide and had received livery of his lordship[29] less than a year previously. Those in charge of the young heir had been warned that his interests in the earldom of Ulster could not be safeguarded unless he

79. These lands of Bruce's Ulster inheritance consumed the family's attention for many years and, since Robert visited Ulster at least twice while a seriously ill man not far from death, his concern must have been to retain the Bruce claim

himself were brought over and installed with a show of force.[30] But there was little forcefulness to be found anywhere in the England of 1328. On the other hand, William had some claim upon Robert Bruce.[31] William presumably came to his cousin's marriage in the hopes that King Robert would intercede for him in Ulster. It was ironic that Bruce, so largely responsible for the unrest in Ulster, should be asked to suppress it.

The immediate concern of de Burgh was to obtain custody of Carrickfergus Castle. But the grasping Queen Isabella seems also to have had designs upon the castle; she also had come to Berwick;[32] and she had enlisted the good offices of King Robert, for it was 'par le Roy Descoce' that she asked that the commissions for the transfer of the castle should be delivered to her 'qu elle les puisse avoir oue ly'.[33] Whether Isabella intended to use the commissions for her own extortionate purposes, or whether there was any intention of offering to transfer the castle to Bruce is not clear. de Burgh in his turn addressed a petition, suggesting that he might in the meantime garrison and victual the castle in readiness for his own arrival there.[34] The result of the earl's petition was a curious compromise: according to the endorsement, commissions were to be sent to the queen mother, while at the same time another commission was to be issued to de Burgh granting him the unpaid ward of Carrickfergus till Michaelmas.[35] Finally, on 15 November 1328, a warrant was issued for the granting to the earl of the custody of Carrickfergus during the king's pleasure.[36]

Whatever part Bruce played in these complex transactions he seems before long to have lent his support to de Burgh. If the terms of the treaty of Northampton forbade the Scots to help the English king's enemies in Ireland, it did not forbid them to help his friends. Thus Bruce, despite his infirmity, made a last descent upon Ulster. This

80. Carrickfergus Castle: Robert Bruce's final journey to Ireland was in 1328, when he personally escorted to Carrickfergus the new earl of Ulster, William de Burgh, his nephew by marriage

time he came in peace, escorting William de Burgh to his heritage with a company that included the earl of Menteith and other Scottish magnates.[37]

In return for this demonstration Bruce doubtless demanded full payment of the tribute promised under the Mandeville indenture. In addition, he might be expected to secure for the abbot of Dundrennan the restoration of the former lands of his house in Burtonstown, County Meath.[38] Moreover, as late as the reign of Henry III of England, the lord of Galloway and his kinsmen, the earls of Atholl and Carrick, had been possessed of extensive lands in Ulster.[39] Whether Murdoch, earl of Menteith, could substantiate a claim to any of these grants is uncertain. Bruce himself, however, was by descent earl of Carrick; and shortly before his trip to Ulster in 1328 he had bestowed the family earldom upon his son, David, so that he might be dignified by a title before his marriage to the sister of Edward III. If, with de Burgh's acquiescence, the Carrick lands in Ulster could be regained, David's appanage would be augmented.

But more than the revival of old claims may have been envisaged. Once Bruce and de Burgh had landed peacefully at Carrickfergus, they are said to have written to Roger Outlaw, the acting justiciar of Ireland, inviting both him and his council to attend a meeting at Greencastle (County Down), ostensibly to treat of peace between Scotland and Ireland.[40] In view of the 'final peace' of Northampton, such a meeting and such a topic might seem superfluous; nor could such discussions have been held without derogation to the authority of the king of England. Not surprisingly, the justiciar failed to keep the rendezvous. Instead, William de Burgh went off to attend a parliament in Dublin. Sometime after the middle of August 1328 Bruce retired to

Scotland.[41] His last visit to Ulster was the last notable enterprise of his career. Within a year he was finally overcome by the sickness that had encouraged his foes to look for his early death.

Had they occurred at an earlier stage of his career, Bruce's 'two curious reappearances in Ulster'[42] might have been dismissed as mere feints. The fact that they occurred in his most experienced years, and despite his grave infirmity, suggest that their significance was weightier. After a decade's absence from Ireland, did Bruce in 1327 think once more of a confederation of the Celtic west? Whether or not he did, his arrival in Ulster demonstrated that there was a power vacuum in the north of Ireland that could be filled only by the Scots or by those who the Scots tolerated. Bruce's trip to Ulster in 1328 doubtless helped William de Burgh to install himself in his heritage, but it also gave Bruce a chance to put forth his power and enhance Scottish prestige. Although outwardly observing the terms of the 'final peace' he thrust upon one of Edward III's dominions peaceful but forceful attentions, that were all the more insulting in so far as they pre-supposed that the English king was unable to do for one of his own subjects what the Scottish king was both willing and able to do. The demonstration was all the more necessary because Scotland would soon be faced with a long minority. Edward III's aversion to the treaty of Northampton had not gone unnoticed; a scrap of parchment was no real safeguard for the throne of David Bruce; King Robert's last concern was to try to prove that the initiative still lay with the Scots, and that the English would be well advised to content themselves with the 'final peace'.

Appendix I

I am indebted to Professor A.A.M. Duncan for drawing my attention to the formulary contained in an Edinburgh University Library MS volume of *Regiam Majestatem* (Edin. Univ. Lib., Borland MSS, no. 207). Among the early material preserved in this formulary is the following undated diplomatic document (fo. 150v), which seems certainly to relate to Robert Bruce's preparations for intervention in Ireland. In its assertion of a common racial origin of Scots and Irish it significantly recalls the Irish Remonstrance of 1317 addressed to Pope John XXII, with its mention of the 'reges minoris Scociae, qui omnes de majori Scocia sanguinem originalem sumpserunt, linguam nostram et condiciones quodammodo ferentes.' (See the version in *Liber Pluscardensis,* Historians of Scotland series, i, 250). As is usual in formularies, the text of the letters in MS Borland 207 is often corrupt. In the following extract the text has, where possible, been restored; but some difficulties still remain.

Littera directa ad Yberniam

Rex omnibus et singulis regibus Ybernie, prelatis quoque et clero eiusdem, ac incolis tocius Ybernie, nostris amicis, salutem.

Cum nos et vos, populus noster et vester, ab olim liberi, ab uno processimus germine nacionis, quos tam lingua communis quam ritus fervencius venerandi excitant in amorem grato animo stimulari, dilectos consanguineos nostros, A, B, et C, latores presencium, vestrasque presencias duximus transmittendos ad tractandum vobiscum et singulis vestrum, nomine nostro, super consideracione amicicie specialis inter nos et vos perpetue convectende et inviolabiliter observanda, per quam, Deo disponente, nostra nacio in antiquam reduci valeat libertatem.

Ratum igitur habemus et habuimus in futuris quicquid predicti T et A et eorum alter, nomine nostro vobiscum tractando et firmando, faceret vel facerent in premissis. In cuius rei.

Appendix II

(i) Public Record Office, Chancery Miscellanea, C. 47 bundle 10, file 19, no. 8 (a): This is a royal writ dated at Nottingham on 17 August 1331 and directed to the justiciar, chancellor and treasurer of Ireland. Allusion is made to a petition of John, son of William Jordan. The officials are requested to forward information as to John's alleged good services when Robert Bruce landed in Ireland in 1327. In particular, they are to inform the king whether John had been promised a reward of 100 librates, and whether or not he had received it.

(ii) Ibid., bundle 10, file 19, no. 8 (b): This is the return to the above writ (complete transcript).
Huius brevis vestri pretextu, nos, justiciarius, cancellarius, & thesaurarius vestri Hibernie, inspecto tenore eiusdem & quosdam de consilio vestro & alios quos evocandos esse videbamus fecimus evocari & cum eis nos super contentis in eodem diligenter informavimus, et primo comperimus quod Robertus de Bruys anno regni vestri primo circa Pascha in terra vestra Hibernie in [por] tu de Wolrynforth applicvit, & ex consensu quorumdam Hibernicorum ulterius in William processisse & ibidem cum excercitu applicuisse & terram vestram Anglie more guerrino invasisse disposuit; quodque Johannesfilius Willelmi Jordan, in hoc brevi nominatus, propter ipsius fidelitatem & industriam, per comitem Kildar tunc justiciarium terre vestre Hibernie missus fuit ad ipsum Robertum & complices suos impediendum a proposito suo predicto, & quod mediante missione illa per ipsuis Johannis subtilitatem, industriam & laborem, dictus Robertus preconceptum in illa parte propositum reliquit omnino & ad Scociam remeavit. Comperimus eciam quod ad premissa facienda & explenda prefati Johannis industria specialiter fuit perlecta. Set utrum & justiciario vestro & aliis de consilio vestro in terra predicta probono servicio suo promittebatur quod provideretur sibi de centum libratis terre per annum de terris & tenementis in manu vestra existentibus habendis ad totam vitam suam necnon, nec si quid aliud ei promittebatur pro servicio illo, nec si aliquam inde remuneracionem unquam esset assecutus non comperimus. Est tamen consilium nostrum quod regia liberalitas sibi aliqua competenti remuneracione si placet provideat, ut alii inde sumentes exemplum animentur ad aggrediendum consimilia vel maiora.

(iii) As a result of this inquest and the return it appears that John was granted fifty librates for life; but despite further faithful service he had difficulty in obtaining possession of the whole of the grant: see Bain, J., *Calendar of Documents relating to Scotland,* iii, no. 1191, pp. 217–18.

Appendix A

The Brus
The History of Robert the Bruce King of Scots

by John Barbour
Translated by George Eyre-Todd

Book XIV

Sir Edward Bruce, the earl of Carrick, who was bolder than a leopard, and had no desire to be at peace, thought Scotland too small for his brother and himself; therefore he set his purpose to be king of Ireland. To this end he entered into treaty with the Irish, and they on their honour undertook to make him king, provided that he, by hard fighting, could overcome the English then dwelling in the country; and they promised to help him with all their might.

When he heard this promise he had great joy in his heart, and with consent of the king gathered to him men of great valour, and taking ship at Ayr in the next month of May, sailed straight to Ireland.

He had in his company the valiant Earl Thomas, and good Sir Philip the Mowbray, trusty in hard assault; Sir John Soulis, a good knight; and the doughty Sir John Stewart, as well as the Ramsay of Auchterhouse, right able and chivalrous, with Sir Fergus of Ardrossan, and many another knight.

They arrived safely in Wavering Firth[1] without skirmish or attack, and sent their ships every one home. It was a great enterprise they undertook, when, few as they were, being no more than 6,000 men, they set out to attack all Ireland, where many thousands were ready armed to fight them. But though they were few, they were valiant, and without doubt or fear they set forth in two battles towards Carrickfergus, to spy it.

But the lords of that country, Mandeville, Bysset and Logan, assembled their men every one. De Savage also was there. Their whole gathering was wellnigh 20,000 men.

When they knew that the Scottish host had arrived in their country, they hastened towards it with all their following. And when Sir Edward knew of a certainty that they were coming near him, he set his men in their strongest array. The Earl Thomas had the vanguard, and the rear-guard was under Sir Edward.

Their enemies drew near to battle, and they met them without pinching. Then was to be seen a great mêlée. Earl Thomas and his host drove so doughtily at their foes, that, in a short time, 100 were to be seen lying all bloody. The Irish horses, when they were stabbed, reared and flung, and made great room, and threw their riders. Sir Edward's company then stoutly joined the battle, and all their enemies were driven back. If a man happened to fall in that fight, it was a perilous chance if he rose again. The Scots bore themselves so boldly and well in the encounter that their foes were overwhelmed, and altogether took flight. In that battle were taken or slain the whole flower of Ulster. The earl of Moray won great praise there, for his right valiant feats of arms encouraged his whole company.

That was a right fair beginning; for being but newly arrived, Sir Edward's host defeated in open battle enemies who were four for their one. Afterwards they went to Carrickfergus, and took quarters in the town. The castle was at that time well and newly furnished with victual and men, and the Scots forthwith set siege to it. Many a bold sally was made while the siege lasted, till at length they made a truce.

When the folk of Ulster came wholly to his peace, and Sir Edward undertook to raid the land further, there came to him some ten or twelve of the chiefs of that country, and gave him their fealty. They kept faith with him, however, only a short while; for two of them, one MacCoolechan and another MacArthy, beset a place on his way where he must needs pass.

2,000 spearmen were got together there and as many archers; and all the cattle of the country were drawn thither for safety. Men call that place Endwillane,[2] in all Ireland there is none more strait. There the Irish kept watch for Sir Edward, believing he should not escape. But he soon set forth and went straight towards the spot.

Sir Thomas, earl of Moray, who ever put himself first in attack, alighted on foot with his company, and boldly assailed the fastness. The Irish chiefs of whom I spoke, and all the folk with them, met him right stubbornly; but he with his host made such an attack, that despite their efforts he won the place. Many of the Irish were slain there, and the Scots chased them throughout the wood, and seized an abundance of prey. So great was this that all the Scottish host was refreshed well for a week and more.

Sir Edward lay at Kilnasagart, and there presently he heard that at Dundalk the lords of that country were assembled for war. There was, first, Sir Richard of Clare, lieutenant of all Ireland for the king of England.[3] The earl of Desmond also was there, and the earl of Kildare as well, with de Bermingham and Verdon, lords of great renown.

Butler also was with them, and Sir Maurice fitz Thomas. These were come thither with their men, and were in truth a right great host.

And when Sir Edward knew of a surety that there was such a knightly company, he forthwith arrayed his force and set out thither, and took quarters near the town. But because he knew full well that a great host was in the town, he arrayed his men, and kept in battle order, to meet the enemy if they should attack.

And when Sir Richard of Clare, and the other lords in that place, knew that the Scottish battle were come so near, they took counsel and agreed not to fight that night, because it was late, but determined that on the morrow, immediately after sunrise, they should sally forth with their whole force. Accordingly that night they did no more, but each side kept its quarters.

That night the Scottish company kept right careful watch, all in order, and on the morrow at daylight they arrayed themselves in two battles, and stood with banners all displayed, ready prepared for the fight.

Those within the town, when the sun was risen and shining clear, sent forth fifty of their number to spy the order and advance of the Scots. These rode forth and soon saw them; then came again without delay. And when they were alighted together they told their lords that the Scots seemed to be valiant and of right great nobleness. 'But of a surety,' they said, 'they are not half a dinner for us here!'

The lords at these tidings were greatly rejoiced and reassured, and caused the order to go throughout the city that all should quickly arm themselves. And when they were armed and ready and all arrayed for the fight, they went forth in good order.

They soon came in touch with their foes, who were watching for them right boldly. Then a fierce battle began, for either side set all its strength to overwhelm its foes in the fight, and each charged the other with all its force. The furious struggle lasted long, while none could see or know who was likely to be uppermost. From soon after sunrise till after midday the fighting lasted thus doubtful; but at length the stout Sir Edward, with the whole of his company, rushed so furiously upon the enemy that they could no longer endure the battle. With broken ranks they all took flight, followed right keenly by the Scots. Mixed all together the two hosts entered the town. There a cruel slaughter was to be seen, for the right noble Earl Thomas followed the chase with his host, and made such a butchery in the place, and such fierce slaughter, that the streets were all bloody with slain men. But the English lords got all away.

When the town, as I have told, was stormed, and all their foes were fled or slain, the Scots quartered in the place. There was in it such plenty of victual, and such great abundance of wine, that the good earl feared greatly lest his men should be drunken, and in their drunkenness come to blows; therefore he appointed a free gift of wine to be paid to each man, and of a surety they had all enough. That night they were right well at ease, and right glad of the great renown begotten by their valour.

After this fight they sojourned there in Dundalk three days and more, then they set forth southward. The Earl Thomas ever rode in front, and as they marched through the country they could see upon the hills a marvellous number of men. But when the earl would sturdily make towards them with his banner, they would flee, all that were there, and none abide to fight.

The Scots rode southward till they came to a great forest, Kilross it was called, and they all took their quarters there.

Meantime, Richard of Clare, the English king's lieutenant over all the baronage of Ireland, had got together a great host. There were five battles great and broad, and they sought Sir Edward and his men, and were by this time come very near him.

He soon got knowledge that they were coming upon him, and were so near, and he led his men against them, and boldly took the open field. Then the earl rode forward to espy, and he sent Sir Philip the Mowbray and Sir John Stewart forward to discover the way the English were taking. Soon they saw the host coming at hand. They were, at a guess, 50,000 strong. Then the knights rode back to Sir Edward, and said the enemy were right many.

'The more they be,' he answered, 'the more honour altogether have we, if we bear us manfully. We are set here at bay, and to win honour or die. We are too far from home to flee; therefore let each man be valiant. Yonder host are the scourings of the country, and if they be manfully assailed they shall easily, I trow, be made to flee.'

All then said they should do well. With that the English battles, 10,000 strong, approached near, ready to fight, and the Scots met them with great force. The Scots were all on foot, and their enemies on steeds well equipped, some covered wholly with iron and steel. But the Scots at the encounter pierced the English armour with spears, and stabbed the horses, and bore down the men. A fierce battle then took place. I cannot tell all their strokes, nor who caused his enemy to fall in the battle; but in a short time, I warrant, the English were so overwhelmed that they durst no more abide, but scattered all of them and fled, leaving dead on the battlefield very many of their good men. The field was all strewn with weapons, armour and dead men.

That great host was fiercely overthrown, but Sir Edward let no man pursue. With the prisoners they had captured the Scots went again to the wood, where their harness was left, and that night they made merry cheer, and praised God earnestly for His grace.

This good knight, who was so valiant, might well be likened in that fight to Judas Maccabaeus. No number of enemies caused him to retreat so long as he had one man against ten.

Thus was Richard of Clare repulsed with his great host. Nevertheless he kept diligently gathering men about him, for he thought still to recover his overthrow. It grieved him wondrous much that he had been twice discomfited in battle by a small company.

And the Scots, who had ridden into the forest to take rest, lay there two nights, and made themselves mirth, solace and play. Then they rode to meet O Dempsey, an Irish chief who had made oath of fealty to Sir Edward; for previously he had prayed him to visit his country, and had promised that no victual nor anything that could help should be lacking to the Scottish host.

Sir Edward trusted in his promise, and rode straight thither with his rout. O Dempsey caused him to cross a great river, and in a right fair place, low by a lough edge,[4] he made them take their quarters, and said he would go and have victual brought to them. He departed without more delay, for his plan was to betray them. He had brought them to a place from which all the cattle had been withdrawn full two days' journey and more, so that in all that country they could get nothing sufficient to eat. His plan was to weaken them with hunger, then bring their enemies upon them.

This false traitor had caused his men to dam the outlet of a lough a little above the place where he had quartered Sir Edward and the Scots, and in the night he let it out. The water then came down on Sir Edward's men with such force that they were in peril of being drowned ere they knew they were in the midst of a flood. With great difficulty they got away, and by God's grace kept their lives, but much of their armour was lost there.

Of a truth O Dempsey made them no brave feast, nevertheless they had enough. For though they lacked meat, I warrant they had plenty to drink. They were bested there in great distress, for they had great want of victual, being set between two rivers, and able to cross none of them. The Bann, which is an arm of the sea, and cannot be crossed with horses, was betwixt them and Ulster. They had been in great peril there, were it not for a rover of the sea, Thomas of Down he was called. He heard that the host was thus straitly bested, and he sailed up the Bann till he came very near the place where they lay. They knew him well, and were glad. With four ships that he had seized he set them every one across the Bann; and when they came to inhabited land they found victual and meat enough, and quartered themselves in a wood. None of the Irish knew where the Scots lay, and Sir Edward's men took their ease, and made good cheer.

At that time Richard of Clare and the great chiefs of Ireland were quartered with a vast host on a forest side near the Scots. Each day they sent riders to bring victual of many kinds from the town of Connor, full ten Irish miles away. Each day, as these riders came and went, they passed within two miles of the Scottish host. And when Earl Thomas had knowledge of their coming and their gathering, he got him a good company of 300 active and bold horsemen. There were Sir Philip the Mowbray, and also for certain Sir John Stewart, with Sir Allan Stewart, Sir Gilbert Boyd and others. They rode to meet the victuallers, who were making their way with the provisions from Connor to their host, and so suddenly dashed on them that they were wholly discomfited, and let fall all their weapons, and piteously cried for mercy. Thereupon the Scots gave them quarter, but made such clean capture that not one of them all escaped.

The earl learned from them that a part of their host would come out in the evening at the woodside, and ride towards their victual. He thought then upon an exploit. He caused his whole following to dress themselves in the prisoners' array. Their pennons also they took with them, and waited till it was near night, and then rode towards the English host. Some of the host saw them coming, and fully supposed they were their victuallers. Therefore they rode in disorder towards them, having no suspicion that they were their enemies, and being sore hungered besides. For that reason they came on recklessly. And when they were near, the earl and all who were with him rushed upon them at great speed with bare weapons, shouting their battle-cries. And the English, seeing their foes thus suddenly drive at them, were affrighted, and had no heart to help themselves, but made off towards their host.

The Scots made chase and slew many, so that all the field was strewn with them, more than 1,000 being slain. They chased them right up to their host, and then again went their way. In this fashion the victual was seized, and many of the English were slain. Then the earl and his company brought the prisoners and provisions to Sir Edward, who was blithe of their coming. That night the Scots made merry cheer, being all then fully at their ease, and guarded securely.

Their enemies, on the other hand, when they heard how their men had been slain, and their victual all seized, took counsel, and determined to set out towards Connor and take quarters in the city. They did this in great haste, and rode to the city by night. There they found provisions in great plenty, and made good and merry cheer, for all trusted in the town where they were.

Upon the morrow they sent to espy where the Scots had taken quarters. But the spies were all met and seized, and brought to the Scottish host. The earl of Moray quietly asked one of their company where their host was, and what they planned to do, telling him if he found that he told him the truth he should go home ransom free.

'Of a truth,' the man said, 'I shall tell you. Their plan is, to-morrow at daybreak, to seek you with their whole host if they can get knowledge where ye be. They have sent word throughout the country that all the men of this region, on right cruel pain of their lives, betake themselves this night to the city. Of a truth there shall be so many that ye shall in no wise cope with them.'

'Par Dieu,' said the earl, 'that may be so!'

With that he went to Sir Edward and told him the whole tale. Then they took counsel all together, and determined to ride to the city that same night, so as to lie with all their host between the town and those outside. They did as they devised; they came presently before the town, and rested but half a mile from it.

And when daylight dawned, fifty Irish on active ponies came to a little hill a short space from the town, and saw Sir Edward's place of quartering. They marvelled at the sight, how so few durst in any wise undertake so high an enterprise as to come thus boldly upon the whole great chivalry of Ireland to do battle. This was the truth without fail, for opposed to them were gathered there with the warden, Richard of Clare, the Butler, and the two earls, of Desmond and Kildare, with Bermingham, Verdon, and Fitz-Warenne, as well as Sir Pascal, a Florentine, and knight of Lombardy, renowned for feats of arms. The Mandevilles were also there, the Byssetts, Logans and others besides, the Savages as well, and one called Sir Nicol of Kilkenan. And with these lords were so many men that, I trow, for one of the Scots they were five or more.

When the scouts had thus seen the Scottish host, they went in haste, and told their lords all plainly how the Scots were come near, so that there was no need to go far to seek them.

And when the Earl Thomas saw that these men had been on the hill, he took with him a good company of horsemen – there might be 100 of them – and made his way to the hill. They made an ambush in a hollow place, and in a short time they saw a company of scouts come riding from the city. At that they were blithe, and kept themselves secret till the scouts were come near. Then with a rush all who were there dashed boldly upon them.

The scouts, seeing them thus suddenly come on, were dismayed. Some of them kept their ground stoutly to make fight, while the others fled; but in a right short time those who made halt were overcome so that they altogether turned their backs. The Scots pursued right to the gate, and slew a great number, then went again to their host.

Book XV

When the Irish within the town saw their men thus slain and chased home again, they were all downcast, and in great haste called loudly to arms. All armed themselves and made ready for the battle, and they marched forth all in fair array, with banners displayed, ready in their best fashion to attack their enemies.

And when Sir Philip the Mowbray saw them come forth in such brave array, he went to Sir Edward the Bruce, and said, 'Sir, it is good that we devise some stratagem which may avail to help us in this great battle. Our men are few, but their will is greater than their power. Therefore, I counsel that our baggage, without man or page, be arrayed by itself, and it shall seem a host far more in number than we. Set we our banners in its front, and yonder folk who come out of Connor, when they see them, shall believe that we for certain are there, and shall charge thither. Let us then come on their flank, and we shall have the advantage, for if they be entered among our baggage they shall be entangled, and then we with all our strength may lay on and do all we can.'

They did as he proposed, and the host that came out of Connor made at the banners, and, spurring their steeds, dashed at full speed amongst the baggage. The water carts there greatly cumbered the riders. Then the earl came upon them with his battle, and made grievous attack. Sir Edward also, a little way off, joined battle right boldly, and many foes fell under foot. The field soon grew all wet with blood. Both sides fought with great fierceness, and dealt mighty blows and thrusts, dashing forward and drawing back, as either side beat the other. It was dreadful to see how they kept up that great struggle in knightly fashion upon either side, giving and taking wide wounds. It was past prime before it could be seen which were to be uppermost. But soon after prime the Scots drove on so desperately, and charged so recklessly, each man like a champion, that all their foes took flight. None was able to stand by his comrade, but each fled his different way, most making for the town.

The Earl Thomas and his host so eagerly chased them with naked swords, that, being all mingled among them, they came together with them into the place. There the slaughter was so fierce that all the streets ran with blood. Those the Scots took they put all to death, so that well nigh as many were slain in the town as in the field of battle. Fitz-Warenne was taken; but so affrighted was Richard of Clare that he made for the south country. All that month, I trow, he was to have no great stomach for fighting. Sir John Stewart, a noble knight, was wounded with a spear that pierced him sharply right through the body. He went to Montpelier, and lay there long in healing, and at last recovered.

Then Sir Edward, with his host, took quarters in the town. That night they were blithe and jolly over the victory they had got. And forthwith, on the morrow, Sir Edward set men to discover what provisions were in the city. And they found in it such abundance of corn and flour, wax and wine, that they marvelled greatly. Sir Edward caused the whole to be carted to Carrickfergus. And he went thither with his men, and set close and vigorous siege to the castle till Palm Sunday was past. Then a truce was made on either side till the Tuesday in Easter week,[5] so that they might spend that holy time in penance and prayer.

But upon Easter Eve, during the night, there arrived safely at the castle fifteen ships from Dublin loaded with armed men. 4,000 all told, I trow, they were, and they all privily entered the castle. Old Sir Thomas the Mandeville was captain of that host.

They had espied that many of Sir Edward's men were scattered over the country, and they planned to sally forth in the morning, without waiting longer, and suddenly surprise the Scots, who, they believed, would be lying trustfully because of the truce. But I trow falseness shall ever have foul and evil result.

Sir Edward knew nothing of this, for he had no thought of treason; but he ceased not because of the truce to set watches upon the castle. Each night he caused men to watch it well, and that night Neil Fleming kept guard with sixty valiant and active men.

As soon as the day became clear those within the castle, having armed themselves and made ready, let down the draw-bridge, and sallied forth in great number. And when Neil Fleming saw them he sent a messenger to the king[6] in haste, and said to those beside him, 'Now I warrant shall men see who dares to die for his lord's sake! Bear ye yourselves well, for of a surety I will fight with all this host. We shall hold them in battle till our master be armed.'

With that they joined battle. They were, of a truth, altogether too few to fight with such a great host. Nevertheless, they drove at them boldly with all their might, and their foes marvelled greatly that they were of such manhood, and had no dread of death. But their fierce enemies attacked in such number that no valour could avail them, and they were every man slain, and none at all escaped.

Meanwhile the man who went to the king to warn him of the Irish coming out, apprised him in the greatest haste. Sir Edward, then commonly called the king of Ireland, when he heard of such pressing business on hand, in right great haste got his gear. Twelve active men were in his chamber, and they armed themselves with the greatest speed. Then boldly, with his banners, he took the middle of the town.

With that his enemies were drawing near. They had divided their whole host in three parts. The Mandeville, with a great following, held his way right through the town. The rest went on either side of the place to intercept those that should flee. They planned that all whom they found there should die without ransom.

But otherwise went the game; for Sir Edward, with his banner and the men of whom I have spoken, made such bold attack on that host as was a marvel to see. In front of him went Gib Harper, the doughtiest of deed then living in his degree, and with an axe made room before him. He felled the foremost to the ground, and afterwards, in a little space, he knew the Mandeville by his armour, and dealt him such a swinging blow that he went headlong to the earth. Sir Edward, who was near by, turned him over, and with a dagger took his life on the spot.

With that Fergus of Ardrossan, who was a right courageous knight, joined the battle with sixty men and more. Then they pressed their foes right hard, and they, seeing their lord slain, lost heart, and would have drawn back. But ever as fast as the Scots could arm they came to the melee, and they drove so at their foes that these altogether turned their backs. The Scots chased them to the gate, and a hard fight and great struggle took place there. There, with his own hand, Sir Edward slew a knight who was called the best and most valorous in all Ireland. His surname was Mandeville, his proper name I cannot tell. The assault then waxed so hard that those in the donjon durst neither open gate nor let down bridge. Sir Edward so fiercely pursued those that fled there for refuge that, for certain, of all who sallied forth against him on that day never a one escaped. They were all either taken or slain. MacNicol then joined the fight with 200 good spearmen, who slew all they could reach. This same MacNicol, by stratagem, took four or five of the English ships, and slew the whole crews.

When an end was made of this fighting, Neil Fleming was still alive, and Sir Edward went to see him. About him, all in a heap on either hand, lay his followers slain, and he himself was in the throes of death. Sir Edward pitied him and mourned him greatly, and lamented his great manhood and his valour and doughty deeds. So greatly did he make lament that his men marvelled, for he was not wont to lament for anything, nor would he hear men make lament. He stood by till Fleming was dead, then had him to a holy place, and caused him to be buried with honour and great solemnity.

In this wise Mandeville sallied forth. But of a surety, as was well seen by his sallying, falsehood and guile shall ever have an evil end. The English made their attack in time of truce, and on Easter day, the day on which God rose to save mankind from the stain of old Adam's sin. For this reason this great misfortune befell them, each and all, as I have said, being taken or slain. Those in the castle were thrown into such affright forthwith, seeing not where any succour could come to them, that they presently made treaty, and, to save their lives, yielded the stronghold freely to Sir Edward. He kept his covenant with them to the utmost. He took the castle and victualled it well, and set in it a good warden to keep it, and rested there for a time.

Of him we shall relate no more at present, but go to King Robert; whom we have left long unspoken of.

When he had convoyed to the sea his brother Edward and his host, the king made ready with his ships to fare into the Isles. He took with him Walter Stewart, his kinsman, and a great host, with other men of great nobleness. They made their way to Tarbert in galleys prepared for their voyage. There they had to draw their ships. Between the seas lay a mile of land sheltered all with trees. There the king caused his ships to be drawn across, and since the wind blew strong behind them as they went, he had ropes and masts set up in the ships, and sails fastened to the tops, and caused men to go drawing alongside. The wind that was blowing helped them, so that in a little space the whole fleet was safely drawn across.[7]

And when the men of the Isles heard tell how the good king had caused ships with sails to go between the two Tarberts, they were all utterly dismayed. For they knew by ancient prophecy that whoever should thus make ships go with sails between the seas should have the dominion of the Isles, and that no man's strength should stand against him. Therefore they all came to the king. None refused him obedience except only John of Lorne. But very soon afterwards he was taken and brought to the Bruce; and those of his men who had broken faith with the king were all slain and destroyed.

The king took this John of Lorne, and presently sent him to Dumbarton, where he was kept in prison for a time. Afterwards he was sent to Loch Leven, and was long there in captivity, and there I trow he died. The king, when all the Isles, greater and less, were brought to his pleasure, spent the rest of that season in hunting and games and sport.

Book XVI

When Sir Edward by his valiant prowess had three times defeated Richard of Clare and the whole baronage of Ireland, and afterwards, with all his men of might, was come again to Carrickfergus, Thomas, the good earl of Moray, took his leave to pass into Scotland. Sir Edward gave him leave reluctantly, and charged him especially to pray the king to come to see him in Ireland, for were they both in that country, he said, none should withstand them.

The earl took his departure and went to his ships, and passing over sea, soon arrived in Scotland. Forthwith he went to the king, who received him gladly, and inquired how his brother fared and of his doings in Ireland; and the earl told him truly all that had taken place.

When the king had done asking, the earl gave him his message, and the Bruce said he would gladly see his brother, and also all belonging to that country and the war there. He then gathered a great host, and appointed two lords of great valour, Walter Stewart and James of Douglas, to be wardens in his absence, and to defend the country. Then he set out for the sea, and at Lochryan in Galloway took ship with all his following, and soon came to Carrickfergus.

Sir Edward was blithe at his coming, and went swiftly down to meet him, and welcomed him with gladsome cheer. He did the same to all who were with the king, and especially his nephew Thomas, earl of Moray. And they went to the castle, and he made them much feasting and good fare. They sojourned there for three days in great mirth and royal state.

In this wise King Robert arrived in Ireland, and when he had sojourned with his men three days in Carrickfergus, they took counsel, and determined to make their way with their whole host through all Ireland from one end to the other.

Sir Edward, the king's brother, rode in front with the vanguard. The king himself had the rearguard, and in his company had the valiant Earl Thomas. They took their way forth, and soon passed Endwillane. It was the month of May, when birds on the bough sing many a different note for the softness of that sweet season, when the branches are covered with leaves and bright blossoms, the fields are gay with sweet-smelling many-coloured flowers, and all things become blithe and glad. At that season the good king rode forth.[8]

The warden, Richard of Clare, knew that the king had arrived, and learned that he purposed to march towards the south country. He gathered to him out of all Ireland a right great armed host of squires, burghers and yeomanry, to the number of nigh 40,000. Yet he would not venture to fight his enemies all together in open field, but bethought him of a stratagem. He planned that he, with all that great host, should privily make ambush in a wood by the way side, where the Scots must march, and that they should let the vanguard pass to a distance, and then fall boldly with all their men upon the rearguard.

They did as he devised, and took ambush in a wood. The Scottish van rode past them close at hand, while the Irish made no showing of themselves. Sir Edward rode a long way to the front with his host, taking no heed to the rearguard. And when Sir Edward had passed by, Sir Richard of Clare sent active yeomen who could shoot well to skirmish on foot with the rearguard. Now, two of the men sent out skirmished at the wood-side, and shot arrows among the Scots.

The king had with him 5,000 active and bold men, and when he saw these two come so nigh, and recklessly shoot among them, he judged right well that of a certainty they had support very near. Accordingly he gave order that no man should be so reckless as ride at them, but that all should keep close together, and ride ever in battle order, ready to make defence if they should be attacked, 'For we shall soon, I warrant, have to deal with more of them.'

But Sir Colin Campbell,[9] who was near by the place where these two yeomen were boldly shooting, spurred on them at full speed, and soon overtook one and slew him with his spear. The other turned, and shot again, and slew Sir Colin's horse. With that the Bruce came hastily, and, in great displeasure, with a truncheon that was in his hand, gave Sir Colin a stroke that sent him crashing down on his saddle-bow. Then he bade them quickly pull him down; but other lords who were there in some measure appeased the king. 'Disobedience,' said the Bruce, 'might bring about our discomfiture. Think ye yonder rascals durst assail us so near our host unless they had support at hand? Right well am I assured that we shall have enough to do presently; therefore let each man look to it that he be ready.'

With that some thirty bowmen came and skirmished, and hurt a number of the king's men; till the Bruce caused his archers to drive them back with arrows. By this time the Scots entered an open field, and saw 40,000 men arrayed in four battles against them.

'Now, sirs,' said the king, 'let us see who shall prove valiant in this fight! On them forthwith!'

So stoutly then did the Scots ride at them, and so hardily did they join battle, that a great number of their foes were brought to the ground at the first encounter. Then was heard a dreadful breaking of spears, and mighty noise of onset, as each side rode against the other. Horses came crashing head against head, so that many fell lifeless to the ground. Many an active and valiant man, as one ran upon the other, was stricken dead to the earth. The red blood poured from many a wound in such great quantity that the streams ran with it. Both sides, filled with rage and hate, drove at each other boldly with their bare flashing weapons, and many a strong man was slain on the spot. For those that were bold and active pressed to be foremost, and fight face to face with their foes. There, I warrant, many a cruel conflict and stern battle was to be seen.

In all the Irish war was no such hard fighting known. In less than three years Sir Edward won nineteen great victories, and in sundry of these battles he vanquished 20,000 men and more, with horses mailed to the feet. But at all these times he had at least one against five. In this struggle the king had always eight enemies to one of his own men. But he so bore himself that his brave feats and his valour encouraged all his host, and the most faint-hearted was made bold. Wherever he saw the battle thickest he rode most boldly into it, and ever made room about him, slaying all he could overtake, and furiously driving them back.

The valiant Earl Thomas was at all times near him, and fought as if he were mad. From the prowess of these two their men took mighty hardihood. They shunned no danger, but demeaned themselves most stoutly, and so boldly drove at the enemy that their foes were all dismayed. Then the Scots, seeing by their looks that the enemy somewhat avoided the fight, dashed against them with all their strength, and pressed them so hard with blows, that at last they gave way. And now, seeing them take flight, they charged them with all their force, and slew many as they fled.

The king's men so pursued them that they were every one scattered. Richard of Clare made his way at the utmost speed to Dublin, with other lords that fled beside him. There they garrisoned both the castle and the towns in their possession.

So desperately were they daunted that I trow Richard of Clare had no desire to prove his strength in battle or skirmish while King Robert and his host tarried in that country. They kept within garrison in this fashion.

And the king, who was so much to be prized, saw in the field right many slain. And one of the prisoners, who was bravely arrayed, he saw weep wondrous tenderly. He asked him why he made such cheer, and the prisoner answered, 'Sir, of a surety it is no marvel that I weep. I see here stricken under foot the flower of all the North of Ireland, boldest of heart and hand, and most doughty in fierce attack.'

'By my faith,' said the king, 'thou art wrong. Thou hast more cause to make mirth, since thou hast thus escaped death.'

In this fashion Richard of Clare and all his following were overthrown by a slender host. And when the bold Edward Bruce knew that the king had fought thus with so great a host and he away, there could have been seen no more wrathful man. But the good king told him the fault lay in his own folly, by reason that he rode so heedlessly and far ahead, and made no vanguard to them of the rear. 'In war,' he said, 'those who ride in the van should at no time press far from sight of the rear, else great peril may befall.'

Of this battle we shall speak no more. The king and all who were with him rode forward in better array and nearer together than they did before. They rode openly through all the land, but found none to say them nay. They rode even before Drogheda and before Dublin, but found none to give battle. Then they went further inland, and held their way south to Limerick, which is the south-most town in Ireland. There they lay for two or three days, and got ready again for the march.

And when they were all ready the king heard a woman's cry, and forthwith asked what that was.

'Sir,' said some one, 'it is a laundress who just now has been seized with labour, and whom we must leave here behind us. For this reason she makes yonder evil cheer.'

'Certes,' said the king, 'it were shame that she should be left in that strait! Of a surety he is no man I trow who will not pity a woman then.'

At that he halted his whole host, and caused a tent to be pitched, and made her go into it, and bade other women stay beside her till her child was born, and gave order before he left how she should be carried with the host. Then he rode forward on his way. It was a right sovereign courtesy for so great and so mighty a king to cause his men to tarry in this fashion for a poor humble laundress.

They marched northward again, and passed athwart all Ireland, through Munster and Connaught right to Dublin, and through all Meath and Uriel,[10] as well as Leinster, and afterwards through the whole of Ulster to Carrickfergus. They fought no battle in all that march, for there was none that durst attack them. And all the Irish chiefs, except one or two, came to Sir Edward and did homage to him. Then they each went home again to their own districts, undertaking to do in everything the bidding of Sir Edward, whom they called their king.

He was now well on the way to conquer the whole land, for he had the Irish and Ulster on his side, and he was so far advanced in his war that he had passed with force of arms through all Ireland from end to end. Could he have governed himself with reason, and not followecl his impulses too fast, but have been moderate in his actions, it seems almost certain that he should have conquered the whole country of Ireland. Rut his extravagant pride and his wilfulness, which was more than boldness, prevented his intent, as I shall hereafter describe.

Meanwhile the Bruce had made his way through all Ireland, and come again to Carrickfergus.

And when Sir Edward, in royal fashion, had all the Irish at his bidding, and all Ulster as well, the king made ready to return home. A great number of his men, the boldest and most approved in feats of war, he left with his brother. Then he passed to the beach, and when their leaves were taken on either side, he went on board, carrying the Earl Thomas with him, and, setting sail forthwith, arrived without mishap in Galloway.

Book XVIII

Sir Edward Bruce, ever irking at rest, and eager to be at work, a day before the succours arrived that had been sent him by the king, and despite the counsel of all who were with him, set forth upon the march. Besides the Irish chiefs, who rode with him in great bands, he had not in all in the country at that time, I trow, 2,000 men.

He set out towards Dundalk. And when Richard of Clare heard that he marched with a small following, he gathered together out of the whole of Ireland all the armed men he could. Thus he had with him at that time 20,000 equipped horsemen, besides a host of men on foot, and he set out towards the north. When Sir Edward heard that he was come near, he sent out as scouts the Soulis and the Stewart and Sir Philip the Mowbray, and when these three had seen the enemy's advance, they returned and told the king that their foes were in right great number. Sir Edward made answer quickly, and said he should fight that day though the enemy were three times or four times as many.

'Of a surety,' said Sir John Stewart, 'I council ye, fight not in such haste. They say my brother is coming, and near at hand, with 1,500 men. Were they joined with you ye could with more confidence abide the battle.'

Sir Edward looked right wrathful, 'What sayest thou?' he asked Soulis.

'I' faith, sir,' said he, 'I say as my friend has said.'

The king then asked Sir Philip, and he answered, 'Sir, as our Lord sees me, methinks it no foolishness to await your friends, who make speed to ride hither. We are few; our foes are many. God may grant us good fortune, it is true, but it were a miracle if our strength should overcome so many in battle.'

'Alas,' said Sir Edward, in great wrath, 'I never thought to hear that from thee! Now, help who will, assuredly without longer tarrying I will fight this day. While I live, no man shall say that any force made me flee. God save us from the charge of fouling our fair name!'

'So be it then,' said they, 'we shall take what God sends.' When the Irish chiefs beard what had passed, and knew for certain that their king, with his small following, would fight against so great and mighty a host, they came to him with the utmost speed, and counselled him most earnestly to await his friends. They would, they said, keep the enemy engaged all that day, and the morrow as well, with their attacks.

But no counsel could prevail; the king's mind was set always upon the battle. And when they saw he was so stubbornly set to fight, they said, 'Ye may indeed go to battle with yonder great host, but we account ourselves free utterly, and none of us will stand to fight. Set no store, therefore, by our strength. For our custom in this country is to follow and fight, and to fight fleeing, and not to stand in open battle till one side be discomfited.'

'Since that is your custom,' he said, 'I ask of you no more than this, that ye and your host stand all together in battle array at a distance, without leaving the field, and see our fight and our ending.'

They said of a surety they should do this; then they withdrew to their men, who were well-nigh 40,000 strong.

The king and those about him, not 2,000 in all, arrayed themselves stalwartly to do battle with 40,000 and more. Sir Edward that day would not put on his coat armour, but Gib Harper, whom men held without peer in his estate, wore the whole of Sir Edward's array.

In this wise they awaited the battle, and, their enemies coming at great speed all ready for the encounter, right boldly they met them. So few were the Scots, of a truth, that they were overwhelmed by their foes. Those of them that endeavoured most to make a stand were cut down, and the rest fled for succour to the Irish host. Sir Edward, despite his valour, was slain, and Sir John Stewart as well, with Sir John de Soulis, and others besides of their company. So suddenly were they overcome that few were slain on the spot; the rest made their way to the Irish chiefs who, in battle order, were waiting at hand. John Thomasson, leader of the men of Carrick in the host, when he saw the discomfiture, withdrew to an Irish chief of his acquaintance, who received him loyally. And when he was come to that chief he saw being led away from the battle the stout Sir Philip the Mowbray. He had been stunned in the fight, and was led by the arms by two men on the causeway that stretched in a long straight line between the place of battle and the town. They held their way towards the town; but when they were midway on the road Sir Philip overcame his dizziness, and perceived he was seized and led away by two of the enemy. In a moment he hurled from him first the one and then the other, then swiftly drew his sword and set out along the causeway towards the fight. The road was full of a multitude of men going towards the town, and he as he met them dealt such blows that against their will he made a full hundred leave the causeway. This was told for a certainty by John Thomasson, who saw the whole achievement.

Mowbray went straight towards the battle, but Thomasson, taking certain heed that the Scots were all completely overthrown, called hastily to him, and said, 'Come here, for there is none alive; they are every one slain.'

Then Sir Philip stood still awhile, and saw that his friends were all done to death, and he came and joined company with him.

This John Thomasson afterwards wrought so shrewdly that all who had fled to the Irish host, though they had lost part of their weapons, reached Carrickfergus safe and whole. Meanwhile the English who had been in the battle sought among the dead to find Sir Edward, to get his head, and they found Gib Harper in his coat of mail. Then, because of the arms he wore, they struck off his head, and salted it in a bucket, and sent it afterwards to England as a present to King Edward. They supposed it Sir Edward's head, but were deceived because of the splendour of the armour. Nevertheless Sir Edward died there.

In this wise through wilfulness were all these nobles at that time lost, which was afterwards a great regret. Had their extraordinary valour been guided with sense and moderation, unless the greater misfortune befell them, it should have been a right hard task to bring them to disaster. But great and extravagant pride caused them all to pay dear for their bravery.

Those who fled from the battle sped in haste towards the sea-coast, and came to Carrickfergus. And those on the way from King Robert to Sir Edward, when they heard of the discomfiture, returned to the same place. This retreat was not made without difficulty, for many times that day the Irish attacked them; but they held together in close order, defending themselves cautiously, and, sometimes by force, sometimes by craft, and sometimes giving bribes to be allowed to pass scatheless, they made their escape. Then in boats and ships they set forth and arrived all safely in Scotland.

When the people of Scotland had knowledge of Sir Edward's overthrow, the whole land mourned full tenderly for him and for those who were slain with him.

After Edward the Bruce had been discomfited in the manner I have described, and the field had been entirely cleared, so that no resisters were to be seen, the warden, Richard of Clare, and all the hosts with him set out towards Dundalk. They made no direct encounter at that time with the Irish, but hastened to the town. Then they sent oversea to the king of England Gib Harper's head in a bucket. John Maupas carried it to the king, who received it with great delight, and was right blithe at the gift, being full glad to be delivered of so fierce a foe. His heart was so filled with pride because of this that he formed a plan to ride with a great host into Scotland, to avenge himself with a strong hand for the vexation, trouble, and harm that he had swered there. He gathered a vast host, and sent his ships by sea with great abundance of victual. On that occasion he thought to destroy the whole of Scotland so utterly that none should be left alive therein, and with his people in great array he set forth towards the north.

Appendix B

The Remonstrance of the Irish Princes to Pope John XXII, 1317

To the most holy Father in Christ, John, by the grace of God sovereign Pontiff, his devoted children, Donald O Neill, king of Ulster and by hereditary right true heir to the whole of Ireland and also the under-kings and nobles and the whole Irish people, with humble recommendation of themselves and devout kisses of his blessed feet.

Lest the sharp-toothed and viperous calumny of the English and their untrue representations should to any degree excite your mind against us and the defenders of our right, which God forbid, and so that there may be no ground for what is not well known and is falsely presented to kindle your displeasure, for our defence we pour into yours ears with mighty out-cry by means of this letter an entirely true account of our origin and our form of government, if government it can be called, and also of the cruel wrongs that have been wrought inhumanly on us and our forefathers by some kings of England, their evil ministers and English barons born in Ireland, wrongs that are continued still; and this we do in order that you may be able to approach the subject and see in which party's loud assertion the truth bears company. And thus being carefully, and sufficiently informed so far as the nature of the case demands, your judgment, like a naked blade, may smite or correct the fault of the party that is in the wrong.

Know then, most Holy Father, that since the time when our early ancestors, the three sons of Milesius or Micelius of Spain, by God's will came into Ireland (then destitute of all inhabitants) with a fleet of thirty ships from Cantabria, a city of Spain standing on the bank of the river Ebro or Hiberus (from which we take the name we bear), 3,500 years and more have passed, and of those descended from these men 136 kings without admixture of alien blood assumed the monarchical rule over all Ireland down to king Legarius, from whom I, Donald, have derived my descent in a straight line. It was in days that our chief apostle and patron S. Patrick, sent us at the inspiration of the Holy Ghost by your predecessor Celestine in the year CCCCXXXV [*recte* CCCCXXXII] taught the truths of the Catholic faith with the fullest success to our fathers.

And after the faith had been preached and received, 61 kings of the same blood, without intervention of alien blood, kings admirably in the faith of Christ and filled with works of charity, kings that in temporal things acknowledged no superior, ruled here uninterruptedly in humble obedience to the Church of Rome until the year 1170.

And it was they, not the English nor others of any nation who eminently endowed the Irish Church with lands, ample liberties and many possessions, although at the present time she is, for the most part, sadly despoiled of those lands and liberties by the English.

And although for so long a time those kings with their own power had stoutly defended against tyrants and kings of divers countries the inheritance that God had given them and had always kept their birthright of freedom unimpaired, yet at last, in the year of the Lord MCLXX,[1] at the false and wicked representation of King Henry of England, under whom and perhaps by whom St Thomas of Canterbury, as you know, in that very year suffered death for justice and defence of the church, Pope Adrian, your predecessor, an Englishman not so much by birth as by feeling and character, did in fact, but unfairly, confer upon that same Henry (whom for his said offence he should rather have deprived of his own kingdom) this lordship of ours by a certain form of words, the course of justice entirely disregarded and the moral vision of that great pontiff blinded, alas! by his English proclivities. And thus, without fault of ours and without reasonable cause, he stripped us of our royal honour and gave us over to be rent by teeth more cruel than any beast's; and those of us that escaped half-alive and woefully from the deadly teeth of crafty foxes and greedy wolves were thrown by violence into a gulf of doleful slavery.

For, from the time when in consequence of that grant the English iniquitously but with some show of religion entered within the limits of our kingdom, they have striven with all their might and with every treacherous artifice in their power, to wipe our nation out entirely and utterly to extirpate it. By base and deceitful craftiness they have prevailed against us so far that, with no authority from a superior, they have driven us by force from the spacious places where we dwelt and from the inheritance of our fathers; they have compelled us to seek mountains, woods, bogs, barren tracts and even caverns in the rocks to save our lives, and for a long time back to make our dwellings there like beasts. Yet even in such places as these they harass us continually and endearour all they can to expel us from them and seek unduly to usurp to themselves every place we occupy, mendaciously asserting in their blind madness that there is to be no free abode for us in Ireland but that all the land is entirely theirs by right.

Whence, by reason of all this and much more of the same kind, relentless hatred and incessant wars have arisen between us and them, from which have resulted mutual slaughter, continual plundering, endless rapine, detestable and too frequent deceits and perfidies. But alas! all correction and due reform fail us, for want of a head. And so for many years the native Irish clergy and people have stood in too serious and terrible danger not alone as regards what is perishable and bodily, but further still, through this want, the greatest danger, that of souls, is hanging over them, and that beyond an ordinary degree. For we hold it as an established truth that more than 50,000 human beings of each nation, in addition to those cut off by famine, distress and prison, have fallen by the sword in consequence of that false representation and the grant resulting from it, since the time when it was made. Let these few general particulars of the origin of our ancestors and the wretched position in which a Roman Pontiff placed us suffice on this occasion.

Know, most holy Father, that King Henry of England, who was authorised in the manner already stated to enter Ireland, and also the four kings his successors have clearly gone beyond the limits of the grant made them by the Pope's bull in certain definite articles, as appears plainly from the very text of the bull.

For the said Henry, as is embodied in the bull, undertook to extend the bounds of the Irish Church, to preserve its rights uninjured and entire, to bring the people under the rule of law and to train them in a good way of life, to implant virtue and to root out the weeds of vice and to make a yearly payment of one penny from every house to blessed Peter the apostle.

Henry himself, as well as his aforesaid successors and their wicked and crafty English ministers in no respect indeed keeping this promise, but departing altogether from the terms of the grant, have of set purpose and design accomplished in fact the opposite of all the foregoing engagements. For by them the bounds of the Church have been so far restricted, curtailed, and cut down that some cathedral churches have been forcibly despoiled of a half of their lands and possessions and even more, while nearly every liberty of the Church has been by these same persons cast adrift. For bishops and dignitaries are summoned, arrested, taken and imprisoned without respect by the king of England's ministers in Ireland; and though they suffer repeated and serious wrongs of this kind they are so overpowered with slavish fear that they in no wise dare to intimate them to your Holiness, and since they themselves are shamefully mute, we also will keep silent in this matter.

Likewise, the Irish people, whom in set terms they had promised to shape to good morals and to bring under laws, they so shape that its holy and dove-like simplicity has been surprisingly altered into a serpentine craftiness through daily life with them and through their bad example; and they also deprive it of the written laws by which, for the most part, it was formerly governed, and of all other law, save what could not be uprooted, enacting for the extermination of our race most pernicious laws, beyond measure wicked and unjust, some of which are here inserted as instances.

In the king of England's court in Ireland these laws are rigidly observed, viz. that any person that is not an Irishman may bring any Irishman into court on any cause of action without restriction; but every Irishman, cleric or lay, excepting only prelates, is refused all recourse to law by the very fact [of being Irish].

Also, as usually happens for the most part when by perfidy and guile some Englishman kills an Irishman, however noble and inoffensive, whether cleric or lay, regular or secular, even if an Irish prelate should be killed, no punishment or correction is inflicted by the said court on such a nefarious murderer; nay more, the better the murdered man was and the greater the place he held among his people, the more his murderer is honoured and rewarded by the English, not merely by the populace but even by English religious and bishops, and most of all by those to whom it falls through their positions to inflict just punishment and due correction on such evil-doers.

Also, every Irishwoman, whether noble or otherwise, who marries any Englishman, is entirely deprived, after her husband's death, of the third part of his lands and possessions, her rightful dowry, precisely because she is Irish.

Likewise, wherever the English can oppress an Irishman by main force they in no way suffer the Irish to dispose of their property by their last wishes or to make a last will and testament; nay, they appropriate to themselves all the goods of those persons, and deprive the Church of its right and of their own authority make serfs by violence of the blood that has been free from all antiquity.

Likewise, by the common council of this king of England and also by the action of certain English bishops, of whom the chief is a man of small wit and no learning, the archbishop of Armagh, an unjust statute has been lately made in the city of Kilkenny in this form of deformity:

> It is agreed that it be enjoined on all religious that abide in the land of peace among the English that they do not receive into their order or religion any except those that are English by nation; and if they do otherwise the Lord King will take them as contemners of his command, and their founders and patrons will take them as disobedient and in opposition to this ordinance made by the common counsel of the whole land of Ireland among the English.[2]

And even before this statute was made, and afterwards, the friars, preachers, minorites, monks, canons and other English religious have been observing it strictly enough, in the highest degree being acceptors of persons; yet the monasteries of monks and canons where at the present day the Irish are refused were, generally speaking, founded by them.

Likewise, where they were bound to implant virtues and root up the weeds of vice, they have cut out by the root the virtues already planted and of themselves have brought in vices.

Also of the same and the banquets of the English. For the English inhabiting our land, who call themselves of the middle nation, are so different in character from the English of England and from other nations that with the greatest propriety they may be called a nation not of middle [*medium*], but of utmost, perfidy. For, from of old they have had this wicked unnatural custom, which even yet has not ceased among them but every day becomes stronger and more established, viz. when they invite noblemen of our nation to a banquet, during the very feast or in the time of sleep they mercilessly shed the blood of their unsuspicious guests, and in this way bring their horrible banquet to an end. When this has been thus done they have cut off the heads of the slain and sold them for money to their enemies, as did the baron Peter Brunechehame [Bermingham], a recognised and regular betrayer, in the case of his gossip Maurice de S.[3] and his brother Caluache, men of high birth and great name among us. Inviting them to a banquet on Trinity Sunday, on that same day when the repast was finished, as soon as they had risen from the table he cruelly murdered them with twenty-four of their following and sold their heads dear to their enemies. And when he was afterwards accused to the king of England, the present king's father, of this crime, the king inflicted no punishment on so nefarious a traitor.

Likewise Sir Thomas de Clare, brother of the earl of Gloucester, summoning to his house Brian Ruadh, prince of Thomond, his gossip, though as a token of closer confederacy and friendship he had communicated of the same host divided into two parts, at last by counsel of the aforesaid unspeakable nation he suddenly tore him from the table and the feast, had him dragged at horses' tails, and having cut off his head had the headless corpse hung by the feet from a beam.[4]

Likewise, Geoffrey de Pencoyt, of the same nation, after a feast which he had made for them in his house, on that same night, as they were sleeping in their beds, killed Maurice, king of Leinster, and Arthur, his father, men of very high nobility and authority.

Likewise, John fitz Thomas, earl of Kildare, three days after the killing, had the head of an Irish nobleman, his gossip (accidentally slain not by him, but by others), cut off in order to basely sell it. And likewise, the same Earl John, after the execrable death of the father as above narrated, thrust into a filthy prison John, son of the aforesaid most distinguished Caluache, a handsome youth who, from the time when he had been lifted from the baptismal font by the earl himself, had been reared continuously in his house; and after a few days he had the guiltless youth not guiltlessly put to death in the prison.

Let these few cases, notorious to everyone, out of the countless misdeeds of that nation suffice as instances, on this occasion. And though acts of this kind apppear horrible and detestable to all Christians, yet to those of that oft-mentioned nation, as by too hard a daily experience we feel, they seem honourable and praiseworthy, since those that do them reap not at all the punishment of which they are deserving, but by a too flagrant antithesis the reward of praise which they do not merit is heaped upon them. For not only their laymen and secular clergy but some also of their regular clergy dogmatically assert the heresy that it is no more sin to kill an Irishman than a dog or any other brute. And in maintaining this heretical position some monks of theirs affirm boldly that if it should happen to them, as it does often happen, to kill an Irishman, they would not on that account refrain from saying mass, not even for a day.

And as, beyond all doubt, the monks of the Cistercian order of Granard, in Ardagh diocese, so too the monks of Inch, of the same order, in Down diocese, shamelessly fulfil in deed what they proclaim in word. For, bearing arms publicly, they attack the Irish and slay them, and nevertheless they celebrate their masses.

And in like manner friar Simon of the Order of Friars Minors, brother of the bishop of Connor, is the chief formulator of this heresy; and in the year just passed, unable from the fulness of his malignant heart to keep silent he shamelessly burst out in words into a declaration of this kind in the court of Lord Edward de Broyse (Bruce), earl of Carrick and in the presence of the said lord, as he himself testifies, viz. that it is no sin to kill a man of Irish birth and if he were to commit it himself he would none the less for that celebrate mass.

And falling out of this heresy into another error, all of them indifferently, secular and regular, assert with obstinacy that it is lawful for them to take away from us by force of arms whatever they can of our lands and possessions, of every kind, making no conscientious scruple about it even when they are at the point of death. And all the land they hold in Ireland they hold by usurpation in this way.

And of whatever condition or station he may be that should withstand this error or preach in opposition to them, for that alone he is proclaimed an enemy to the king and kingdom of England, as guilty of death and outlawed by the king's council. For, lusting eagerly for our lands, they it is that, to the no small loss of the kings and kingdom of England, by sowing perpetual dissensions between them and us, have craftily and deceitfully kept us apart from them, lest of our own free will we should hold from the king directly the lands that are rightfully our due.

That this is a characteristic policy of theirs is well established, and from it spring frequent acts of bad faith and treachery. For they never cease from sowing similar dissensions not merely between persons of remote consanguinity but even between brothers and near relations. And as in way of life and speech they are more dissimilar from us and in their actions from many other nations than can be described by us in writing or in words, there is no hope whatever of our having peace with them. For such is their arrogance and excessive lust to lord it over us and so great is our due and natural desire to throw off the unbearable yoke of their slavery and to recover our inheritance wickedly seized upon by them, that as there has not been hitherto, there cannot now be or ever henceforward be established, sincere good will between them and us in this life. For we have a natural hostility to each other arising from the mutual, malignant and incessant slaying of fathers, brothers, nephews and other near relatives and friends so that we can have no inclination to reciprocal friendship in our time or in that of our sons.

Likewise it cannot escape you, since it is manifest to everyone, that the Roman curia does not receive a penny from every house in Ireland as was promised.

In this way then, and no other nor otherwise, have the kings of England and their often-mentioned subjects observed the articles of the above-said Bull to the Irish church and nation.

Since then such injustices and abominations of the said nation were clearly and openly intimated to that king's [Edward II] counsel and also to the king himself about two years past in letters of several noblemen of our nation by means of John de Hutome (now, as we have understood, bishop of Ely), in order to have redress, and as we also offered him [i.e. the king] generally that, to his greater advantage and to our peace we would hold our land, due by right to us alone, from him immediately without any opposition, according to the conditions and articles laid down and contained in Adrian's bull (of which we transmit you a copy) or that he should make a friendly arrangement between our said adversaries and us, himself dividing up reasonably with consent of the parties and to avoid unlimited bloodshed our own land that belonged to us; put since then we have received no answer from him or his council in that matter.

Let no one wonder then that we are striving to save our lives and defending as we can the rights of our law and liberty against cruel tyrants and usurpers, especially since the said king, who calls himself lord of Ireland, and also the said kings his predecessors have wholly failed in this respect to do and exhibit orderly government to us and several of us.

Wherefore, if for this reason we are forced to attack that king and our said enemies that dwell in Ireland, we do nothing unlawful but rather our action is meritorious and we neither can nor should be held guilty of perjury or disloyalty on this account, since neither we nor our fathers have ever done homage or taken any other oath of fealty to him or his fathers. And therefore, without any conscientious misgivings, so long as life endures we will fight against them in defence of our right and will never cease to attack and assail them until through want of power they shall desist from unjustly injuring us and the justest of Judges shall take evident and consign vengeance upon them for their tyrannous oppression and other most wicked deeds; and this with a firm faith we believe will soon come to pass.

Furthermore, we are ready and prepared to maintain by the testimony of twelve bishops at least and of many other prelates the articles here set forth and to prove the wrongs herein recited, lawfully in due time and place and by way of law which is due to us of right; not like the English, who in the time of their prosperity and power will never stand to any due course of proceedings or process of law; and if prosperity and power were with them now they would have been far from taking shelter under the wings of the Roman Curia, nay rather would they be fiercely afflicting all nations round about with their wonted tyranny, despising the power of God and that of the Roman Curia, which we declare to be one and the same ordinance. Whence, if the said Curia were fully instructed concerning their deeds, they would be ill satisfied by the comfort they would receive from it, for comfort is not merited by their wickedness.

Therefore, on account of the aforesaid wrongs and infinite other wrongs which cannot easily be comprehended by the wit of man and yet again on account of the [injustice] of the kings of England and their wicked ministers and the constant treachery of the English of mixed race, who, by the ordinance of the Roman curia, were bound to rule our nation with justice and moderation and have set themselves wickedly to destroy it; and in order to shake off the hard and intolerable yoke of their slavery and to recover our native liberty, which for a time through them we lost, we are compelled to wage deadly war with them, aforesaid, preferring under stress of necessity to put ourselves like men to the trial of war in defence of our right, rather than to bear like women their atrocious outrages.

And that we may be able to attain our purpose more speedily and fitly in this respect, we call to our help and assistance Edward de Bruyis, illustrious earl of Carrick, brother of Robert by the grace of God most illustrious king of the Scots, who is sprung from our noblest ancestors.

And as it is free to anyone to renounce his right and transfer it to another, all the right which is publicly known to pertain to us in the said kingdom as its true heirs, we have given and granted to him by our letters patent, and in order that he may do therein judgement and justice and equity which through default of the prince [i.e. the king of England] have utterly failed therein, we have unanimously established and set him up as our king and lord in our kingdom aforesaid, for in our judgment and the common judgement of men he is pious and prudent, humble and chaste, exceedingly temperate, in all things sedate and moderate, and possessing power (God on high be praised) to snatch us mightily from the house of bondage with the help of God and our own justice, and very willing to render to everyone what is due to him of right, and above all is ready to restore entirely to the Church of Ireland the possessions and liberties of which she was damnably despoiled, and he intends to grant greater liberties than ever otherwise she has been wont to have.

May it please you therefore, most Holy Father, for the sake of justice and general peace mercifully to approve what we have done as regards our said lord and king, forbidding the king of England and our aforesaid adversaries henceforward to molest us, or at least be pleased to render us with fitting favour our due complement of justice in respect of them.

For know, our revered Father, that besides the kings of lesser Scotia who all drew the source of their blood from our greater Scotia, retaining to some extent our language and habits, 197 kings of our blood have reigned over the whole island of Ireland.

Here ends the process set on foot by the Irish against the king of England.

NOTES

1 – THE BRUCE INVASION OF IRELAND: A REVISED ITINERARY AND CHRONOLOGY

1. Barrow, G.W.S., *Robert Bruce and the community of the realm of Scotland* (3rd edn, 1988), chap. 13.
2. See McNamee, C., *The Wars of the Bruces. Scotland, England and Ireland, 1306–1328* (East Linton, 1997), 169; Reid, W.S., 'Seapower and the Anglo-Scottish war, 1296–1328', *The Mariner's Mirror*, 46 (1960), 7–23.
3. Duncan, A.A.M. (ed.), *Regesta regum Scottorum V. The acts of Robert I* (Edinburgh, 1988), 135–36; idem, 'The Scots' invasion of Ireland, 1315', in Davies, R.R., *British Isles 1100–1500* (Edinburgh, 1988), 103.
4. Gilbert, J.T. (ed.), *Chartularies of St Mary's Abbey, Dublin*, 2 vols (London, 1884), ii, 344.
5. Barbour, J., *The Bruce*, ed. A.A.M. Duncan (Edinburgh, 1997), 564; above, pp. 169–70.
6. Barbour, *The Bruce*, ed. Duncan, 520; above, p. 161.
7. *Chartul. St Mary's, Dublin*, ii, 344.
8. Orpen, G.H., *Ireland under the Normans*, 4 vols (Oxford, 1911–20), iv, 162.
9. Duncan (ed.), *Regesta regum Scottorum V*, 575.
10. Greeves, J.R.H., 'Robert I and the de Mandevilles of Ulster', in *Dumfriesshire & Galloway Nat. Hist. & Antiq. Soc. Trans.*, 3rd ser., 34 (1955–56), 59–73; idem, 'The Galloway lands in Ulster', 6 (1957–58), 115–22.
11. Barbour, *The Bruce*, ed. Duncan, pp. 520–22; above, p. 161.
12. Otway-Ruthven, A.J., *A history of medieval Ireland* (London, 1968), 226; Frame, R., 'The Bruces in Ireland, 1315–1318', *Irish Historical Studies,* 19 (1974), 26; *Chartul. St Mary's, Dublin*, ii, 345.
13. Barbour, *The Bruce*, ed. Duncan, 522; above, p. 162; *Chartul. St Mary's, Dublin*, ii, 350.
14. Sayles, G.O., 'The siege of Carrickfergus, 1315–16', *Irish Historical Studies*, 10 (1956–57), 94–100.
15. Barbour, *The Bruce*, ed. Duncan, 522; above, p. 162; see, for example, Freeman, A.M. (ed.), *The annals of Connacht* (Dublin, 1944), s.a. 1315.
16. See, e.g., below pp. 117, 132; but cf. Duffy, S., 'The Gaelic account of the Bruce invasion *Cath Fhochairte Brighite*: medieval romance or modern forgery?', *Seanchas Ard Mhacha*, 13, no. 1 (1989), 59–121.
17. *Annals of Connacht*, s.a. 1315.
18. Duncan, 'The Scots' invasion of Ireland, 1315', pp. 107–08.
19. See Reeves, W., *Ecclesiastical antiquities of Down, Connor, and Dromore* (Dublin, 1847), 281.

20. Sweetman, H.S. (ed.), *Calendar of documents relating to Ireland, 1171–1307*, 5 vols (London, 1875–86), ii, 432.
21. *Chartul. St Mary's, Dublin*, ii, 385.
22. See Frame, R., 'The justiciarship of Ralph Ufford: warfare and politics in fourteenth-century Ireland', *Studia Hibernica*, 13 (1974), 23.
23. Mac Iomhair, D., 'Bruce's invasion of Ireland and first campaign in County Louth', *The Irish Sword*, 10 (1972), 188–212; Smith, B., 'The Bruce invasion and County Louth, 1315–18', *County Louth Arch. & Hist. Soc. Journ.*, 22 (1989), 7–15.
24. Otway-Ruthven, A.J., 'The partition of the de Verdon lands in Ireland in 1332', *Royal Irish Academy Proc.*, 66 (1968), 421.
25. *Chartul. St Mary's, Dublin*, ii, 345.
26. Butler, R. (ed.), *The annals of Ireland by Friar John Clyn* (Dublin, 1845), 12.
27. *Annals of Connacht*, s.a. 1315.
28. Mac Airt, S. (ed.), *The annals of Inisfallen* (Dublin, 1951), s.a. 1315.
29. Philips, J.R.S. (ed.), 'Documents on the early stages of the Bruce invasion of Ireland, 1315–1316', *Roy. Ir. Acad. Proc.*, 79 (1979), 258.
30. *Annals of Inisfallen*, s.a. 1315.
31. *Annals of Inisfallen*, s.a. 1315.
32. Barbour, *The Bruce*, ed. Duncan, 540; above p. 165.
33. *Chartul. St Mary's, Dublin*, ii, 346.
34. Phillips (ed.), 'Documents on the Bruce invasion', 263; *Chartul. St Mary's, Dublin*, ii, 346.
35. Phillips (ed.), 'Documents on the Bruce invasion', 263.
36. *Annals of Connacht*, s.a. 1315.
37. *Chartul. St Mary's, Dublin*, ii, 346.
38. Phillips, J.R.S., 'The mission of John de Hothum to Ireland, 1315–1316', in Lydon, J. (ed.), *England and Ireland in the later middle ages* (Dublin, 1981), 63.
39. Richardson, H.G. & Sayles, G.O., *The Irish parliament in the middle ages* (Philadelphia, 1952), 335; but cf. Phillips, 'Mission of John de Hothum', 68.
40. *Chartul. St Mary's, Dublin*, ii, 347.
41. *Chartul. St Mary's, Dublin*, ii, 348.
42. A point first made in Phillips, 'Mission of John de Hothum', 68.
43. *Chartul. St Mary's, Dublin*, ii, 347.
44. See above, p. 181.
45. *Chartul. St Mary's, Dublin*, ii, 347.
46. *Chartul. St Mary's, Dublin*, ii, 407–09.
47. Barbour, *The Bruce*, ed. Duncan, 536–38; above, p. 164–65.
48. *Chartul. St Mary's, Dublin*, ii, 347; Otway-Ruthven, *Medieval Ireland*, 228.
49. *Chartul. St Mary's, Dublin*, ii, 347; Frame, 'The Bruces in Ireland', 32.
50. Phillips (ed.), 'Documents on the Bruce invasion', 251–52.
51. *Chartul. St Mary's, Dublin*, ii, 347.
52. Otway-Ruthven, *Medieval Ireland*, 229.
53. Phillips (ed.), 'Documents on the Bruce invasion', 251–53.
54. *Chartul. St Mary's, Dublin*, ii, 349–50.
55. *Chartul. St Mary's, Dublin*, ii, 349.

56. Frame, 'The Bruces in Ireland', p. 29, note 114.
57. Barbour, *The Bruce*, ed. Duncan, 553, 580; above, p. 168.
58. Sayles, 'Siege of Carrickfergus'.
59. *Chartul. St Mary's, Dublin*, ii, 345, 349.
60. Duncan (ed.), *Regesta regum Scottorum V*, 378.
61. See McNamee, *Wars of the Bruces, passim*; Duffy, S., 'The Bruce brothers and the Irish Sea world, 1306–29', above, pp. 49–50.
62. Duffy, S., 'The 'Continuation' of Nicholas Trevet: a new source for the Bruce invasion', *Roy. Ir. Acad. Proc.*, 91, C (1991), 314.
63. Smith, 'The Bruce invasion and County Louth', 9–10.
64. *Annals of Connacht*, s.a. 1316.
65. *Chartul. St Mary's, Dublin*, ii, 348, 349.
66. Gilbert, J.T. (ed.), *Historic and municipal documents of Ireland, AD 1172–1320* (London, 1870), 457.
67. *Chartul. St Mary's, Dublin*, ii, 348.
68. See Frame, 'The Bruces in Ireland', 21, note 79.
69. Frame, 'The Bruces in Ireland', 22.
70. *Cal. Patent rolls, 1313–17*, 551.
71. *Chartul. St Mary's, Dublin*, ii, 298.
72. Barbour, *The Bruce*, ed. Duncan, 580; above, p. 170; Butler (ed.), *Annals of Clyn*, 13.
73. *Annals of Connacht*, s.a. 1317.
74. Barbour, *The Bruce*, ed. Duncan, 582; above, p. 171.
75. *Chartul. St Mary's, Dublin*, ii, 298, 352.
76. *Chartul. St Mary's, Dublin*, ii, 299.
77. See Duffy, S., 'The Anglo-Norman era in Scotland and Ireland: convergence and divergence', in *Celebrating Columba. Irish-Scottish connections 597–1997*, ed. T.M. Devine & J.F. McMillan (Edinburgh, 1999), 15–34.
78. See Duffy, 'Bruce brothers', above, p. 51–52.
79. *Chartul. St Mary's, Dublin*, ii, 353.
80. Gilbert (ed.), *Historic & municipal documents*, 392–93.
81. *Chartul. St Mary's, Dublin*, ii, 299–300, 353.
82. See Frame, R., 'The campaign against the Scots in Munster, 1317', *Irish Historical Studies*, 24 (1985), 361–72.
83. Frame, 'The Bruces in Ireland', 22–23.
84. *Caithréim Thoirdhealbhaigh*, ed. S.H. O'Grady, 2 vols (London, 1929), ii, 83.
85. *Annals of Inisfallen*, s.a. 1317.
86. See Simms, K., 'The battle of Dysert O'Dea and the Gaelic resurgence in Thomond', *Dál gCais*, 5 (1979), 59–66; Ghiollamhaith, A.N., 'Dynastic warfare and historical writing in North Munster, 1276–1350', *Cambridge Medieval Celtic Studies*, 2 (1981), 73–89.
87. The details of the various troop movements are in Frame, 'Campaign against the Scots'.
88. Orpen, *Ireland under the Normans*, iv, 192.
89. *Chartul. St Mary's, Dublin*, ii, 301.
90. Barbour, *The Bruce*, ed. Duncan, 594; above, p. 173.
91. See above, pp. 177–84.
92. *Chartul. St Mary's, Dublin*, ii, 407.

93. Duffy, 'Continuation of Nicholas Trevet', 309.
94. Otway-Ruthven, 'Partition of the de Verdon lands'.
95. Tresham, E. (ed.), *Rotulorum patentium et clausorum cancellariae Hiberniae calendarium* (London, 1828), 13; *Cal. close rolls, 1307–13*, 188.
96. Butler (ed.) *Annals of Clyn*, 13.
97. Mac Niocaill, G., 'Cáipéisí ón gceathrú céad déag', *Galvia*, 5 (1958), 33–35.
98. See above, pp. 107–18.
99. Barbour, *The Bruce*, ed. Duncan, 667; above, p. 174.
100. *Chartul. St Mary's, Dublin*, ii, 360.

2 – The Bruce Brothers and the Irish Sea World, 1306–29

1. To the works cited in Asplin, P.W.A., *Medieval Ireland* c.*1170–1495: A Bibliography of Secondary Works* (Dublin, 1971), nos 279–86, add: Frame, R., 'The Bruces in Ireland, 1315–18', *Irish Historical Studies,* 19 (1974–75), 3–37; Phillips, J.R.S., 'Documents on the Early Stages of the Bruce Invasion of Ireland, 1315–1316', *Proceedings of the Royal Irish Academy*, 79, Section C (1979), 247–70; O Murchadha, D., 'Select Documents XXXVI: Is the O Neill-MacCarthy Letter of 1317 a Forgery?', *IHS,* 23 (1982–83), 61–67; Lydon, J.F., 'The Impact of the Bruce Invasion, 1317–27', in Cosgrove, A. (ed.), *A New History of Ireland,* II (Oxford, 1987), Chapter X; Duncan, A.A.M., 'The Scots' Invasion of Ireland, 1315', in Davies, R.R. (ed.), *The British Isles 1100–1500: Comparisons, Contrasts and Connections* (Edinburgh, 1988), pp. 100–17; Duffy, S., 'The Gaelic Account of the Bruce Invasion, *Cath Fhochairte Brighite:* Medieval Romance or Modern Forgery?', *Seanchas Ard Mhacha,* 13 (1988–89), 59–121, *Cambridge Medieval Celtic Studies* 21 (Summer 1991).
2. The best recent survey of the subject is perhaps Barrow, G.W.S., *Kingship and Unity: Scotland 1000–1306* (Edinburgh, 1981), Chapter 6.
3. O'Donovan, J. (ed.), *The Annals of the Kingdom of Ireland by the Four Masters*, 7 vols (Dublin, 1848–51), ii, s.a. 1060; Stokes, W. (ed.), 'The Annals of Tigernach', *Revue celtique,* 17 (1896), s.a. 1061.
4. Hennessy, W.M. & MacCarthy, B. (eds), *The Annals of Ulster*, 4 vols (Dublin, 1887–1901), ii s.a. 1073; Hennessy, W.M. (ed.), *The Annals of Loch Cé*, Rolls Series, 2 vols (London, 1881), i, s.a. 1073; *Annals of the Four Masters,* s.a. 1096; Seán Mac Airt (ed.), *The Annals of Inisfallen*, (Dublin, 1959), s.a. 1111.5; *Cronica Regum Mannie & Insularum,* transcribed and translated by George Broderick (Belfast, 1979), fol. 33v.
5. Ibid., fol. 36r.
6. Scott, A.B. & Martin, F.X. (eds), *Expugnatio Hibernica: The Conquest of Ireland by Giraldus Cambrensis*, translated by A.B. Scott and F.X. Martin (Dublin, 1978), pp. 78–79. Ruaidrí Ó Conchobair's reliance on Hebridean support was inherited by his sons. In their struggles for kingship in Connacht against Ruaidrí's brother, Cathal Crobderg, Ruaidrí's sons relied on the backing of the descendants of Somerled of Argyll (d. 1164), while Cathal Crobderg looked to the descendants of Fergus of Galloway (d. 1161). When Cathal Crobderg was banished to Ulster to join John de Courcy in 1200 he may there have met and enlisted the services as seneschal (or

reachtaire) of one Toirbert son of the Galloway man *(Annals of Loch Cé,* s.aa. 1200 and 1210), since de Courcy, not King John as is usually claimed, was responsible for initiating Gallovidian seisin in Ulster (Stubbs, W. (ed.), *Chronica Magistri Rogeri de Houedene,* 4 vols, RS (London, 1871), iv, 25), and we find that when Ruaidrí Ó Conchobair's son Diarmait went to the Hebrides in 1221 and collected a fleet for the purpose of acquiring the kingship of Connacht, he was intercepted and killed by Thomas of Galloway, earl of Atholl (*Annals of Loch Cé,* s.a. 1220; see also *Annals of the Four Masters,* s.a. 1220). Diarmait's brother, Toirrdelbach, married his daughter off to Maelmuire son of Suibne (or Svein), probably the first of the MacSweeneys of Kintyre to become linked (or more correctly, re-linked) with Ireland *(Annals of Loch Cé,* s.a. 1269).

7. Bliss, W.H. (ed.), *Calendar of Entries on the Papal Registers Relating to Great Britain and Ireland: Papal Letters,* 5 vols, (London, 1893–1904), *1198–1304,* p. 69, 883–1904).
8. See the remarks of Cheney, C.R., 'Manx Synodal Statutes, A.D. 1230(?)–1351, Part I: Introduction and Latin Texts', *Cambridge Medieval Celtic Studies,* 7 (summer 1984), 63–89 (pp. 64–65 and n. 7).
9. Sheehy, M.P. (ed.), *Pontificia Hibernica: Medieval Papal Chancery Documents Relating to Ireland, 640–1261,* 2 vols (Dublin, 1962–65), I, no. 11. The editor takes this to be Glendalough, very occasionally referred to as *Insula Sancti Salvatoris,* but it seems more likely that the diocese of Sodor is intended, and that Glendalough was deliberately excluded from the list, the Anglo-Norman archbishops of Dublin being busy annexing it to the archdiocese (see Orpen, G.H., *Ireland under the Normans, 1169–1333,* 4 vols (Oxford, 1911–20), ii 71–73; Ronan, M.V., 'The Union of the Dioceses of Glendalough and Dublin', *Journal of the Royal Society of Antiquaries of Ireland, 60* (1930), 56–72).
10. *Cronica Regum Mannie,* 50 and 51; though Bangor's links with St Malachy may offer another explanation.
11. *Calendar of Papal Letters, 1198–1304,* p. 74.
12. Haddan, A.W. & Stubbs, W. (eds), *Councils and Ecclesiastical Documents relating to Great Britain and Ireland,* 3 vols (London, 1884), ii, 246 and 249.
13. Luard, H.R. (ed.), *Matthaei Parisiensis, Monachi Sancti A!bani, Chronica Majora,* 7 vols, RS (London, 1872–83), ii, M *358.*
14. Gilbert, J.T. (ed.), *Chartul. St Mary's, Dublin,* 2 vols, RS (London, 1884), ii, 263 and 265.
15. *Calendar of Papal Letters, 1305–42,* p. 102.
16. Sweetman, H.S. (ed.), *Calendar of Documents Relating to Ireland,* 5 vols (London, 1875–86), I, no. 429.
17. Ibid., no. 976.
18. Bain, J., Simpson, G.G. & Galbraith, J.D. (eds.), *Calendar of Documents Relating to Scotland,* 5 vols (Edinburgh, 1881–1988), v, Part 2, no. 9, p. 136. Where a Gaelic orthographic equivalent is in common usage I have in general chosen to apply it to the personal names of individuals mentioned in the text, when such seems applicable. Lest I be accused of giving a misleading Gaelic 'tint' to their appearance in order to assist the argument of the paper, I may point out that Olaf the Black, for instance, is referred to in an English official document as 'Olave Duff', his son is there called 'Magnus Mac Olave Duff' *(Calendar of Documents, Ireland, I,* no. 3206), while the Latin Manx *Chronicle* refers to his nephew as 'Gotredus Don' *(Cronica Regum Mannie,* fol. 44v), employing epithets and a patronymic that clearly indicate a Gaelic-speaking milieu.
19. *Calendar of Documents, Ireland,* I, no. 2381.

20. Simpson, G.G. (ed.), *Handlist of the Acts of Alexander III* (Edinburgh, 1960), no. 171.
21. Stevenson, J. (ed.), *Documents Illustrative of the History of Scotland 1286–1306*, 2 vols (Edinburgh, 1870), I, 156–57.
22. See, for example, Gilbert, J.T. (ed.), *Historical and Municipal Documents of Ireland* (London, 1870), no. LXXXI, p. 336.
23. *Calendar of the Fine Rolls, 1272–[1509]*, 22 vols (London, 1911–62), *1307–19*, p. 332; *Rotuli Scotiae*, 2 vols, Record Commission (London, 1814–19), i, 173. Incidentally, some indication of who the public perceived to be most at risk from Scottish control of the Irish Sea perhaps comes from the fact that it was to Dublin that the decapitated head of Thomas Dun was brought for public display *(Chartul. St Mary's, Dublin*, ii, 355).
24. Stubbs, W. (ed.), *Memoriale Fratris Walteri de Coventria*, 2 vols, RS (London, 1873), ii, 206; see also 'The Melrose Chronicle', s.aa. 1215 and 1235, printed in translation in *Early Sources of Scottish History A.D. 500 to 1286*, collected and translated by A.O. Anderson, 2 vols (London, 1922), ii, 404 and 496–98.
25. *Calendar of Documents, Ireland*, I, no. 3206.
26. This is a subject Professor J.F. Lydon has made his own: see, for example, his 'Irish Levies in the Scottish Wars, 1296–1302', *The Irish Sword*, 5 (1961–62), 207–17.
27. London, PRO, E. 372/152 (Pipe roll 1 Edward II), membrane 35d; Mills, J. (ed.), *Calendar of Justiciary Rolls preserved in the Public Record Office of Ireland*, 2 vols (Dublin and London, 1905–14), ii 354; *Calendar of Documents, Ireland*, v, no. 633.
28. Discovered by Professor A.A.M. Duncan, it was first printed by Nicholson, R.G., in 'A Sequel to Edward Bruce's Invasion of Ireland', *Scottish Historical Review*, 42 (1963), 30–40 (Appendix I, pp. 38–39). It is available in translation in Barrow, G.W.S., *Robert Bruce and the Community of the Realm of Scotland*, first edition (London, 1966), p. 434 (see also third edition (Edinburgh, 1988), p. 379, n. 9, for a crucial emendation by Professor Barrow of his earlier translation, acknowledging that the text of the letter does indeed intend 'nostra nacio' to refer to a single Gaelic 'nation' dwelling in Ireland and Scotland). The original has also been printed twice by Professor Duncan, in *Formulary E. Scottish Letters and Brieves 1286–1424*, Scottish History Department Occasional Papers (Glasgow, 1976), no. 94, p. 44, and in *The Acts of Robert I, Regesta Regum Scottorum*, v (Edinburgh, 1988), no. 564.
29. For the campaign, see Barrow, G.W.S., *Robert Bruce*, third edition, especially pp. 163–73.
30. See n. 26 above.
31. *Calendar of Justiciary Rolls*, II, 74.
32. *Calendar of Documents, Scotland*, III, no. 190. Three months before the launch of Edward Bruce's invasion, several individuals, including Thomas of Lancaster and the Abbot of Furness, were granted a safe conduct for two years for their servants and mariners going to obtain supplies in Ireland, 'provided that they are not carried to the King's Scotch enemies, or they hold communion with them in any manner' *(Calendar of the Patent Rolls, 1232–[1509]*, 53 vols (London 1891–1971), 1313–17, pp. 218, 219, 221 and 470).
33. The best account of this campaign is in Stanford Reid, W., 'Sea-power in the Anglo-Scottish War, 1296–1328', *Mariner's Mirror*, 46 (1960), pp. 7–23.
34. *Chartul. St Mary's, Dublin*, II, 346.
35. *Cronica Regum Mannie*, fol. 33.
36. See, for example, *Annals of the Four Masters*, s.aa. 1094 and 1095.

37. See Curtis, E., 'Murchertach O'Brien, High King of Ireland, and his Norman Son-in-Law, Arnulf de Montgomery, *circa* 1100', *JRSAI*, 51 (1921), 116–21; Power, R., 'Magnus Barelegs' Expeditions to the West', *SHR*, 65 (1986), 107–32; Candon, A., 'Muirchertach Ua Briain: Politics and Naval Activity in the Irish Sea, 1075 to 1119', in Mac Niocaill, G. *et al.* (eds), *Keimelia: Essays in Memory of Tom Delaney* (Galway, 1989), pp. 397–415.
38. See, for example, *Annals of the Four Masters,* s.a. 1102; Anderson, A.O., *Early Sources,* II, 127.
39. *Cronica Regum Mannie,* fol. 37r.
40. Ó Cuív, B., 'A Poem in Praise of Ragnall, King of Man', *Eigse*, 8 (1956–57), 283–301.
41. *Calendar of Documents, Ireland,* I, nos 428 and 898.
42. Orpen, G.H., *Ireland under the Normans*, ii, 11, n. 2.
43. 'Tangadar teachd ó Temhraigh Domhnall mac Ragnaill do ghabh cennas Innsi Gall 7 urmhór Gaoidheal'. The quotation is from 'The Book of Clanranald: The Macdonald History', printed in Cameron, A. (ed.), *Reliquiae Celticae*, 2 vols (Inverness, 1894), ii, 156–57.
44. *Annals of Ulster,* s.a. 1212; *Annals of the Four Masters* and *Annals of Loch Cé, s.a.* 1211.
45. See for example, *Annals of the Four Masters, s.a. 1247.*
46. Bergin, O., *Irish Bardic Poetry* (Dublin 1970), no. 45.
47. Calendar of Documents, Scotland, I, no. 2041.
48. Ibid., no. 2185; *Calendar of Documents, Ireland,* ii no. 652.
49. Mac Néill, E., *Phases of Irish History* (Dublin, 1937), pp. 330–31.
50. *Calendar of Documents, Ireland,* i, no. 1179; *Calendar of Documents, Scotland,* I, no. 852; see also Frame, R., 'Aristocracies and the Political Configuration of the British Isles', in *The British Isles,* by Davies, R.R., pp. 142–59 (p. 150).
51. See, for example, *Annals of Loch Cé,* s.aa. 1258 and 1259. The 'Frisbok' *Haakon Haakonsson's saga* is translated in Anderson, A.O., *Early Sources,* ii 611, 617, 625–26 and 635.
52. Anderson, A.O., *Early Sources*, ii, 622 and 634.
53. Stuart, J. & Burnell, G. (eds.), *Rotuli Scaccarii Regum Scotorum: The Exchequer Rolls of Scotland*, 23 vols (Edinburgh, 1878–1908), I, 27–28.
54. Hall, A. (ed.), *Nicolai Triveti Annalium Continuatio* (Oxford, 1722). A better text than that printed by Hall can be found in Arundel MS 18 in the Library of the College of Arms, London.
55. McDiarmid, M.P. (ed.), *Barbour's Bruce: A Fredome is a Noble Thing*, 3 vols, Scottish Text Society (Edinburgh, 1980–85), ii, Book xv. 267–300. The 'ancient prophecy' is perhaps nothing more than a twist in the traditional tale linking Magnus Barelegs' alleged acquisition of Kintyre with the accomplishment of the same feat; see also the discussion of the motif by Cheape, H., 'Recounting Tradition: A Critical Review of Medieval Reportage', in Fenton, A. & Pilsson, H. (eds), *The Northern and Western Isles in the Viking Age* (Edinburgh, 1984), pp. 197–222.
56. *Regesta Regum Scottorum,* v, no. 101.
57. Wilson, J., 'The Passage of Malachy through Scotland', *SHR,* 18 (1921), 69–82; Reid, R.C., 'Caput of Annandale or the Curse of Malachy', *Transactions of the Dumfriesshire and Galloway Natural History and Antiquarian Society,* third series, 32 (1954), 155–66; Barrow, G.W.S., *Robert Bruce,* third edition, pp. 24–25 and 318.
58. *Barbour's Bruce*, ii Book iii. 67–70.
59. Ibid., Book vi.581; see the extract, apparently out of the *Chronicle* of John of Tynemouth, printed in Phillips, J.R.S., 'Documents on the Early Stages of the Bruce Invasion', pp. 269–70.

60. Rothwell, H. (ed.), *The Chronicle of Walter of Guisborough*, Camden Society (London, 1957), p. 370 ('... dominum scilicet Thomam de Brus qui Anglicos semper odio habuerat').
61. *The Chronicle of Lanercost,* translated by Herbert Maxwell (Glasgow, 1913), p. 188.
62. *Rotuli Scotiae*, i, 96 ('Intelliximus a nonnullis quod Robertus de Brus inimicus et preditor noster mititur pro viribus et proponit totum navigium suum de Insulis Forinsecis usque ad Insulam nostram de Man in presenti hiemi transmittere ad insulam illam destruendam...').
63. *Regesta Regum Scottorum,* v, 379. See, for example, Freeman, A.M. (ed.), *The Annals of Connacht* (Dublin, 1944), s.a. 1318.8; and compare *Annals of Inisfallen,* s.a. 1318.4.
64. The two Hebridean commanders killed with Edward Bruce may have been Alexander son of Aengus Mór mac Domnaill and Ruaidrí son of Alain mac Ruaidrí; their identity remains a matter of conjecture.
65. Walsh, P., 'O'Donnell Genealogies', *Analecta Hibernica,* 8 (1938), 377.
66. *Annals of Connacht,* s.aa. 1290.7 and 1291.3 and .4.
67. Ibid., s.a. 1318.6.
68. Ibid., s.a. 1303.6.
69. *Calendar of Documents, Scotland,* ii, no. 1255; Walsh, P. (ed.), *Leabhar Chlainne Suibhne: An Account of the Mac Sweeney Families in Ireland, with Pedigrees* (Dublin, 1920), p. 16.
70. *Calendar of Documents, Scotland,* iii, no. 415; *Calendar of the Close Rolls, 1272–[1509],* 47 vols (London, 1892–1963), *1313–18,* p. 153.
71. *Calendar of Documents, Scotland,* iii, no. 420.
72. Ibid., no. 857.
73. Ibid., no. 521; 'Accounts of the Great Rolls of the Pipe of the Irish Exchequer for the Reign of Edward II', *Report of the Deputy Keeper of the Public Records of Ireland,* 42 (Dublin, 1911), p. 17; PRO, E. 101/237/2.
74. Thomson, J.M. *et al.* (eds), *Registrum Magni Sigilli Regum Scottorum,* 11 vols (Edinburgh, 1882–1914), i, Appendix 2, nos 56–58; the sources for Aengus Og's marriage, all late, are listed in Steer, K.A. & Bannerman, J.W.M., *Late Medieval Monumental Sculpture in the West Highlands* (Edinburgh, 1977), p. 203, n. 3.
75. Lloyd, J.E., *A History of Wales from the Earliest Times to the Edwardian Conquest,* 2 vols (London, 1911), I, 183–84.
76. *Calendar of Papal Letters, 1198–1304,* pp. 8, 13, and 19.
77. See Davies, R.R., *Conquest, Coexistence and Change: Wales 1063–1415* (Oxford, 1987), p. 10, n. 5
78. *Cronica Regum Mannie,* fol. 45r.
79. *Calendar of Documents, Scotland, I,* no. 1917; see also the letters of protection, dated 21 April 1256, to King Magnus of Man, forbidding Henry III's 'bailiffs and lieges of West, South and North Wales' from harbouring Harald, grandson of the former King Ragnall, or his accomplices, who had killed Magnus's brother in 1249 (ibid., no. 2046).
80. *Calendar of Close Rolls, 1313–18,* p. 6.
81. *Calendar of Documents, Scotland,* iii, no. 562.
82. For an important series of essays on this subject, see now Davies, R.R., *Domination and Conquest: The Experience of Ireland, Scotland and Wales 1100–1300* (Cambridge, 1990).
83. Duncan, A.A.M., *Scotland: The Making of the Kingdom,* Edinburgh History of Scotland, 1 (Edinburgh, 1975), pp. 522–25; Treharne, R.F., 'The Franco-Welsh Treaty of Alliance in 1212', *Bulletin of the Board of Celtic Studies,* 18 (1958–60), 60–75, prints the text of Llywelyn ap

Iorwerth's letter to Philip Augustus claiming to have 'made neither truce nor peace, nor even parley, with the English, but that, by God's grace, I and all the princes of Wales unanimously leagued together have manfully resisted our – and your – enemies, and by God's grace we have recovered by force of arms from the yoke of their tyranny a large part of the land and the strongly defended castles which they, by fraud and deceit, had occupied, and having recovered them, we hold them strongly in the might of the Lord' (pp. 63 and 74).

84. *Matthaei Parisiensis Chronica Majora*, iii, 372–73.
85. Chaplais, P. (ed.), *Treaty Rolls Preserved in the Public Record Office, 1234–1325*, 2 vols (London, 1955–72), 2, no. 29; see also Davies, R.R., *Domination and Conquest*, p. 78.
86. Shirley, W.W. (ed.), *Royal and Other Historical Letters Illustrative of the Reign of Henry III*, 2 vols, RS (London, 1862–66), i, no. 211; *Calendar of Documents, Scotland*, v, Part 2, no. 6, p. 135.
87. Wright, T. (ed.), *Matthaei Parisiensis Chronica Majora*, iv, 489; *The Political Songs of England from the Reign of John to that of Edward II*, CS (London, 1839), pp. 19–20.
88. *Calendar of Documents, Ireland*, II, no. 661; *Annals of Connacht*, s.a. 1258.9; at his death Brian is again called *ri Gaídil Érenn* ('king of the Gaels of Ireland') ibid., s.a. 1260.2.
89. Jones, T. (ed.), *Brenhinedd y Saesson, or, the Kings of the Saxons*, translated by T. Jones, Board of Celtic Studies History and Law Series, 25 (Cardiff, 1971), pp. 241–42 (s.a. 1256); for earlier use of the Welsh title, see Richter, M., 'David ap Llywelyn, the First Prince of Wales', *Welsh History Review*, 5 (1971), 205–19.
90. Edwards, J.G. (ed.), *Littere Wallie preserved in Liber A in the Public Record Office*, Board of Celtic Studies History and Law Series, 5 (Cardiff) pp. 184–86.
91. Calendar *of Documents, Scotland*, I, no. 2163.
92. *Miscellaneous Irish Annals A.D. 1114–1437*, translated by S. Ó hInnse (Dublin, 1947), pp. 102–03.
93. Chaplais, *Treaty Rolls*, no. 153; see also no. 177.
94. Fryde, N., *List of Welsh Entries in the Memoranda Rolls, 1282–1343* (Cardiff, 1974), no. 317, p. 39.
95. *Calendar of Documents, Ireland*, iii, no. 366.
96. *Calendar of Various Chancery Rolls, 1277–1326* (London, 1912), p. 323.
97. Gransden, A. (ed.), *Chronica Buriensis 1212–1301: The Chronicle of Bury St Edmunds 1212–1301*, translated by A. Gransden (London, 1964), pp. 128–29.
98. Wright, T., *Political Songs of England*, pp. 19–20. The phrase is Professor Barrow's.
99. *Robert Bruce,* third edition, p. 52; see also p. 63.
100. *Chronicle of Guisborough*, pp. 325–26, translated in Barrow, G.W.S., *Robert Bruce,* third edition, p. 68
101. *Calendar of Documents, Ireland, IV*, no. 506
102. Wright, T., *Political Songs of England*, pp. 300–01. A strong parallel is found in some 'prophetic' verses composed perhaps during or just after the Bruce invasion, which describe an imagined visit by Edward II to Ireland in 1320, after a certain crisis, to bring peace between the English and the Irish; from there, he will go to Scotland, bringing with him English, Irish and Welsh, to subdue the Scots rebels and put Robert Bruce to flight, who will end his days as a wanderer (Phillips, J.R.S., 'Edward II and the Prophets', in Ormrod, W.M. (ed.), *England in the Fourteenth Century: Proceedings of the 1985 Harlaxton College Symposium* (Woodbridge, 1986), pp. 189–201 (p. 194); my thanks are due to Professor Phillips for providing me with a copy of his paper).
103. *Calendar of Documents, Scotland,* v, Part 2, no. 694, p. 254.
104. Ibid., no. 1926.
105. *Regesta Regum Scottorum,* v, no. 571; the first modern printing is by Beverley Smith, J., 'Gruffydd

Llwyd and the Celtic Alliance, 1315–18', *BBCS,* 26 (1974–76), 463–78 (p. 478), where there is a full discussion.

106. A case for setting the invasion in the 'mainstream' of Scottish policy is made in Frame, R., 'The Bruces in Ireland', p. 15; Professor Barrow remains dubious: *Robert Bruce,* third edition, p. 317.
107. Duncan, A.A.M., 'The Scots' Invasion of Ireland', p. 115.
108. Maxwell, H., *Chronicle of Lanercost,* p. 253.
109. See Nicholson, R.G., 'A Sequel to Edward Bruce's Invasion', p. 32 and Appendix II, p. 39; and also Frame, R., *English Lordship in Ireland 1318–1361* (Oxford, 1982), pp. 138–42, for further discussion.
110. Duncan, A.A.M., 'The Scots' Invasion of Ireland', p. 114.
111. Earlier versions of this paper were read to meetings of the Irish Historical Society and the Dublin University History Society; I am grateful to both bodies, and to Professor J.F. Lydon for his help and encouragement.

3 – The Bruce Invasion of Ireland: an Examination of Some Problems

1. Warner, Sir G. (ed.), *The Libelle of Englyshe Polycye,* II. 698–701.
2. *Statutes of the Realm,* i, 157.
3. See my unpublished Ph.D. thesis, *Ireland's Participation in the Military Activities of English Kings in the Thirteenth and Early Fourteenth Century* (London, 1955).
4. PROI, Memoranda roll 5 Edward II, m.26 (Record Commission's Calendar, vi, 187–89).
5. *Caithr. Thoirdh.,* ii. 83. For this and other bibliographical abbreviations I have used the forms listed in 'Rules for the guidance of contributors', *Irish Historical Studies,* iv, no. 13.7–33 (March 1944).
6. For the history of the invasion see Chapter 1 above and Armstrong, O., *Edward Bruce's Invasion of Ireland*; Orpen, G.H., *Normans,* iv, ch. 37; Curtis, E., *Med. Ire.* (2nd ed., 1938), pp. 180–97; Dunlop, R., 'Some notes on *Barbour's Bruce,* Bks xiv–xvi, and xviii'; Little, A.G. & Powicke, F.M., (eds), *Essays presented to T.F. Tout,* pp. 277–90.
7. Barbour, J., *The Bruce,* in Skeat, W. (ed.) (1894), xiv, ll.4–7; above p. 161.
8. The number of men with Bruce was said to be 6,000 *(Chartul. St Mary's, Dublin,* ii, 303). While this figure cannot be accepted literally, all the other authorities agree that the Scottish army was a large one.
9. This is quite clear from the accounts of the receivers of victuals at Carlisle and elsewhere in Scotland. See for examples PRO, E. 101/7/20, f. 10; B.M., Add. MSS., 7966A, ff. 17, 66v–67v; 8835, f. 35; 35291, f. 54v.
10. See my Ph.D. thesis, ch. V.
11. At least one English chronicler asserts that the purpose of the invasion was to weaken the army of Edward II by diverting it to Ireland: Trokelowe, J., in Riley, H.T. (ed.) *Annales* (1886), p. 91.
12. MacNeill, E., *Phases of Irish History,* ch. XII, on Bruce's supposed inauguration at Faughart, see above, pp. 14–15.
13. The remonstrance is printed in Fordun, J., *Scotichronicon,* Hearne, J. (ed.), iii, 908–26. An English translation will be found in Curtis, E. & McDowell, R.B., *Irish Historical Documents, 1172–1922,*

pp. 38–46, and above, pp. 177–84. For the papal reaction see Watt, J., 'Negotiations between Edward II and John XXII concerning Ireland', *I.H.S.*, x, no. 37, 1–20 (March 1956).

14. O'Donovan, J. (ed.), *Tribes and Customs of Hy-Many* (Irish Archaeological Society, 1843), pp. 136–37.
15. Rymer, *Foedera* (London, 1818), ii, part 2, 122.
16. Barbour, J., *The Bruce*, iii, 11. 680 ff; McL. Barron, E., *The Scottish War of Independence*, ch. XXII, argues that Bruce had fled either to Norway or the Orkney Islands; but I see no. reason to doubt the evidence of Barbour on this point. Certainly Edward I (whose spies, as Barron admits, were everywhere) believed that Bruce was hiding on some island between Scotland and Ireland – *Cal. doc. Scotland, 1272–1307*, no. 1888.
17. *Gal. doc. Irel.*, 1293–1301, no. 555; *Cal. justic. rolls Irel., 1295–1303*, p. 218.
18. Rothwell, H. (ed.), *The Chronicle of Walter of Guisborough* (Camden Society, 1957), p. 329.
19. *Chartul. St Mary's, Dublin*, ii, 344; *Cal. pat. rolls, 1317–21*, pp. 271, 313.
20. PRO, E. 372/152 (Pipe roll I Edward II), m. 35d; see above, pp. 51–53.
21. PROI, Mem. roll 31–35 Edward I (Calendar, p. 169); Mem. roll 8 Edward II (Rec. Comm. Cal., x, 81); *Gal. close rolls*, 1308–13, p. 339.
22. B.M., Add. MSS., 22923, fol. 14v; *Cal. doc. Scotland, 1272–1307*, nos 1905, 1915; *Chronicon de Lanercost* (Bannatyne Club), p. 205.
23. *Cal. close rolls, 1313–18*, p. 355.
24. PRO, E. 101/237/2.
25. Fitzmaurice, E.B. & Little, A.G., *Materials for the history of the Franciscan Province of Ireland*, 1230–1450, pp. 95 ff.; PROI, Plea roll 9–11 (Calendar, pp. 49–50).
26. *Cal. close rolls, 1313–18*, p. 561; full text in Rymer, *Foedera*, ii, part 2, 339. No record of the inquiry by Mortimer into the Bishop's conduct has survived; but on Pipe roll 9 he is allowed £26 13s 4d. Edward II pardoned him for his good service in repressing the Irish of Wexford – *P.R.I. rep. D.K.* 39, p. 70.
27. PROI, Plea roll 8–9 Edward II (Calendar, pp. 58–59).
28. *Chartul. St Mary's, Dublin*, ii. 342; *Ann. Conn.*, p. 229; *Ann. Loch Cé*, i. 561.
29. *Cal. doc. Scotland, 1307–57*, nos 922, 1191; *Chartul. St Mary's, Dublin*, ii, 367; see above, Chapter 7.
30. PROI, Plea roll 8–9 Edward II (Calendar, pp. 31–32).
31. Previous to 1315 many of the Anglo-Irish had fought among themselves, sometimes with Irish allies. During the Bruce war and after, the activities of the de Lacy family, the Cogans and others was obviously the result of discontent with existing settlements – Genealogical Office, MS. 190 (Betham Collection), pp. 135–36, 179; *Chartul. St Mary's, Dublin*, ii, app. ii–iii.
32. *Cal. close rolls, 1313–18*, p. 333.
33. PRO, E. 101/237/5/ 8–9; Society of Antiquaries London, MS. 122, Wardrobe Book II Edward II, fol. 33v.
34. *Cal. pat. rolls, 1317–21*, p. 535. A notification of good behaviour, on behalf of the earl of Ulster, was issued by the king in September 1322. But it is obviously connected with the rebellion of Lancaster and was issued with similar notifications on behalf of other people at the same time – *Cal. pat. rolls, 1321–24*, p. 203.
35. Ibid., *1307–13*, p. 189. In September 1286 de Burgh had been party to an interesting agreement with a number of leading Scots, Robert Bruce the elder and his son among them, Stevenson, J., *Documents Illustrative of the History of Scotland*, i, 22–23.
36. *Chartul. St Mary's Dublin*, ii, 342.

37. Ibid., 296–97; *Ann. Loch Cé,* i. 565; Armstrong, O., *Bruce Invasion,* pp. 79–87, 95–96.
38. *Hist & mun. doc. Ire.,* pp. 397–401; Armstrong, O., op. cit., pp. 203–04. The king was obviously uncertain of de Burgh's loyalty and fearful lest he should exacerbate the bad feeling between the citizens of Dublin and the magnates. Eventually, to get de Burgh out of the way, he summoned him to England: *Cal. pat. rolls, 1313–17,* p. 465.
39. *Hist. & mun. doc. Ire.,* pp. 270–84; Jope, E.M. & Seaby, W.A., 'A New Document in the Public Record Office: Defensive Houses in Medieval Towns', *U.J.A.*, xxii. (1959), 115–18.
40. *Cal. anc. rec. Dublin,* i, 132; *Hist. & mun. doc. Ire.,* p. 389.
41. *Cal. anc. rec. Dublin,* i, 113.
42. *Hist. & mun. doc. Ire.,* pp. 391–92.
43. See, for example, PROI, Plea roll 8–9 Edward II (Calendar, pp. 52–53).
44. PRO, E.101/237/4–5
45. PRO, E.101/237/5 – payments to Martin de Fyssacre and 5 *balistarii,* 30 April 1316–31 March 1317.
46. PRO, E. 101/237/8 – payments for houses hired 2 April 1317–Easter 1318. That the exchequer was destroyed as a result of the burning of the suburbs appears likely from PRO, S.C.8/118/5881. (I am indebted to Miss J. Otway-Ruthven for this reference.) See also Armstrong, O., *Bruce Invasion,* p. 104.
47. *Hist. & mun. doc. Ire.,* pp. 402–12; *P.R.I. rep. D.K.* 42, P. 47; Armstrong, O., *Bruce Invasion,* pp. 104–05.
48. *P.R.I. rep. D.K.* 42, pp. 33–34.
49. Ibid. 39, p. 65.
50. Ibid., p. 71; *Hist. & mun. doc. Ire.,* pp. 392–93.
51. The accounts of the royal purveyors based in Dublin show this; see, for example, PRO, E.102/16/21.
52. B.M., Add. MSS., 7966A, f. 67; *Cal. doc. Scotland, 1272–1307,* p. 190; Johnstone, H. (ed.), *Annales Gadenses* (London, 1951), pp. 4–6; *Hist. & mun. doc. Ire.,* p. 378. Frequently the Irish purveyors had to employ special guards to protect victuals against theft – see, for example, PROI 101/14/40, payments to three 'garcionibus vigilantibus' guarding wine for eight nights in Dublin 'inter aquam et castrum propter exercitum versus Ultoniam' and to others guarding it by day.
53. *Cal. justic. rolls Ire., 1305–07,* p. 198.
54. *Cal. close rolls, 1313–18,* p. 476; full text in *Hist. & mun. doc. Ire.,* pp. 401–02.
55. Palgrave, *Parliamentary Writs,* i, 458, no. 11.
56. *Cal. close rolls, 1318–23,* pp. 529, 708, 719–20; *Cal. pat. rolls, 1321–24,* p. 205; Palgrave, *Parliamentary Writs,* i, 680–81, nos 160–61.
57. Denholm Young, N. (ed.), *Vita Edwardi Secundi,* p. 61.
58. The earl served in the campaign of 1296 and had been commander of the Irish contingent in the campaign of 1303–04; but afterwards he would never serve in Scotland, despite repeated requests by the king – see especially the king's letter to the earl in *Cal. close rolls, 1302–07,* p. 436, and Palgrave, *Parliamentary Writs,* i, 392, nos 63–64; 400–01, no. 13; 423, no. 12; 425, no. 25; *Cal. close rolls, 1318–23,* p. 529.
59. Huge debts had been contracted by the exchequer as a result of the Scottish campaigns, many of these sums due to the magnates who had served in Scotland. But in addition there was no money to meet renewed demands from the king – see especially *Cal. justic. rolls Ire., 1305–07,*

p. 269.

60. PROI, Memoranda rolls 3–6 Edward II (Rec. Comm. calendar, v–vi), passim; *P.R.I. rep. D.K.* 39, p. 32.
61. PROI, Memoranda roll 5 Edward II (Rec. Comm. calendar, vi, pp. 255–56); *Cal. close rolls, 1307–13*, pp. 412–13; for supplies procured see PRO, E. 101/14/25, fol. 7/15, 238/24, 236/3, 236/7, 375/8, in 21–21v.
62. PRO, E.101/235/14, receipts at the exchequer 1–7 Edward II, calculated at £19,245, which shows a considerable fall on those for Edward I.
63. *Hist. & mun. doc. Ire.*, pp. 327–28; see also pp. 342–50; PRO, E. 101/14/40 and other purveyors' accounts.
64. *Cal. doc. Scotland, 1307–57*, no. 469. None of Balscote's particular accounts have survived, but see payments on issue rolls 8–11 Edward II (PRO, E. 101/237/2, 4, 5, 8) and Pipe roll 14 Edward II, m. 25–25d (PRO, E.372/166). So serious was the shortage of money that the government resorted to the device of pardoning debts, many of them very large, for service *about* to be rendered against the Scots PROI, Plea roll 9–11 Edward II (Calendar, pp. 54–64).
65. The returns were as follows: PRO, E. 101/237/1–8 Edward II £46 13s 4d; E.101/237/3–9 Edward II £65 2s 6d; E. 101/237/7–11 Edward II £49 16s 7½d; E. 101/237/11–13 Edward II £22 19s 8d; E.101/237/13–14 Edward II £3 15s 6¾d.
66. PROI, Memoranda roll 8 Edward II (Rec. Comm. calendar, x, pp. 177–78); *Rotuli Scotie*, i, 188; *Hist. & mun. doc. Ire.*, pp. 336–37.
67. *Cal. chancery warrants, 1244–1326*, p. 436.
68. *Cal. pat. rolls, 1313–17*, p. 608; *Cal. close rolls*, 1313–18, p. 391.
69. *Close rolls, 1234–37*, pp. 163, 362; *Pat. rolls, 1216–25*, p. 337; PRO, Chancery Miscellanea, Bdl. 2, no. 1, m. 9.
70. PROI, Memoranda rolls 4–5 Edward II (Rec. Comm. calendar, v, pp. 653–54), 9 Edward II (Rec. Comm. calendar, x, pp. 653–54); *Rotuli Scotie*, i, 138.
71. See my Ph.D. thesis, chs. IV–V passim.
72. PRO, E.101/237/4–5; E.372/171, mm. 25–26; W. Laird Clowes, *The Royal Navy*, i, 325–27; Reid, W.S., 'Trade, Traders and Scottish Independence', *Speculum*, xxxix (1954), 220–21.
73. For the capture of Man see Moore, A.W., 'The Connexion between Scotland and Man', *Scottish Historical Review*, iii, no. 12 (July 1906), 405.
74. Sayles, G.O., 'The Siege of Carrickfergus Castle, 1315–16', *I.H.S.*, x. no. 37 (March 1956), 98–99.
75. PRO, E101/309/19, m. 3 – for particulars of de Hothum's account of his expenses for his mission to Ireland.
76. *Ann. Loch Cé*, i, 595.
77. *Tribes and Customs of Hy-Many*, p. 137.
78. PRO, S.C. 8/130/6480. I am indebted to Dr Geoffrey Hand for this reference.
79. *Cal. doc. Scotland, 1307–57*, no. 922.
80. The huge quantity of supplies sent from Ireland for the Scottish campaign of 1322 and afterwards suggests this – Stowe, B.M., MSS., 553, ff 47–48v; PRO, E.101–16/7–8, 20–21, 238/5.
81. Butler, R. (ed.), *The Annals of Ireland by Friar John Clyn* (Irish Archaeological Society, 1849), p. 12.

4 – The Scottish Soldier Abroad: the Bruce Invasion and the Galloglass

1. The full text is printed by Bryan, D., *The Great Earl of Kildare* (Dublin, 1933), 18–19. There is an important correction from the original MS in Otway-Ruthven, A.J., *A History of Medieval Ireland* (hereafter *Med. Irel.)* (London, 1968), 396, n. 34.
2. Nicholson, R.G., *Scotland in the Later Middle Ages* (Edinburgh, 1974), 478–79.
3. The standard accounts are Armstrong, O., *Edward Bruce's Invasion of Ireland* (London, 1923); Orpen, G.H., *Ireland Under the Normans* (Oxford, 1920), iv, ch. xxxvii; Otway-Ruthven, *Med. Irel.,* 224–38; Lydon, J.F. in Cosgrove, A. (ed.), *A New History of Ireland* (hereafter *New Hist. Irel.)* (Oxford, 1987), 281–94, for which see Chapter 6 above.
4. Lydon, J.F., 'The Bruce Invasion of Ireland', in Hayes-McCoy, G.A., (ed.), *Historical Studies,* i (London, 1963), 111–25, and Chapter 3 above.
5. Berry, H.F. (ed.), *Statutes and Ordinances of Ireland, King John to Henry V* (Dublin, 1907), p. 245.
6. De Passagno certainly received payment and later contracted with 'Jordano de Insula' to go to Ireland with 200 men-at-arms and 20,000 foot (PRO, E. 159/93, m. 76).
7. Lydon, J.F., *New Hist. Irel.,* 197–201, above, pp. 119–22.
8. Frame, R., 'The Bruces in Ireland' (hereafter Frame, R., 'Bruces'), *Irish Historical Studies,* xix (1974), 224–51.
9. Nicholson, R.G., 'A sequel to Edward Bruce's invasion of Ireland', *Scottish Historical Review* (hereafter *SHR),* xiii (1963), 38–39; see Chapter 7 above.
10. Freeman, A.M. (ed.), *Annála Connacht: the Annals of Connacht* (hereafter *An. Con.),* (Dublin, 1944), 249.
11. Duffy, S., 'The Bruce brothers and the Celtic alliance', *Cambridge Medieval Celtic Studies,* 21, (1991), 64–65; see Chapter 2 above.
12. Barrow, G.W.S., *Robert Bruce* (3rd edn, Edinburgh, 1988), 169.
13. Bain, J., *et al.,* (eds), *Calendar of Documents relating to Scotland* (5 vols., Edinburgh, 1881–1986), iv. p. 489; v. no. 492 (xvi).
14. Frame, R., 'Bruces', 5.
15. Phillips, J.R.S., 'Documents on the early stages of the Bruce invasion of Ireland, 1315–16', *Proceedings of the Royal Irish Academy,* 79 (1979), nos 10, 15, 16.
16. Duncan, A.A.M., 'The Scots invasion of Ireland, 1315' in Davies, R.R. (ed.), *The British Isles 1100–1500* (Edinburgh, 1988), 103, 113.
17. Gilbert, J.T. (ed.), *Chartul. St Mary's, Dublin* (London, 1884), ii, 346, 34.
18. Rothwell, H. (ed.), *The Chronicle of Walter of Guisborough* (London, 1957), 397.
19. Stevenson, J. (ed.), *Chronicon de Lanercost* (Edinburgh, 1839), 205.
20. Frame, R., 'Bruces', 35–36.
21. Phillips, J.R.S., 'Documents', (as above, n. 15), nos 4, 7.
22. Lydon, J.F., *New Hist. Irel.,* 291–92; above, p. 138.
23. Douglas, A.A.H. (ed.), *The Bruce... by John Barbour,* translated by A.A.H. Douglas (Glasgow, 1964), 528; above, p. 163. Uniquely, the government gave financial assistance to the 'community of Dundalk', late in 1315, to help 'relieve and repair' the damage caused by the Scots (PRO, E. 101/237/4).
24. Butler, R. (ed.), *The Annals of Ireland by Friar John Clyn* (hereafter Clyn) (Dublin, 1849), 12.

25. *Chartul. St Mary's, Dublin*, ii, 345.
26. Clyn, 12.
27. Mac Airt, S. (ed.), *The Annals of Inisfallen* (Dublin, 1951), 419.
28. *An. Con.*, 253; but cf. above, p. 44.
29. Lucas, H.S., 'The great European famine of 1315, 1316 and 1317' in Carus-Wilson, E.M. (ed.), *Essays in Economic History* (London, 1962), ii, 40–72. In Ireland the famine lasted a year longer to 1318.
30. *Chartul. St Mary's, Dublin*, ii, 349.
31. Tresham, E. (ed.), *Rotulorum Patentium et Clausorum Cancellarie Hibernie Calendarium* (Dublin, 1828), 30, no. 2; PRO, E.101/238/17.
32. PRO, E.101/237/9; *Chartul. St Mary's, Dublin*, ii, cxxviii.
33. Ibid., 360.
34. MacCarthy, B. (ed.), *Annals of Ulster* (Dublin, 1893), ii, 433.
35. Nicholson, R.G., 'Sequel' (as above, n. 9), 33; above, p. 155.
36. PRO, E.101/239/5; Frame, R., *English Lordship in Ireland 1318–61* (Oxford, 1982), 141.
37. Nicholson, R.G., 'Sequel' (as above, n. 9), 34; above, pp. 156–57.
38. *Chartul. St Mary's, Dublin*, ii, 367.
39. Clyn, 20.
40. Berry, H.F., *Statutes,* (as above, n. 5), 485.
41. The justiciar in August led a force to recover parts of Ulster 'lately destroyed and devastated by Irish and Scots of the outer isles' (MacNeill, C., 'Lord Chancellor Gerrard's Notes of his Report on Ireland', *Analecta Hibernica, 2* (1931), 206).
42. Otway-Ruthven, A.J., *Med. Irel.*, 368.
43. *An. Con.*, 249.
44. Ibid., 185.
45. Hennessy, W.M. (ed.), *The Annals of Loch Cé* (London, 1871), i, 451.
46. Ibid., 435.
47. *An. Con.*, 91. This 'king of Argyll' is quite probably Somerled's grandson, Duncan, lord of Lorn in Argyll, who is known to have died between 1244 and 1248 (Duncan, A.A.M. & Brown, A.L., 'Argyll and the Isles in the earlier Middle Ages', *Proceedings of the Society of Antiquaries of Scotland,* xc, (1956–57), 197 (table), 200, 202). I am indebted to Dr Grant G Simpson for this reference.
48. Simms, K., *From Kings to Warlords* (Cambridge, 1987), 118.
49. Ibid., ch. viii.
50. Candon, A., 'Muirchertach Ua Briain, politics, and naval activity in the Irish Sea, 1075–1119' in Mac Niocaill, G. & Wallace, P.F. (eds), *Keimelia* (Galway, 1988), 411.
51. Lydon, J.F., 'The hobelar: an Irish contribution to medieval warfare', *Irish Sword,* ii (1954), 12–16.
52. O'Meara, J.J., *The First Version of the Topography of Ireland by Giraldus Cambrensis* (Dundalk, 1951), 85.
53. The classic text is Hayes-McCoy, G.A., *Scots Mercenary Forces in Ireland* (Dublin, 1937). Despite the publication of McKerral, A., 'West Highland mercenaries in Ireland', *SHR,* xxx (1951), 1–14, the subject has been almost totally ignored by Scottish historians.
54. Curtis, E., *Richard II in Ireland* (Oxford, 1927), 58, 87–88, 150, 175–76.
55. Ibid., 98, 185.
56. Ibid., 228.
57. Lawlor, H.J., 'Fragments of a lost register of the diocese of Clogher', *County Louth Archaeological*

Journal, 4 (1916–20), 250.

58. Simms, K., *Kings to Warlords,* 122.
59. Ibid., 105, 131, 135–36, 139.
60. Hayes-McCoy, G.A., (as above, n. 553, ch. 2).
61. *Chartul. St Mary's, Dublin,* ii, 340.
62. *Annals of Inisfallen,* (as above, n. 27), 407.
63. *An. Con.,* 223.
64. Sayles, G.O., 'The rebellious first earl of Desmond', in Watt, J.A., Morral, J.B. & Martin, F.X., (eds), *Medieval Studies Presented to Aubrey Gwynn, SJ* (Dublin, 1961), 209.
65. Sayles, G.O., 'The legal proceedings against the first earl of Desmond', *Analecta Hibernica,* 23 (1966), 20–21.
66. Ibid., 17.
67. PRO, E. 101/28/21, fo. 8, in Connolly, P.M., 'Lionel of Clarence and Ireland 1361–66' (Ph.D, University of Dublin, 1977), 135.
68. Empey, C.A. & Simms, K., 'The Ordinances of the White earl and the problem of coign in the later Middle Ages', *Proceedings of the Royal Irish Academy,* 75 (1975), 186.
69. Otway-Ruthven, A.J., *Med. Irel.,* 353.
70. Curtis, E. (ed.), *Calendar of Ormond Deeds 1509–47* (Dublin, 1937), 44–45.
71. *State Papers Henry VIII* (hereafter *S.P. Hen. VIII*), ii, part III (London, 1834), 502.
72. Hayes-McCoy, G.A., *Irish Battles* (London, 1969), 48–67.
73. Ellis, S. (ed.), *Calendar of State Papers Ireland: Henry VIII* (forthcoming), nos 83, 98 (ii).
74. Curtis, E., (as above n. 70), 357.
75. Conway, A., *Henry VII's Relations with Scotland and Ireland* (Cambridge, 1932), 196–97; Gairdner, J. (ed.), *Letters and Papers Illustrative of the Reigns of Richard III and Henry VII* (London, 1863), ii, 312, 316.
76. *S.P. Hen. VIII,* ii, part III, 13.
77. Ibid., 507.
78. Ellis, S., (as above, n. 73), no. 1109; *S.P. Hen. VIII,* iii, 173, 318 n. 1.
79. Ibid., 146, 133; Price, L., 'Armed forces of the Irish chiefs in the early sixteenth century,' *Journal of the Royal Society of Antiquaries of Ireland,* 62 (1932), 201–07.
80. Dorrian, D., 'The Cockpit of Ireland: Northwest Ulster 1540–1603 (BA, University of Dublin, 1985), 5.
81. Dawson, J.E.A., 'Two kingdoms or three?' in Mason, R.A. (ed.), *Scotland and England, 1286–1815* (Edinburgh, 1987), 113–15.
82. *S.P. Hen. VIII,* ii, 25.
83. Ibid., iii, 444.
84. Ibid., ii, 1, 5, 6.

5 – The Battle of Faughart

1. The script of a lecture broadcast by Radio Éireann in 1955–56. For contemporary evidence for Edward Bruce's activities in Ireland, see Sayles, G.O., *Documents on the Affairs of Ireland before the*

King's Council (Irish Manuscripts Commission, 1979), pp. 72–76, 78–80, 90, 94, 97–98, 101, 103–06.

6 – The Impact of the Bruce Invasion, 1315–27

1. Lydon, J.F., 'Edward I, Ireland and Scotland', p. 54.
2. *Cal. justic. rolls Ire., 1305–07,* pp. 268–69.
3. *Cal. doc. Ire., 1302–07,* no. 515.
4 Lydon, J.F., 'Edward I, Ireland and Scotland', p. 56.
5. Lydon, J.F., 'Enrolled account of Bicknor', p. 13.
6. PROI, RC 8/6 (mem. roll 5 Edw. II), *passim.*
7. PROI, RC 8/9 (mem. roll 7 Edward II), p. 9. Two years previously the Irish council had ordered an inquiry into such defects, but nothing had been done (RC 8/6 (mem. roll 5 Edward II), pp. 221–22).
8. *Cal. close rolls, 1308–13,* p. 484.
9. *P.R.I. rep. D.K. 39,* p. 32.
10. For this and what follows see Lydon, J.F., 'Edward II and the revenues of Ireland'.
11. PRO, E. 101/236/3; 236/7.
12. PRO, R.C. 8/6 (mem. roll 5 Edward II), pp. 255–56; *Rot. Scotie,* i, 24.
13. *Cal. pat. rolls, 1313–17,* p. 234.
14. *Rot. Scotie,* i, 138. In July a clerk was sent to Ireland 'with divers sums of money' for wages *(Cal. pat. rolls, 1313–17,* p. 333).
15. PRO, E. 101/238/1, 238/6.
16. PRO, E. 101/16/16. With the earl of Louth, it included four bannerets, six knights, sixty-three men at arms, 189 hobelars, and ninety-three foot. Of the £1,249 received for wages, only £526 came from the Irish exchequer.
17. *Stat. Ire., John-Hen. V,* p. 265.
18. Richardson & Sayles, *Ir. Parl. in Middle Ages,* p. 292.
19. Cole, H. (ed.), *Documents illustrative of English history in the thirteenth and fourteenth centuries* (London, 1844), p. 71.
20. *Cal. justic. Rolls Ire., 1305–07,* p. 252.
21. *Stat. Ire. John-Hen. V,* p. 307.
22. Richardson & Sayles, *Ir. Parl. in Middle Ages,* p. 129.
23. *Stat. Ire. John-Hen. V,* p. 271.
24. *Chartul. St Mary's, Dublin,* ii, 194.
25. Hand, G.J., *Eng. Law in Ire.,* p. 172.
26. *Chartul. St Mary's, Dublin,* ii, 294.
27. *Cal. justic. rolls Ire., 1308–14,* p. 200.
28. PRO, E. 101/235/24.
29. *Cal. justic. rolls Ire., 1308–14,* pp. 145–46, 199–200, 247.
30. *Rot. pat. Hib.,* p. 14, no. 222.
31. *Cal. justic. rolls Ire.,* 1308–14, pp. 159–60.

32. *Cal. close rolls, 1307–13*, p. 181.
33. Ibid., pp. 413, 416, 422.
34. The main outline is in Otway-Ruthven, A.J., *Med. Ire.,* pp. 222–23.
35. *Chartul. St Mary's, Dublin*, ii, 340.
36. *Cal justic. rolls Ire., 1308–14*, p. 278.
37. *Chartul. St Mary's, Dublin*, ii, 341. Many were killed by the rebels.
38. Richardson & Sayles, *Admin. Ire.*, p. 83.
39. *Chartul. St Mary's, Dublin*, ii, 341.
40. Butler, R. (ed.), *Annals of Ireland by Thady Dowling* (Dublin, 1849), p. 19.
41. *Chartul. St Mary's, Dublin*, ii, 342.
42. Ibid., p. 344. Most authorities accept Larne as the actual landing place. There is a basic narrative in Armstrong, O., *Edward Bruce's Invasion of Ireland* (London, 1923); Orpen, G.H., *Normans*, iv, 160–206; Otway-Ruthven, A.J., *Med. Ire.*, pp. 224–56. Especially important is Frame, R., 'The Bruces in Ireland' in *IHS.,* xix, no. 73 (Mar. 1974), pp. 3–37. See also Lydon, J.F., 'The Bruce invasion of Ireland' in *Hist. Studies*, iv (1963), pp. 111–25 (Chapter 3 above), and the important collection of documents, Phillips, J.R.S. (ed.), 'Documents on the early stages of the Bruce invasion of Ireland', 1315–16, in *R.I.A. Proc.,* ixxix (1979), sect. C, pp. 247–70.
43. Barrow, G.W.S., *Robert Bruce and the community of the realm of Scotland* (2nd ed., Edinburgh, 1976), pp. 411–12.
44. Phillips, J.R.S., 'Documents', p. 269.
45. The text will be found in Nicholson, R.G., 'A sequel to Edward Bruce's invasion of Ireland' in *Scot. Hist. Rev.*, xiii, no. 133 (April 1963), pp. 38–39 above Chapter 7. A convenient translation is in Barrow, G.W.S., *Robert Bruce*, p. 434. But by rendering *nostra natio* as 'your nation' Barrow has completely altered the meaning of Bruce's appeal.
46. *Hist. & mun. doc. Ire.,* pp. 377–78; for a suggested re-dating of the document, see above pp. 51–52.
47. *Ann. Conn.,* p. 249. In a letter to the king, Nicholas de Verdon also reported that the Scots intended to conquer Ireland with the aid of the Irish (Phillips, S.R.S., 'Documents', no. 15).
48. Appendix B above.
49. The annals in recording the invasion of Robert Bruce in 1317 say that he brought 'many gallowglasses with him' (*Ann. Conn.*, p. 249).
50. Wood, H., 'Letter from Domnall O Neill to Fineen Mac Carthy, 1317' in *R.I.A. Proc.,* xxxvii (1926), sect. C, p. 143. This was not the first time an appeal had been made. In the mid-thirteenth century Gilla Brigte Mac Con Midhe addressed a poem to O Domhnaill appealing for unity between Cenél Eoghain and Cenél Conaill against 'the foreigner' (Mac Con Midhe, *Poems*, pp. 12–21).
51. *A.L.C,* i, 579.
52. Pipe roll 9 Edward II in *P.R.I. rep. D.K. 39*, p. 65.
53. *Ann. Conn.,* p. 253.
54. Ibid., p. 241.
55. *Chartul. St Mary's, Dublin,* ii, 345.
56. For a detailed account of the invasion and Edward's first campaign see Mac Iomhair, D., 'Bruce's invasion of Ireland and first campaign in County Louth' in *Ir. Sword,* x (1971–72), pp. 188–212.
57. PRO, E. 101/237/4.

58. Clyn, *Annals*, p. 12.
59. PRO, E. 101/237/4.
60. *Chartul. St Mary's, Dublin*, ii, 345.
61. *Ann. Inisf*, p. 419.
62. Pipe roll 10 Edward II in *P.R.I. rep. D.K. 39*, p. 71.
63. *Cal. Close rolls, 1313–18*, p. 186.
64. Phillips, J.R.S., 'Documents', p. 249.
65. *Cal. doc. Scot. 1307–57*, no. 448.
66. For de Hothum's embassy, and the Bruce invasion in general, see the important paper by Phillips, J.R.S., 'The mission of John de Hothum to Ireland, 1315–16' in Lydon, J.F., *Eng. & Ire.*, pp. 62–85.
67. Phillips, J.R.S., 'Documents', p. 251.
68. PRO, E. 101/237/2 (issue roll 1314–15). Total receipt for the year came to only £2,968 (E. 101/237/1; receipt roll 1314–15). So money was scarce.
69. *Hist. & mun. doc. Ire.*, pp. 327–28, 334–37, 340–52.
70. PROI, KB 1/2 (plea roll 1312–18), m. 17. Fitz Thomas later told the king that the Irish in Desmond had united against him because of the invasion (Phillips, J.R.S., 'Documents', no. 14).
71. *Chartul. St Mary's, Dublin*, ii, 347.
72. *Cal. close rolls, 1313–18,* p. 189. The full text is in Phillips, J.R.S., 'Documents', no. 5.
73. Clyn, *Annals*, p. 16.
74. Sayles, G.O., 'The siege of Carrickfergus castle, 1315–16' in *I.H.S.*, x, no. 37 (March 1956), pp. 94–100.
75. Phillips, J.R.S., 'Documents', no. 47.
76. PRO, E. 101/237/4 (issue roll 1315–16). The following year only £262 was given to de Balscot and £40 to Adam de la More, clerk of the wages in the Leinster army (E. 101/237/5 (issue roll 1316–17)).
77. *Hist. & mun. doc. Ire.*, pp. 372–86.
78. PRO, E. 101/309/19, m. 3, now in Phillips, J.R.S., 'Documents', p. 267.
79. Barrow, G.W.S., *Robert Bruce*, pp. 25–26.
80. Thompson, E.M. (ed.), *Adae Murimuth continuatio chronicarum* (Rolls Series, London, 1889), p. 30.
81. *Hist. & mun. doc. Ire.*, pp. 359–65.
82. Sayles, G.O., *Affairs of Ire.*, no. 140.
83. PRO, S.C. 6/1239/13, now edited by Robin Frame as 'The campaign against the Scots in Munster, 1317' in *I.H.S.*, xxiv, no. 95 (May 1985), pp. 362–72.
84. Watt, J.A., 'Negotiations between Edward II and John XXII concerning Ireland' in *I.H.S.*, x, no. 37 (Mar. 1956), pp. 1–20; Watt, J.A., *Ch. & two nations*, pp. 183–89.
85. *Cal. doc. Scot., 1307–57*, no. 480.
86. For a view of this important document in another context see Muldoon, J., 'The remonstrance of the Irish princes and the canon law tradition of the just war' in *Amer. Jn. Legal. Hist.*, xxii (1978), pp. 309–25.
87. *Chartul. St Mary's, Dublin*, ii, 359.
88. *Ann. Conn.*, p. 253.
89. Ibid.
90. PRO, E. 101/237/9. The news was then added to the Red Book of the exchequer (*Chartul. St*

Mary's, Dublin, ii, p. cxxviii, n. 2).

91. *Chartul. St Mary's, Dublin*, ii, 360.
92. *Ann. Conn.*, p. 253; bu cf. above, p. 44.
93. O'Donovan, J. (ed.), *The tribes and customs of Hy Many, commonly called O'Kelly's country* (Irish Archaeological Society, Dublin, 1843), p. 137.
94. *Caithr. Thoirdh.*, ii, 83.
95. Sayles, G.O., *Affairs of Ire.*, nos 127–28.
96. *Hist. & mun doc. Ire.*, pp. 456–62.
97. Hand, G.J., 'The dating of the early fourteenth-century ecclesiastical valuations of Ireland' in *Ir. Theol. Quart.*, xxix (1957), p. 273.
98. Sayles, G.O., *Affairs of Ire.*, p. 228.
99. Pipe roll 12 Edward II in *P.R.I. rep. D.K. 42*, pp. 33–34.
100. Clyn, *Annals*, p. 12. See, too, the letter of Maurice fitz Thomas that reported that all the Irish were united by the invasion and were ready for war (Phillips, J.R.S., 'Documents', no. 14).
101. *Cal. pat. rolls, 1317–21*, p. 535.
102. Sayles, G.O., *Affairs of Ire.*, no. 151.
103. Hand, G.J., *Eng. Law in Ire.*, pp. 35–36, 141.
104. Ibid., p. 36.
105. *Ann. Conn.*, pp. 263, 265.
106. *Chartul. St Mary's, Dublin*, ii, 361.
107. Gwynn, A., 'The medieval university of St Patrick's, Dublin' in *Studies*, xxvii (1938), pp. 199–212, 437–54.
108. *Stat. Ire., John-Hen.* V, pp. 281–91.
109. Ibid., p. 307.
110. Sayles, G.O., 'The rebellious first earl of Desmond' in *Med. studies presented to A. Gwynn*, pp. 203–27. An indispensable commentary is provided by Frame, R., *Eng. lordship*, especially pp. 157–95.
111. Sayles, G.O., 'The legal proceedings against the first earl of Desmond' in *Anal Hib.*, no. 23 (1966), p. 8.
112. Ibid., pp. 8–9, 17–28.
113. Ibid., p. 8.
114. Ibid., p. 6. For the date see Frame, R., *Eng. lordship*, p. 180, n. 101.
115. Frame, R., *Eng. lordship*, pp. 169–73.
116. Ibid., pp. 176–82.
117. *Chartul. St Mary's, Dublin*, ii, p. 365.
118. *Chartul. St Mary's, Dublin*, p. 364.
119. Lydon, J.F., 'The Braganstown massacre, 1329' in *Louth Arch. Soc. Jn.*, xix (1977), pp. 5–16.
120. Clyn, *Annals*, p. 20.
121. Orpen, G.H., *Normans*, iv, 245–49.
122. Baldwin, J.F., *The King's Council in England during the middle ages* (Oxford, 1913), p. 473.
123. *Hy Many*, p. 139.
124. Clyn, *Annals*, p. 30.
125. *Chartul. St Mary's, Dublin*, ii, pp. 365–66.
126. Ibid., p. 366.

127. Nicholson, R.G., 'A sequel to Edward Bruce's invasion of Ireland' in *Scot. Hist. Rev.,* xiii (1963), p. 32 (Chapter 7 above); Frame, R., *Eng. lordship,* pp. 138–41.
128. Ibid., p. 141. More important, the king's castle of Leixlip was garrisoned 'contra Scotos felones et inimicos' (PRO, E. 101/239/5).

7 – A Sequel to Edward Bruce's Invasion of Ireland

1. This article has profited from the helpful comments of Dr Geoffrey Hand and Dr James Lydon.
2. Lt. Col. J.R.H. Greeves has already outlined Robert Bruce's 'two curious reappearances in Ulster', in his well-informed article, 'Robert I and the De Mandevilles of Ulster' in *Transactions of the Dumfriesshire and Galloway Natural History and Antiquarian Society*, 3rd series, xxxiv, 59–73.
3. *Foedera* (Record Commission edition), ii, pt i, 523.
4. *Foedera,* ii, pt i, 521.
5. *Chronicon de Lanercost* (Bannatyne Club), 256–57. The Franciscan Friar Henry Cogery might possibly have been sent either to arrange or to countermand this scheme: on 6 February 1327 letters close were issued for payment of forty shillings for his expenses on a mission from Ireland to Scotland on certain special business touching the king. (Tresham, E. (ed.), *Rotulorum Patentium et Clausorum Cancellariae Hiberniae Calendarium,* vol. i, pt i, 36, no. 77).
6. See Appendix 1.
7. Edward Bruce had reputedly held parliaments in Ulster (*Jacobi Grace Kilkenniensis Annales Hiberniae*) afterwards cited as the *Grace Annals* – Butler, R. (ed.), Irish Archaeological Society, 1842, 71).
8. O'Donovan, J. (ed.), *Annals of the Kingdom of Ireland by the Four Masters,* (1848), i, 537.
9. The account of the bailies of Ayr rendered at Dumbarton on 4 February 1327/8 mentions the provision of empty casks 'pro victualibus cariandis vsque in Hibernia' (*Exchequer Rolls of Scotland,* i, 69); among the 'marts' for which the household clerk, John Logan, accounted for the period 17 February 1327/8–12 May 1329 were '*xlvj captis de balliuis Vltonie*' and '*ij de exennio per tempus compoti*' (Ibid., 196).
10. Appendix II.
11. Appendix II.
12. See Armstrong, O., *Edward Bruce's Invasion of Ireland* (1923), 67–68; 97–98.
13. *Lanercost,* 259; *Calendar of Close Rolls, 1327–30,* 157 (18 August 1327), 212 (26 June 1327); *Calendar of Patent Rolls, 1327–30,* 139 (22 July 1327).
14. Appendix II.
15. For his background see Greeves, J.R.H., loc. cit., pp. 59–73.
16. A contemporary transcript of the document exists in the PRO, Diplomatic Documents, Exchequer, Treasury of Receipt, E. 30, 1536, no. 1. A version in a modern transcript is contained in British Museum, Additional MSS., no. 25,459, ff. 126–33. The indenture, but not the covering letter, is calendared by Bain, J., in *Calendar of Documents relating to Scotland,* iii, no. 922, p. 167.
17. One 'cendre' was equated with ten quarters (British Museum, Additional MSS., no. 25,459, fo. 129v). The twenty-one chalders, nine bolls 'de frumento Hybernie' mentioned in the account of

John of Dunfermline, clerk of the liverance of King Robert's household, were probably forthcoming from these tributary payments (*Exchequer Rolls of Scotland*, i, 186).

18. *Et le dit roy Descoce ad reserue deuers ly en ceste acorde touz les Hyrois Duluestre qi volent estre les soens e a sa foi de quele condicioun qe il soyent enclos dedentz ceste sa suffraunce*' (PRO, Diplomatic Documents, Exchequer, Treasury of Receipt, E. 30, 1536, no. 1).
19. See Armstrong, O., op. cit., 135.
20. *Rotulorum Patentium et Clausorum Cancellariae Hiberniae Calendarium, i,* pt i, 35, no. 47 (14 August 1326).
21. See *Rotulorum Patentium et Clausorum Cancellariae Hiberniae Calendarium, i,* pt i, 83 and 34.
22. See Public Record Office, Diplomatic Documents, Exchequer, Treasury of Receipt, E. 30, 1536, no. 1, and British Museum, Additional MSS., no. 25,459, ff. 126–33.
23. British Museum, Additional MSS., no. 25,459, fo. 132v.
24. British Museum, Additional MSS., no. 25,459, fo. 130.
25. See Nicholson, R.G., 'The Last Campaign of Robert Bruce' in *English Historical Review*, lxxvii (1962), 233–46.
26. See Stones, Prof. E.L.G., 'The Anglo-Scottish Negotiations of 1327', *Scottish Hist. Rev.*, xxx (1951), 49–54.
27. *Foedera*, ii, pt ii, 740–41.
28. The Bruce (Scottish Text Society), ii, 174.
29. See the *Laud Annals* (p. 367) printed in vol. ii of the *Chartul. St Mary's, Dublin* (Rolls Series); also the *Grace Annals*, 108–09.
30. Supra, p. 156.
31. Bruce's second wife was Elizabeth de Burgh, daughter of the Red Earl of Ulster, so that she was aunt to William, and her son, David Bruce, was his full cousin. She died on 26 October 1327.
32. For the diplomatic mission entrusted to her at this time see Stones, Prof. E.L.G., 'An Addition to the 'Rotuli Scotiae', *Scottish Hist. Rev.*, xxix (1950), 24–51.
33. PRO, Chancery Warrants, C. 81, file 154, no. 1880.
34. PRO, Chancery warrants, C. 81, file 154, no. 1880. The petition is calendared by Bain, J., op. cit., iii, no. 963, p. 174.
35. PRO, Chancery Warrants, C. 81, file 154, no. 1880, dorse.
36. PRO, Chancery Warrants, C. 81, file 157, no. 2195.
37. See the *Grace Annals,* 108–11; *Laud Annals,* 367; *The Annals of Loch Cé* (Rolls Series), i, 607. The only surviving Scottish record suggestive of this episode seems to be the account of John Logan rendered at Scone on 24 August 1329, which mentions a present of 200 stock-fish made by Bruce to the earl of Ulster *(Exchequer Rolls of Scotland,* i, 199).
38. The treaty of Northampton had stipulated that the rights of the church should be safeguarded. A number of Scottish religious houses accordingly petitioned for the restitution of the lands and possessions of which they had been deprived by English kings. On 28 October 1328 the justiciar of Ireland was instructed to take action in favour of the abbot of Dundrennan *(Foedera,* ii, pt ii, 758). A further order under the privy seal was addressed to the justiciar on 5 December 1328, but the justiciar neglected to comply with it, ostensibly because a grant of 9 May 1328 had conveyed a liferent of the lands to Thomas de Warilowe at the request of Roger Mortimer (PRO, Chancery Miscellanea, C. 47, bundle 10, file 10, no. 1).

39. King John had granted these lands to Alan of Galloway (Bain, J., *Calendar of Documents relating to Scotland,* i, nos 578, 58S, 625,764, 890, 905), Thomas of Atholl (ibid, i, nos 585, 586, 627, 722, 830, 857, 891) and Duncan of Carrick (ibid., i, nos 874, 878, 879).
40. *Grace, Annals*, 108–11; *Laud Annals*, 367.
41. *Grace, Annals*, 108–11; *Laud Annals*, 367.
42. Greeves, J.R.H., loc. cit., p. 61.

Appendix A – *The Brus* – the History of Robert the Bruce King of Scots

1. Now Lough Larne.
2. Probably the Moiry Pass, in Killevy parish, Armagh.
3. Edmund Butler was really the Justiciary or Lord-Lieutenant of Ireland at the time, though Richard of Clare was a conspicuous figure; there may also be some confusion with Richard de Burgh.
4. Professor Skeat argues the 'great river' to have been the Blackwater, and the lough edge the western shore of Lough Neagh, but a location in Leinster is preferable.
5. i.e. until 13 April 1316.
7. Fifty years earlier the same feat was done at Tarbert by Hakon of Norway, and two centuries earlier still, Magnus Barefoot drew his galleys across the isthmus.
8. According to Hailes, King Robert's Irish campaign took place in the autumn and early spring of 1316–17.
9. The king's nephew, son of Lady Mary Bruce and Sir Neil Campbell, Bruce's early adherent, ancestor of the house of Argyll.
10. Now the counties of Louth aud Monaghan.

Appendix B – The Remonstrance of the Irish Princes to Pope John XXII, 1317

1. *Recte* 1155, for the Bull of Adrian IV.
2. For this statute of the parliament at Kilkenny in 1310 see Curtis, E., *Medieval Ireland* (1938), I, p. 180. It was immediately revoked by order of the king. The Archbishop of Armagh referred to is Walter Joce or Jorz.
3. Muircheartach O Conchobhair, his kinsman Maelmorda, and Calbhach O Conchobhair with twenty-nine chiefs of his people were slain by Sir Piarus MacFeoruis by treachery and deceit in MacFeorais's castle (F.M. ann. 1305.) For the treacherous murder of Murchertach O Conor of Offaly and his leading men by Piers Bermingham in 1305, see Curtis, E., *Medieval Ireland* (p. 181). Maurice de S. in the text is a scribe's error.
4. 'Brian Ruadh Ua Briain was treacherously taken by the son of the earl of Clare (*sic*) and afterwards drawn between horses, and after this both had entered into gossipred with each other, and taken vows by bells and relics to retain mutual friendship' (F.M. ann. 1277).

This case, or Remonstrance, of the Irish chiefs, led by Donal O Neill, king of Cenél Eoghain or Tyrone, against English oppression, was addressed to the Avignon Pope John XXII in the latter part of 1317, apparently through two papal nuncios, Luke and Gaucelin, who were then in England attempting to make peace between Edward II and Robert Bruce. For a summary of it and a comment upon the charges contained in it against the English and Anglo-Irish, see Curtis, E., *Medieval Ireland*, pp. 191–93.

The Latin original of the Remonstrance is found only in the *Scotichronicon* of John Fordun, a Scottish historian of the Bruce wars, who died about 1384. It was printed, in imperfect form, by Thomas Hearne in 1722 in his edition of the *Scotichronicon*, vol. III, pp. 908–26. My friend Mr Charles MacNeill has compared this with the Harleian text in the British Museum and kindly allowed me to use it as well as his translation (E. Curtis).

Illustration List

Photographs courtesy of Linzi Simpson unless otherwise stated.

1 – The Bruce Invasion of Ireland: A Revised Itinerary and Chronology

an earlier Richard, grandfather of the earl. The photograph shows a medieval ogee-headed window from a house in Barrack Lane in the town.

13. Geoffrey de Joinville inherited by marriage half of the great de Lacy lordship of Meath, which had Trim Castle at its core, and which then passed to the Mortimers. The photograph shows, under excavation, the mural tower on the walls of Dublin which was called after de Joinville and which he may have used as a residence. Photograph courtesy of C. Walsh.
14. After Roger Mortimer's ignominious defeat at the battle of Kells in December 1315 he fled to Dublin and left Trim Castle in the charge of Walter Cusack. The photograph shows the keep of the castle under excavation, with the barbican gate in the background. Photograph courtesy of A. Hayden.
15. Kildare cathedral: not much of the current fabric of Kildare cathedral is old enough to have witnessed the passage of the Scots through the town in January 1316, but the south trancept and part of the tower probably did.
16. Kildare: this largely overlooked remnant of the medieval fortifications of the town of Kildare may have suffered the assault of the Bruce army in January 1316.
17. Lea Castle, County Laois: John fitz Thomas's magnificent castle at Lea in County Laois is testimony to the control he exerted in this frontier area close to the Irish, but Edward Bruce consigned it to the flames in 1316.
18. Edward Bruce in Ireland, 1315-16. After McNamee, 1997, based on a map by J.F. Lydon in *An Historical Atlas of Scotland, c.400–1600* (St Andrews, 1975), pp. 168–69.
19. These de Verdon lands north of Dundalk were the subject of the predations of raids by the native Ó hAnluain (O Hanlon) dynasty in 1316.
20. Kindlestown Castle, County Wicklow, built to protect the southern approaches to Dublin; the manor lands of Kindlestown Castle were probably among those burned by the O Tooles and O Byrnes during the Bruce wars.
21. The medieval Castle d'Exeter at Slane lay in the path of Robert and Edward Bruce and an estimated army of 20,000 Scots and Irish in mid-February 1317, which is said to have ravaged the countryside roundabout.
22. This is one of the few visible stretches of the medieval town walls of Dublin, which were said to be in a very bad state of disrepair when Robert Bruce approached the city in the early weeks of 1316, although however badly defended the town was, he chose not to attempt an assault.
23. Nenagh Castle, County Tipperary: the town of Nenagh, a possession of the chief governor, Edmund Butler, was an inevitable target of Scottish attack in 1317 as they headed west towards Limerick.
24. Castleconnell, County Limerick: if proof was needed of the earl of Ulster's opposition to Bruce's plans for Ireland it was visible for all to see when the Scots burned Castleconnell in March 1317.
25. Although the capture of Limerick seems to have been their goal in early 1317, the Scots never did manage to cross the Shannon, and the defences of the city were not therefore put to the test.
26. The Bruces in Ireland, 1317. After McNamee, 1997, based on a map by J.F. Lydon in *An Historical Atlas of Scotland, c.400–1600* (St Andrews, 1975), pp. 168–69.
27. The local lords, the de Verdons, had earlier established a settlement at Faughart, as their motte still proves, and Bruce may have diverted his army to the location in order to plunder it.
28. From the hilly ground at Faughart the town of Dundalk is visible below. It was a significant vantage point from which to fight against an army approaching from the town, and the defeat of the Scots must by any standard be deemed a shock result.

2 – The Bruce Brothers and the Irish Sea World, 1306–29

29. Robert Bruce's plans for an alliance of Scots, Irish and, if possible, the Welsh, have been the subject of much speculation over the years, but historians have recently come to view his plans as more than mere make believe; this stylised statue at the entrance to Edinburgh Castle is rather more fanciful. Photograph courtesy of S. Foran.
30. Nothing brings home the closeness of the connection between Ireland and Scotland better the clear sight of one country visible from the other: the photograph, taken at the very castle in which Robert Bruce seems to have spent the winter of 1306–07, has Kintyre in the background.
31. It is more than likely the case that Robert Bruce dispatched his now famous letter to the Irish, describing the Scots and Irish as 'our nation', from the Bisset castle on Rathlin island; little remains of it today, as this photograph shows.
32. There can hardly be a rock-sited castle in Ireland more majestic than Dunluce, County Antrim; although what survives is late, its origins lie in antiquity, and there was a castle here in the Anglo-Norman period, possibly constructed by or under the supervision of Richard de Burgh, Robert Bruce's father-in-law. Its location indicates the importance of the sea-route to Scotland.
33. Like most fortresses that cling to the north Irish Sea littoral and the Western Isles, Dunluce Castle was garrisoned and victualled by sea, probably by means of the extraordinary cave immediately below.
34. The extant remnants of Castle Carra, near Cushendun, County Antrim, may now seem of little consequence, but the land was in the possession of the Bisset family from the mid-thirteenth century, who were presumably its builders (though perhaps at a later date); their transference from Scotland to Ulster at this point is an indication of the vitality of the links between the two countries.
35. One of the most dramatically sited castles on the Irish coast, Kinbane in north Antrim, is all but cut off from the landward side and is testimony to the capacity of the sea to act as a means of communication, in this case between Somerled's MacDonnell descendants and their 'new' home in the Glens of Antrim.
36. This O Conor tomb and effigy in the Dominican priory in Roscommon is ornamented with images of galloglass in full battle dress: they personified the military link between Ireland and western Scotland so prominent from the mid-thirteenth century onwards. Photograph courtesy of F. Verstraten.

3 – The Bruce Invasion of Ireland: an Examination of Some Problems

37. The photograph illustrates the sad remains of the formerly impressive sea-girt castle on Rathlin Island, off the coast of County Antrim, probably built by the Bisset family in the thirteenth century.
38. A view from within what remains of the Bisset castle on Rathlin in which Robert Bruce seems to have stayed, with or without its owners' consent for at least part of the winter of 1306–07. Below is the landing-stage for sea-craft.
39. What is commonly called 'Bruce's Castle' can be seen on this promontory, difficult to access by land; this is the view north-west to the Mull of Kintyre.
40. This is the location of 'Bruce's Castle' with the mainland of Antrim in the distance.

41. This is the only remnant of Olderfleet Castle, which guarded the harbour at Larne, where Robert Bruce was present in August 1328.
42. Carrickfergus Castle presented the greatest challenge to Bruce control over Ulster; the garrison's efforts to hold out against the Scots were not helped by the decision of the earl of Ulster, Richard de Burgh, who was Robert Bruce's father-in-law, to divert to his own use supplies intended for the castle's relief.
43. This is what survives of the ditch surrounding the archbishop of Dublin's castle at Castlekevin, County Wicklow, one of the targets of the resurgent Irish of the Wicklow mountains during the course of Bruce's occupation.

4 – The Scottish Soldier Abroad: the Bruce Invasion and the Galloglass

44. Here, at Church Bay, on Rathlin Island, Robert Bruce would have disembarked in the winter of 1306–07, and no doubt from here he dispatched his letter to possible allies on the Irish mainland, visible in the background.
45. Castletown Mount, near Dundalk, was the caput of the de Verdon family, two members of which, Milo and Nicholas, wrote to Edward II in autumn 1315, stating their view that the Bruces intended the conquest of all Ireland, in alliance with the Irish.
46. Ardscull 'motte': in these fields the battle of Skerries (Ardscull) was fought in January 1316; the army of the Anglo-Irish was very substantial but was forced to yield the field to the Scots 'by mischance', probably because of divisions amongst its leaders.
47. The Franciscan friary, Dundalk: Friar Clyn says that in June 1315 the Scots 'burnt Dundalk and the convent of the Friars; they spoiled books, clothes, chalices and vestments, and they killed many'.
48. Kilkenny Castle did not itself suffer at the hands of the Scots, but it had come into the king's hands following the death at Bannockburn of the last de Clare earl of Gloucester, and the steward (or 'seneschal') of the lordship of Kilkenny, Arnold le Poer, was to the fore in opposing Bruce.
49. There seems little to support the local tradition that the burial site of Edward Bruce, 'king of Ireland', lies in Faughart graveyard: in truth, there can have been little of his body to bury after his enemies had vented their revenge – a contemporary chronicler, based in Dublin, reports that after Edward Bruce was killed at Faughart in 1318, his head was sent to Edward II, his body quartered, his heart, hand and one quarter going to Dublin for public display, and the other quarters to 'other places'. It is, however, a firm conviction in local traditional memory, which asserts that he was buried in Faughart graveyard where this memorial was erected in the mid-nineteenth century. The formal marking out of the 'grave' seems to have been undertaken by local nationalist admirers of Bruce, led by the antiquarian Nicholas O'Kearney.
50. Nenagh Castle contains the finest of the round towers attached to medieval Irish castles (although the upper parts are modern); the property of the Butlers, their lordship of Tipperary was host to large contingents of galloglass certainly by the early fifteenth century, part of the personal retinue of the Butler earls of Ormond.

5 – The Battle of Faughart

51. Traditionally regarded as the birth-place of St Brigid, the shrine at Faughart is still a place of deep devotion to this day.
52. In Faughart graveyard, some way distant from the modern shrine to St Brigid, can be found this holy well dedicated to her.
53. There was an Anglo-Norman manor established at Faughart in the thirteenth century, at the core of which stands the motte pictured here.
54. This photograph, taken from the top of the de Verdon motte at Faughart, shows the medieval parish graveyard in the background.
55. What remains of the medieval parish church of Faughart, at the core of the de Verdon manor, and near the field of battle.
56. This is the view south from the ancient shrine of St Brigid at Faughart and may be the battle-site.
57. The approach to Faughart from Dundalk (in the distance): tactically, from the Scots' perspective, this would make the best vantage point from which to counter the approaching Anglo-Irish army.

6 – The Impact of the Bruce Invasion, 1315–27

58. The familiar Sugarloaf Mountain is located in what was the royal manor of Obrun (from Uí Briúin Chualainn) in the northern foothills of the Wicklow mountains. The justiciar, John Wogan, campaigned here in 1306, but the area continued to present the government with problems and was a cause of concern especially during the Bruce wars.
59. Limerick Castle, described in 1314, on the eve of the Bruce invasion, as being 'situated in the dangerous march between the English and the Irish', and 'threatened with ruin and fallen down and broken on all sides'.
60. The site of Carrickmines Castle, in south County Dublin; here the government came face to face with the Irish of the Wicklow mountains, and the rebellious Harold and Archbold families. Only the remains of one wall survive, incorporated into a barn, but recent archaeological excavations have revealed a series of ditches revetted in stone which may have served a defensive purpose.
61. Castleroche, County Louth, one of the principal lines of defence of the English of County Louth, who remained loyal throughout the Bruce invasion even though the family who built Roche, the de Verdons, were themselves in rebellion against the crown as recently as 1312.
62. Trim Castle: the so-called 'de Verdon Rebellion' was only brought to an end by the intervention of the lord of Trim, Roger Mortimer (the photograph shows the barbican gate under excavation). Photograph courtesy of A. Hayden.
63. Roscrea Castle: the Tipperary-based magnate, Edmund Butler, can hardly have anticipated the arduous appointment he accepted when he agreed to become justiciar in August 1313, a position he held for the next six years. The king's grant to him of Roscrea Castle in 1315 was in part compensation for losses sustained as chief governor.

64. Castlekevin, County Wicklow: the latest in a long succession of campaigns against the Irish of Glenmalure took place in 1312. Led by the justiciar, Edmund Butler, as was frequent practice, the base-camp was the archiepiscopal manor at Castlekevin, of which only fragmentary remains of the gate house survive.
65. Dublin Castle: among the prisoners in Dublin Castle at the onset of the Bruce invasion were seven Scots, including a certain Henry, 'messenger of Robert le Bruys'.
66. In the distance stands Moyry Castle, a later tower house guarding the pass of that name, through which Edward Bruce's army made their southerly march in June 1315.
67. Gatehouse of Limerick Castle: a jury in 1318 found that Maurice fitz Thomas of Desmond had been in Dungarvan at the time of the Scots' arrival in Ireland in 1315 but rushed to protect Kerry and Limerick from the Irish who were rising up in revolt in support of Bruce; had he not done so, they agreed that the whole of Kerry and Limerick 'up to the gate of the city' would have been destroyed.
68. Part of Dublin's medieval quay wall with signs of re-facing that can be dated to the fourteenth century; we know that the walls in this area of the city were deemed vulnerable when Edward and Robert Bruce approached Dublin in February 1317 and that buildings were demolished to strengthen the walls.
69. The remains of Isolde's Tower, Dublin, under excavation. A thirteenth-century circular tower at the north-east corner of the medieval town, it was Dublin's bulwark against a sea-borne assault.
70. Leaving Dublin unmolested, the Scots army moved west where, on their way to their next target at Leixlip, they would have passed the modest castle at Ballowen, near Lucan, the earlier phase of which is here shown under excavation.
71. Heading south, the Bruces came to Callan, County Kilkenny, which they proceeded to assault. The motte castle, shown here, about a century old at the stage of this assault, would have been an easy target; it was the property of the de Clare family, who had held the earldom of Gloucester until the last earl was killed by the Scots at Bannockburn two and a half years earlier.
72. Built in the mid-thirteenth century, St Mary's parish church in Callan, County Kilkenny, may also have fallen prey to the Scots' attack.
73. Next in line for a Scots raid was the town of Kells-in-Ossory, County Kilkenny, and although the castle may have been the prime target, the Augustinian canons (whose house appears in the photograph) hardly managed to avoid the enemies' attention, especially as their prior was a spiritual peer of the Irish parliament.
74. Castleconnell, County Limerick, belonging to Richard de Burgh, earl of Ulster, represented the most southerly point reached by the Scots under Robert Bruce in winter 1316–17.
75. The royal castle at Newcastle McKynegan, County Wicklow, was vital to the government's attempts to maintain control over the Leinster Irish. The area between it and Wicklow town was inhabited by the Anglo-Norman family of Lawless, but because of the endemic warfare in the area they were given government authority to deal with the Irish 'in the manner of the marchers' and they themselves were treated as if an Irish sept, so that they were ordered that, 'if any of their name offend against the peace, they may take and imprison them'. The photograph shows the gatehouse on the motte.

7 – A Sequel to Edward Bruce's Invasion of Ireland

Bibliography

Barbour, J., *The Bruce*, ed. A.A.M. Duncan (Edinburgh, 1997).

Barron, E.M., *The Scottish war of independence*, 2nd edn (Edinburgh, 1934).

Barrow, G.W.S., *The kingdom of the Scots* (London, 1973).

– *The Anglo-Norman era in Scottish history* (Oxford, 1980).

– *Kingship and unity. Scotland 1100–1306* (Edinburgh, 1981).

– *Scotland and its neighbours in the middle ages* (London, 1992).

– *Robert Bruce and the community of the realm of Scotland*, 3rd edn (Edinburgh, 1998).

Barry, T.B., Frame, R. & Simms, K. (eds), *Colony and frontier in medieval Ireland. Essays presented to J.F. Lydon* (London, 1995).

Cosgrove, A. (ed.), *A new history of Ireland. II. Medieval Ireland 1169–1534* (Oxford, 1987).

Curtis, E., *A history of medieval Ireland from 1086 to 1513*, 2nd edn (London, 1938).

Davies, R.R., *Domination and conquest: the experience of Ireland, Scotland, and Wales, 1100–1300* (Cambridge, 1990).

Duffy, S., 'The Gaelic account of the Bruce invasion *Cath Fhochairte Brighite*: medieval romance or modern forgery?', *Seanchas Ard Mhacha*, 13 (1988–89), 59–121.

– 'The "continuation" of Nicholas Trevet: a new source for the Bruce invasion', *Proceedings of the Royal Irish Academy*, 91, C (1991), 303–15.

– 'Irishmen and Islesmen in the kingdoms of Dublin and Man, 1052–1171', *Ériu*, 43 (1992).

– *Ireland in the Middle Ages* (London, 1997).

– 'The Anglo-Norman era in Scotland and Ireland: convergence and divergence', in *Celebrating Columba. Irish-Scottish connections 597–1997*, eds T.M. Devine & J.F. McMillan (Edinburgh, 1999), 15–34.

– 'Ireland and Scotland, 1014–1169: contacts and caveats', in *Seanchas. Essays presented to Francis J. Byrne*, ed. A.P. Smyth (Dublin, 2000), 346–56.

– (ed.), *Atlas of Irish history*, 2nd edn (Dublin, 2000).

Duncan, A.A.M. & Brown, A.L., 'Argyll and the Isles in the Earlier Middle Ages', *Proceedings of the Society of Antiquaries of Scotland*, XC (1956–57), 192–219.

Duncan, A.A.M., 'The Community of the Realm of Scotland and Robert Bruce', *Scottish Historical Review*, xlv (1966), 187–88.

– *Scotland: the making of the kingdom* (Edinburgh, 1975).

– 'The Scots Invasion of Ireland, 1315', in *The British Isles: comparisons, contrasts and connections*, ed. R.R. Davies (Edinburgh, 1988), 100–17.

Frame, R., *English lordship in Ireland 1318–1361* (Oxford, 1982).

– *The political development of the British Isles, 1100–1400* (Oxford, 1990).

– *Ireland and Britain 1170–1450* (London, 1998).

N. Fryde, *The Tyranny and Fall of Edward II* (Cambridge, 1979).

Grant, A., *Independence and nationhood. Scotland 1306–1469* (Edinburgh, 1984).

– 'Scotland's "Celtic Fringe" in the late middle ages: the Macdonald lords of the Isles and the kingdom of Scotland', in *The British Isles 1100–1500: comparisons, contrasts and connections*, ed. R.R. Davies (Edinburgh, 1988), 118–14.

– & Stringer, K.J. (eds), *Medieval Scotland: crown, lordship and community* (Edinburgh, 1993).

Goldstein, R.J., *The matter of Scotland* (Lincoln, Nebraska, 1993).

Greeves, J.R.H., 'Robert I and the de Mandevilles of Ulster', *Trans. Dumfriesshire & Galloway Nat. Hist. Soc.*, 3rd ser., 34 (1955–6), 59–73.

– 'The Galloway lands in Ulster', *Dumfriesshire and Galloway Nat. Hist. & Arch. Soc. Trans.*, 3rd ser., 36 (1957–8), 115–22.

Hayes-McCoy, G.A., *Scots Mercenary Forces in Ireland (1563–1603)* (Dublin, 1937; reprint 1996).

Johnson, C., 'Robert Bruce's rebellion in 1306', *English Historical Review*, 33 (1918), 366–67.

Lydon, J., 'An Irish Army in Scotland, 1296', *The Irish Sword*, 5 (1961–62), 184–90.

– 'Irish levies in Scottish Wars, 1296–1302', *The Irish Sword*, 5 (1961–62), 207–17.

– *The lordship of Ireland in the middle ages* (Dublin, 1972).

– 'Edward I, Ireland and the War in Scotland, 1303–1304', in *England and Ireland in the later middle ages*, ed. idem (Dublin, 1981), 43–61.

– *Law and disorder in thirteenth-century Ireland: The Dublin parliament of 1297* (Dublin, 1997).

McDiarmid, M.P. & Stevenson, J.A.C. (eds), *Barbour's Bruce. A Fredome is a Noble Thing!* (Edinburgh, 1985).

McDonald, R.A., *The Kingdom of the Isles: Scotland's western seaboard* c.*1100*–c.*1336* (East Linton, 1997).

McGregor, M., 'Genealogies of the clans: contributions to the study of MS 1467', *The Innes Review*, 51, no. 2 (autumn 2000), 131–46.

McKerral, A., 'West Highland mercenaries in Ireland', *Scottish Historical Review*, 30 (1951), 1–14.

Maclean, L., *The middle ages in the Highlands* (Inverness, 1981).

McNamee, C., *The wars of the Bruces. Scotland, England and Ireland 1306–1328* (East Linton, 1997).

McNeill, P.G.B. & MacQueen, H.L. (eds), *Atlas of Scottish history to 1707* (Edinburgh, 1996).

Nicholls, K., *Gaelic and Gaelicised Ireland in the Middle Ages* (Dublin: Gill & Macmillan, 1972).

Nicholson, R., *Edward III and the Scots, 1327–1335* (Oxford, 1965).

– *Scotland: the later middle ages* (Edinburgh, 1974).

Ó Murchadha, D., 'Is the O'Neill–MacCarthy letter of 1317 a forgery?', *Irish Historical Studies*, 23 (1982–83), 61–67.

Orpen, G.H., *Ireland under the Normans 1169–1333*, 4 vols (Oxford, 1911–20).

– 'The earldom of Ulster, *Journal of the Royal Society of Antiquaries of Ireland*, 43 (1913), 30–46, 133–43; 44 (1914), 51–66; 45 (1915), 123–42; 50 (1920), 167–77; 51 (1921), 68–76.

Otway-Ruthven, A.J., *A history of medieval Ireland* (London, 1968).

Phillips, J.R.S., 'The mission of John de Hothum to Ireland, 1315–1316', in *England and Ireland in the later middle ages*, ed. J. Lydon (Dublin, 1981), 62–85.

– 'The Irish Remonstrance of 1317: an international perspective', *Irish Historical Studies*, 27 (1990), 112–29.

– 'The Remonstrance revisited: England and Ireland in the early fourteenth century', in *Men, women, and war*, eds T.G. Fraser & K. Jeffery (Dublin, 1993), 13–27.

Prestwich, M., *Edward I* (London, 1988).

Reid, W.S., 'Sea power in the Anglo-Scottish war, 1296–1328', *Mariner's Mirror*, 46 (1960), 7–23.

Sellar, W.D.H., 'Hebridean sea kings: the successors of Somered, 1164–1316' in *Celtic Scotland in the Middle Ages*, eds E.J. Cowan & R.A. McDonald (East Linton, 2000), 187–218.

Simms, K., 'The O Hanlons, the O Neills, and the Anglo-Normans in thirteenth-century Armagh', *Seanchas Ard Mhacha*, 9 (1978–79), 70–94.

– 'The battle of Dysert O'Dea and the Gaelic resurgence in Thomond', *Dál gCais*, 5 (1979), 59–66.

– *From Kings to Warlords. The Changing Political Structure of Gaelic Ireland in the Later Middle Ages* (Woodbridge: Boydell & Brewer, 1987).

Simpson, G.G., 'The Declaration of Arbroath Revitalised', *Scottish Historical Review*, lvi (1977), 11–33.

Smith, B., 'A county community in early fourteenth-century Ireland: the case of Louth', *English Historical Review*, no. 428 (July 1993), 561–88.

– *Colonisation and conquest in medieval Ireland. The English in Louth, 1170–1330* (Cambridge, 1999).

Smith, J.B., 'Gruffydd Llwyd and the Celtic alliance, 1315–18', *Bulletin of the Board of Celtic Studies*, 26 (1976), 463–78.

– 'Edward II and the allegiance of Wales', *Welsh History Review*, 8 (1976), 139–71.

Stones, E.L.G. (ed.), *Anglo-Scottish relations 1174–1328* (Oxford, 1965).

Stringer, K. (ed.), *Essays on the nobility of medieval Scotland* (Edinburgh, 1985).

Watt, J.A., 'Negotiations between Edward II and John XXII concerning Ireland', *Irish Historical Studies*, 10 (1956), 1–20.

Webster, B., *Medieval Scotland. The making of an identity* (London, 1997).

Young, A., *Robert the Bruce's rivals: the Comyns, 1212–1314* (East Linton, 1997).

Scottish and Irish history from Tempus

A History of the Black Death in Ireland
Maria Kelly
'A remarkably vivid and perceptive account. Written with verve, it makes a compelling read for anyone interested in the history of Ireland.'
Maurice Keen, author of The Penguin History of Medieval Europe
'A work of meticulous scholarship, this book is the first full-length study of how the bubonic plague reached Ireland in the summer of 1348.'
The Irish Times
176pp 60 illus. (19 col.) Paperback
£15.99/$26.99 ISBN 0 7524 1987 0

The Second Scottish Wars of Independence 1332–1363
Chris Brown
The least well known of Britain's medieval wars, the Second Scottish Wars of Independence lasted for more than thirty years. The Scots were utterly defeated in three major battles. So how did England lose the war?
208pp 100 illus. Paperback
£16.99/$19.99 ISBN 0 7524 2312 6

The Battle of Bannockburn 1314
Aryeh Nusbacher
'The most accessible and authoritative book on the battle.'
Dr Fiona Watson
'The first book on the Bannockburn campaign for almost a century... recommended.'
Historic Scotland
176pp 73 illus. Paperback
£12.99/$18.99 ISBN 0 7524 2326 6

Scotland: A History 8000 B.C. – 2000 A.D.
Fiona Watson
A *Scotsman* Bestseller
'Lavishly illustrated throughout, its trenchant views, surprising revelations and evocative descriptions wi entrance all who care about Scotland.'
BBC History Magazine
A comprehensive history of a proud nation written by Scotland's answer to Simon Schama, Fiona Watson, historian and presenter of BBC Television's landmark history series *In Search of Scotland.*
304pp 100 illus. Paperback
£9.99/$14.99 ISBN 0 7524 2331 2

The Kings and Queens of Scotland
Richard Oram (Editor)
'The colourful, complex and frequently bloody story of Scottish rulers… an exciting if rarely edifying tale, told in a clear and elegant format.'
BBC History Magazine
'Remarkable.'
History Today
272pp 212 illus. (29 col.) Paperback
£16.99/$22.99 ISBN 0 7524 1991 9

UK Ordering

Simply write, stating the quantity of books required and enclosing a cheque for the correct amount, to: Sales Department, Tempus Publishing Ltd, The Mill, Brimscombe Port, Stroud, Glos. GL5 2QG, UK. Alternatively, call the sales department on 01453 883300 to pay by Switch, Visa or Mastercard.

US Ordering

Please call Arcadia Publishing, a division of Tempus Publishing, toll free on 1-888-313-2665